D1556630

WITHDRAWN

Debates in Economic History

Edited by Peter Mathias

Population in Industrialization

Population in Industrialization

edited with an introduction by
MICHAEL DRAKE

METHUEN & CO LTD
11 NEW FETTER LANE LONDON EC4

First published 1969 by Methuen & Co Ltd
Introduction © 1969 by Michael Drake
Printed in Great Britain by
Richard Clay (The Chaucer Press), Ltd,
Bungay, Suffolk

SBN (hardbound) 416 12060 1
SBN (paperback) 416 12070 9

Distributed in the U.S.A.
by Barnes & Noble Inc

Contents

Preface

As this book goes to press, the search for certainty about the causes of demographic change in eighteenth-century England – and in Western Europe as a whole – is more elusive than for any other major issue in economic history. Current research offers almost as many hypotheses as there are contributors to the debate: every hypothesis has invoked a challenge, as Professor Drake's introduction and every contribution to the present volume indicate. Doubtless students (and not only students) find this state of affairs frustrating, even annoying. However, mere annoyance at this 'inadequacy' is a reaction which will only increase the frustration. The intrinsic fascination of the topic should rather be enhanced by the debate: it reveals much about the ways in which advance comes in the social sciences – by new evidence, by asking new questions, by applying new methods, by the double tensions created between new ideas and inadequate existing evidence, between new evidence and old ideas. Irrespective of the 'answers' yet available, the debate thus provides an insight into the evolving methodology of economic history.

The first position, typically, saw conclusions being drawn from a miscellany of mainly printed sources, not offering systematic quantitative data. There was heavy reliance on 'literary' sources – some of them actually fictional from poets, dramatists, and novelists – pamphleteers, and other contemporary commentators. With one or two remarkable exceptions (such as William Petty, Graunt, and Gregory King), such contemporaries were writing without access to systematic data, and without handling the data they had as systematically as we would now demand. The fact that Juliet was married at thirteen could be taken as *prima facie* evidence for an early age of marriage in Shakespeare's England. Nothing could be more misleading. From such impressionistic evidence general conclusions were drawn for the nation as a whole, if not universally valid generalizations. A satisfying single-cause hypothesis about the falling death rate then held the field for a generation, and in elderly textbooks still does.

As research continued, more and more awkward facts were assembled. More rigorous statistical analysis of sources (and the critical evaluation of the older statistical evidence) quite undercut the quantitative basis of the old hypothesis. Beyond a certain degree the original hypothesis could not be adapted to accommodate the deviant data, or new facts glossed to fit the old ideas. At this point the field is thrown open again to a wide range of potential explanations previously discounted by the dominance of received opinion. Dissident voices at last get heard. This is the destructive phase in the historiography of a topic, and through this sequence the demographic debate has recently passed.

The way ahead is very much more complicated than the old-style research which produced the earlier answers. Evidence is now being related rigorously to its precise context, whether of social group, locality, or economic context. Greater critical reticence prevents local studies being accepted too casually as representative samples from which wider generalizations may be drawn. Wholly new forms of statistical analysis, using the latest demographic techniques, are being applied to data. And, most important of all perhaps, a wholly new scale of research is being applied to quantitative data of all sorts, from parish records to national Census and registration material. Collective research and computer processing now give the opportunity for much greater precision of analysis – and doubtless answers, in time, to the mysteries. When new national generalizations are produced they will be derived, not from the old deductive methods of basing the large hypothesis on miscellaneous evidence but rather built up from many micro-studies, with systematic quantitative data analysed in depth. Thus the debate has moved into a wholly new world of historical research. Perhaps the result will be seen as the net effect of very diverse local variables rather than the operation of a major single cause. Certainly the articles printed here, as Professor Drake emphasizes, represent only an interim report.

PETER MATHIAS

Acknowledgements

The editor and publishers wish to thank the following for permission to reproduce the articles listed below:

Professor K. H. Connell for 'Some Unsettled Problems in English and Irish Population History, 1750–1845' (*Irish Historical Studies*, Vol. VII, No. 28, 1951); the Economic History Association for 'Some Neglected Factors in the English Industrial Revolution' by Professor J. T. Krause (*Journal of Economic History*, Vol. XIX, 1959); Dr T. H. Hollingsworth for 'A Demographic Study of the British Ducal Families' (*Population Studies*, Vol. XI, 1957); Professor J. T. Krause for 'English Population Movements between 1700 and 1850' (*International Population Conference, New York, 1961* (London, 1963)); Professor Thomas McKeown and Professor R. G. Brown for 'Medical Evidence Related to English Population Changes in the Eighteenth Century' (*Population Studies*, Vol. IX, 1955); Princeton University Press for 'The Effects of Economic Development on Population Growth' and 'The Effects of Population Growth on Economic Development' by A. J. Coale and E. M. Hoover (*Population Growth and Economic Development in Low-income Countries: a Case Study of India's Prospects*, 1958); P. E. Razzell for 'Population Change in Eighteenth Century England: a Re-appraisal' (*Economic History Review*, Vol. XVIII, 1965) and Dr E. A. Wrigley for 'Family Limitation in Pre-industrial England' (*Economic History Review*, Vol. XIX, 1966).

Editor's Introduction

The debate that forms the subject of this volume centres on the relationship between population growth and economic growth in late eighteenth- and early nineteenth-century England – the period and place of the first Industrial Revolution. For a variety of reasons the debate, which still rages, is an enormously fascinating one. In part this is because the participants have come from such a wide spectrum of the social sciences – history, geography, economics, sociology, social medicine, demography, and social statistics. Population problems, it seems, are more interdisciplinary than most. The pressing nature of the population problems of the currently under-developed world, which have become the focus of so much social scientific inquiry, has imparted an unusual degree of urgency to the study of the historical record of such problems. Also the very intractability of the problems under debate has extended the participants, forcing them to adopt a wide variety of approaches, sometimes involving a methodological ingenuity of a high order, e.g. Dr E. A. Wrigley's 'reconstitution of families'. It is hoped that the contributions collected together in this volume will bring out these features of the debate and, not least, impart some of the excitement (not to say trepidation!) which many of us feel as each new contribution appears on our desks.

The population of England and Wales appears to have grown by about 0·2 per cent per annum in the first half of the eighteenth century, by 0·9 per cent per annum in the second half and by 1·4 per cent per annum in the first half of the nineteenth century. If maintained, rates of growth of this order would lead to a doubling of the population in the course of 350 years, 80 years and 50 years respectively. Obviously, therefore, the change in the rate of growth in the eighteenth and early nineteenth centuries was a remarkable one. It can be explained in terms of a rise in fertility, a fall in mortality, an increase in net immigration, or a combination of all three. As immigration is generally regarded as being of relatively little importance,

attention has been focused on the behaviour of the birth and
death rates.

With reliable population statistics, the mechanism of change
would have been at once apparent. But, as is well known, the
available quantitative evidence is both scanty and deceptive.
The first official census of England and Wales was not taken
until 1801, and civil registration of births, deaths, and marriages
did not begin until 1837. For the eighteenth century we have,
for the country as a whole, only the totals of baptisms, burials,
and marriages recorded in the parish registers kept by the
Church of England clergy. These returns cover only certain
years. Also the rise of non-conformity, the inefficiency of the
clergy, the redistribution of population towards areas badly
served by the Church, all contributed to widening the gap between the actual number of births, marriages, and deaths and
the number recorded in the registers. Just how wide the gap
could be has been shown by Professor Krause, see below
p. 118.

In the absence of reliable statistical series at the national level,
scholars have had to turn to the small-scale study of localities
(see Wrigley, p. 157), sub-groups (see Hollingsworth, p. 73), and
institutions (see Eric Sigsworth, 'A Provincial Hospital in the
Eighteenth and Early Nineteenth Centuries', *College of General
Practitioners, Yorkshire Faculty Journal*, June 1966, pp. 1–8). This
mode of inquiry is not, of course, wholly satisfactory. To show,
for instance, that mortality among ducal families fell sharply
in the middle of the eighteenth century, does not necessarily
mean that it did so among the general population. That birth
control within marriage appears to have been practised widely
in the Devonshire parish of Colyton during the late seventeenth
century does not mean that it was a national phenomenon.
What these studies do provide over the short term are working
hypotheses for further inquiries. Over the long term the steady
accumulation of local studies should, of course, enable us to
perceive more clearly first the regional and later the national
picture.

The production of statistical series over limited periods,
areas, institutions, and themes, or the juggling with the national
data is still an important element in the debate. It is, however,
only a first stage, since it barely touches the core of the problem,

namely whether the jump in the rate of growth of England's population in the eighteenth century was the product of more or less profound social and economic changes, or whether the relationship was reversed. Put more crudely, such inquiries cannot tell us whether the Industrial Revolution brought about a rise in the rate of population growth or whether it was the population growth, independently generated, that facilitated the Industrial Revolution.

These interrelationships are discussed, at a general level, in the opening contribution by A. J. Coale and E. M. Hoover. The other contributions to this volume can be seen as the examination of the factors discussed by them, in the light of the particular situations revealed by historical inquiry. In doing this – in effect, testing theory against historical experience – the contributors bring out the prime purpose of historical inquiry for the social scientist. Take, for instance, the critique in this volume of the theory of the demographic transition.

Coale and Hoover point out that, according to this theory, the pre-industrial society characterized by low incomes has high birth- and death-rates: the former because, among other things, children are valuable as a source of income and security, the latter as a result of food shortages, inadequate sanitation, an inability to deal with disease, and the frequent breakdown of law and order. The economic development of such a society leads to an improvement in the environment, initially through better and more regular food supplies, subsequently through improvements in drainage, water supply, and medicine. These all contribute to a fall in mortality. The factors leading to high birth-rates are not immediately affected, with the result that the natural rate of increase (the gap between the birth- and death-rate) rises. Subsequently urbanization, the restriction of child employment, and greater access to private or state security programmes cause fertility to fall so that a new equilibrium of relatively low fertility, mortality, and natural increase emerges.

At the outset of the present debate, in 1950, most scholars believed the English demographic experience of the previous two hundred years fitted this model. Controversy began, however, when Professor Connell, in the article printed below, pointed out that in his view the very rapid growth of Ireland's population in the late eighteenth and early nineteenth centuries owed little to a fall in the death-rate. On the contrary, he argued, the increase was due to a rise in the birth-rate, consequent upon a fall in the age at marriage, the death-rate meanwhile remaining stable. Connell's findings, presented more fully in his book, *The Population of Ireland, 1750-1845* (Oxford, 1950), put a very big query against the theory of the demographic transition, since they posited a far greater degree of flexibility of the birth-rate, in a pre-industrial context, than the theory allowed for. Also, of course, his findings put historians into the apparently incongruous position of explaining a novel growth of population in two adjacent countries, over approximately the same period, in diametrically opposite ways! Connell went part of the way towards producing a common position by suggesting that further inquiry into the supposed reasons for the fall in mortality in eighteenth-century England (i.e. medical advances, environmental improvements) might show them to be less solidly based than had been supposed.

In 1955 such an inquiry was published by Thomas McKeown and R. G. Brown, see below p. 40. It gave much support to Connell. The alleged advances in surgery, midwifery, medicines, hospitals, and dispensaries appeared, to McKeown and Brown, to be negligible. Indeed, they went further, and suggested that some of the supposed advances probably increased mortality: 'the chief indictment of hospital work at this period, is not that it did no good, but that it positively did harm'. Although they thus dismissed medical effort, with the possible and, as it has turned out, important exception of inoculation against smallpox, they still thought a fall in mortality was the cause of the population rise. They did so because, following the theory of the demographic transition, they believed that birth-rates were high, and therefore any possibility of increase was limited. Further, they thought any increase in family size would all but be nullified by rising infant mortality. In examining other possible causes of a fall in mortality they believed a reduction in the virulence of certain infectious diseases was unlikely, but that an improvement in public health, largely through better nutrition, was probable.

The work of McKeown and Brown was a blow to those

who, taking a lead from Connell's explanation of the growth of
Ireland's population, believed England's population growth
was a product of a rise in the birth-rate, as a result of the
economic changes wrought by the Industrial Revolution. It
was not long, however, before the views of McKeown and
Brown were challenged. First it was shown by Professor
Helleiner, ('The Vital Revolution Reconsidered', *The Canadian
Journal of Economics and Political Science*, XXIII, 1957) that some
diseases ceased to be as effective killers as they had been. For
example, the bubonic plague which had ravaged Europe since
the Middle Ages had all but disappeared from England by the
early eighteenth century. Next Professor Chambers in a regional
study ('The Vale of Trent, 1670–1800', *The Economic History
Review*, Supplement 3, London, 1957) showed that the relationship between food supplies and mortality was by no means as
close as had been supposed, and that major killer diseases such
as typhus, smallpox, and dysentery appeared to operate independently of nutritional conditions. These conclusions confirmed the earlier findings of Utterström ('Some Population
Problems in Pre-industrial Sweden', *Scandinavian Economic
History Review*, II, 1954) so far as Sweden was concerned. They
have subsequently been corroborated in Denmark by Aksel
Lassen (*Fald og Fremgang: træck af befolkningsudviklingen i
Danmark* 1645–1960 (Aarhus, 1965)).

These findings did, of course, punch holes in the McKeown
and Brown analysis, but the paucity of statistical evidence in
England made it extremely difficult to give them any quantitative backing. The appearance, in 1957, of T. H. Hollingsworth's article, 'A Demographic Study of the British Ducal
Families', see below p. 73, provided the first piece of wholly
acceptable, if limited, statistical evidence, and thereby added a
new dimension to the debate. The political and social importance of ducal families meant that their genealogies were all
but complete as far back as the fourteenth century. Thus
Hollingsworth was able to calculate precise age-specific death-
rates. These revealed that in the mid-eighteenth century these
families experienced a striking fall in mortality. An explanation
of this in terms of improved nutrition seemed unlikely. Could
it be explained in terms of specific therapy or the declining
virulence of certain diseases? Whatever the reason, it seemed

unlikely to have any close relationship to the economic developments of the period. The theory of the demographic transition seemed again to be called in question.

The attack on the theory was also being pressed from another quarter. Professor Krause, in a series of articles (two of which appear below), was building up a powerful case in support of the view that in England, as in Ireland, the main cause of population growth was a rise in fertility consequent upon a fall in the age at marriage, in turn brought about by 'early industrialization, with its child labour; the poor laws; enclosure; and mining'. He not only gave examples of a fall in the age at marriage but also, in a massive attack on the credibility of the existing statistics, demonstrated that whatever might have happened to aristocratic mortality, among the common herd it appeared likely that 'death-rates changed but little during the period 1700–1820'.

Krause's position did not, however, go unchallenged, although the attack was an oblique one and took the form of a thrust at the central element of McKeown and Brown's case, namely that specific therapy had little impact on eighteenth-century mortality. Dr Sigsworth, in the article mentioned above, demonstrated that one of their supports, Florence Nightingale, was a most unreliable witness (her statistical apparatus was shot through with error) and that a study of the records of the York County Hospital revealed a much more cheerful picture of institutional conditions than they had painted. The attack was pressed home by Mr Razzell, see below p. 128, who taking the one piece of specific therapy, namely inoculation against smallpox, that McKeown and Brown had recognized, if somewhat reluctantly, might have had a significant impact on mortality, argued that not only could this explain the sharp fall in mortality experienced by Hollingsworth's ducal families but also 'could theoretically explain the whole of the increase in population' of eighteenth-century England.

The final contributor to this volume, Dr E. A. Wrigley, see below p. 157, swings the pendulum yet again. For he shows that in the parish of Colyton not only did the age at marriage of women fluctuate markedly between the sixteenth and the eighteenth centuries but also that these changes were associated with equally marked changes in fertility. Thus, for example, the age at first marriage of women in Colyton fell steadily throughout the eighteenth century, from 31 years in the period 1700–19 to 23 years by 1825–37. During this same period marital fertility rose sharply. Furthermore, Wrigley also demonstrated statistically the existence of birth control within marriage in late-seventeenth-century Colyton. Of course, Colyton is not England, and the techniques of family reconstitution by which these results have been obtained may contain snags. Nevertheless, the findings do suggest that Connell's doubts of 1951, concerning the traditional explanation of England's population growth, were well worth airing.

This bare outline of the main twists and turns of the debate can be fleshed out through a reading of the contributions that follow. Obviously we cannot yet say whether or not the main cause of England's population growth was a rise in the birth-rate or a fall in the death-rate, nor, *a fortiori*, can we say anything very definitive about the effect of economic change upon population change. This lack of finality is as irritating to some as it is exciting and challenging to others. The debate so far has, however, not been entirely without result, for it has revealed a variety of demographic experience undreamed of twenty years ago. It has, too, obviously shattered the *simpliste* notions of the theory of the demographic transition, and in doing so has directed the attention of social scientists to the importance of a society's demographic profile for its economic development. This aspect of the debate has been dealt with below by Coale, Hoover, and Krause, and more briefly by other contributors. It has, however, raised much less controversy. As it may shortly do so, a brief summary of the current position would seem appropriate.

Today the population explosion in the underdeveloped countries of the world is a product of a sharply declining death-rate brought about by western medical science and foreign aid, particularly of food. This fall in the death-rate has thus occurred very largely independently of any changes in the economies or societies of the underdeveloped world. So rapid has been the fall in the death-rate, and so high has been the level at which the birth-rate has been maintained, that populations have grown by as much as 2–3 per cent per annum. The economic effects of this growth appear to have been wholly bad. A rapidly expanding labour supply in areas where it is often already abundant is said to have inhibited the adoption of labour-saving devices and impeded the growth of productivity. In agricultural areas – and, of course, these accommodate the overwhelming bulk of the population – it has encouraged excessive subdivision and over-cropping. Most important of all it has caused funds to be diverted from investment for future growth into current consumption. Finally by increasing the burden of dependency (the load of non-producers that has to be supported by the work-force), a consequence of the biggest cuts in mortality occurring at the lowest age groups, the age distribution of the population has become less conducive to economic growth.

Since it is not uncommon to speak of early eighteenth-century England as an underdeveloped economy, it is pertinent to ask whether population growth had similarly adverse effects there too. Was, in other words, the growth of population a hindrance rather than an aid to industrialization? Did the Industrial Revolution occur in spite of the growth of population?

The first, and most obvious, difference between England's demographic experience in the eighteenth century and that undergone by many underdeveloped countries over the last two decades is that the English rate of population growth was much less rapid – at its highest not above 1·5 per cent per annum. This meant that the possible dislocatory effect of population growth together with its demands on the economy were markedly less. For instance, as Coale and Hoover point out, if a population is growing by 1·0 per cent per annum and the ratio of capital stock to current output is 3 to 1, then it must invest 3 per cent of its current output to maintain its *per capita* income. A country with a population growing at 3 per cent per annum must, under the same conditions, invest 9 per cent of its current output to achieve the same goal: a very much more difficult task.

A perhaps even more important difference between England's eighteenth-century population experience and that of the currently underdeveloped countries might, however, lie in the different mechanism of growth – although, as we have seen, this has yet to be established. If England's population growth was due to advances in medical science bringing down the death-rate, e.g. inoculation against smallpox, then the mechanism of growth would be closely parallel to that operating in the underdeveloped world, e.g. DDT sprayed on malarial swamps. The economic effects of a population growth induced in such ways might then be broadly similar. If, however, the growth of England's population was due to a rise in the birth-rate a very different prospect opens up, as Krause makes clear, see below p. 103. For if fertility rose, it could not have been at its physiological maximum, as it appears to be in many under-developed countries today, where 80 per cent of women in the fertile age groups are married and where birth-rates of 40–50 per 1,000 mean population are common. If, then, the birth-rate was not at its physiological maximum one presumes it must have been restrained, possibly through a late age at marriage, a low incidence of marriage or through birth control within marriage. It follows that if fertility was restrained it was so deliberately, most probably in the interests of maintaining living standards. Now if, under these conditions, fertility rises one can only assume that living standards are improving, otherwise there would be no encouragement to higher fertility. If living standards are rising, then one can assume economic growth is occurring. A growing economy needs the stimulus of rising demand and an adequate supply of labour. The *controlled* expansion of population provides this.

This line of argument does not, of course, rule out the possibility that England's eighteenth-century population growth was the product of a fall in the death-rate. What is important here is the level from which it fell and the contribution made by mortality to the control of population growth prior to its fall. For it could have been the case that the growth of population in England prior to the Industrial Revolution was restrained in large part by the voluntary mechanism operating via the birth-rate, but that the involuntary mechanism operating through the death-rate also played a part, if a lesser one. This might have meant that the population as a whole lived significantly above subsistence level. Thus when the population grew, the capital needs of the Industrial Revolution, which involved a switch of resources from consumption to investment, neither pushed the population below subsistence level nor soaked up too much of the purchasing power needed to provide the domestic demand for manufactured goods, upon which the industrial sector so much depended. The apparent absence of subsistence crises in eighteenth-century England and the impressionistic evidence of contemporaries that living standards were markedly higher there than in the rest of Europe lends support to this hypothesis.

The debate continues!

1 The Effects of Economic Development on Population Growth and The Effects of Population Growth on Economic Development

A. J. COALE and E. M. HOOVER

[First published as chapters 2 and 3 of *Population Growth and Economic Development in Low-Income Countries: a Case Study of India's Prospects*, Princeton University Press, 1958.]

THE EFFECTS OF ECONOMIC DEVELOPMENT ON POPULATION GROWTH

In surveying relations between two complex sets of changes it is natural to begin with the influence of one set on the other, and then to consider influences operating in the opposite direction. Our introductory survey of demographic and economic changes will follow this procedure, beginning in this chapter with a description of how economic development can influence population growth. This influence must operate through one or more of the three determinants of population growth – namely, births, deaths, and migration. Migration as an important cause of economic growth will not be discussed, because in general the substantial international barriers to large-scale migration make it a very uncertain element in the future growth of low-income areas, and in particular international migration seems unlikely to have an important effect on the future growth of the Indian population.

The classical economic theory of population growth (primarily associated with Malthus) held that any rise in incomes (particularly among the poorer classes) tended to increase birthrates and (with more certainty and force) to decrease death-rates.

The course of events since Malthus' time, however, has led

to the gradual evolution of a theory that postulates a more complicated sequence of birth- and death-rates as typically associated with economic development. It is sometimes termed the theory of the 'demographic transition'. According to this theory, an agrarian peasant economy (characterized by a high degree of self-sufficiency within each community and even each family, by relatively slow change in technique, and by the relatively unimportant role of market exchange) typically has high average death-rates. Moreover, these death-rates usually fluctuate in consequence of variations in crops, the varying incidence of epidemics, etc. In such an economy birth-rates are nearly stable at a high level. Death-rates are high as a consequence of poor diets, primitive sanitation, and the absence of effective preventive and curative medical practices. High birth-rates result from social beliefs and customs that necessarily grow up if a high death-rate community is to continue in existence. These beliefs and customs are reinforced by the economic advantages to a peasant family of large numbers of births. The burden of child care rests primarily on the women in a peasant society, and the place of women is typically a subordinate one. The costs of educating children are minimal because of the low level of education given. Children contribute at an early age to agrarian production and are the traditional source of security in the old age of parents. The prevalent high death-rates, especially in infancy, imply that such security can be attained only when many children are born.

In other words, an agrarian low-income society, before it undergoes economic development, has a mortality and fertility pattern that fits pretty closely the conditions which Malthus thought, at least in the first edition of his famous essay, to be a universal tendency: high birth- and high death-rates. Growth of population is usually slow.

Economic development, according to the theory of the demographic transition, has the effect of bringing about a reduction in death-rates. Economic development involves evolution from a predominantly agrarian peasant economy to an economy with a greater division of labour, using more elaborate tools and equipment, more urbanized, more oriented to the market sale of its products, and characterized by rapid and pervasive changes in technique. It also involves improvements in transportation, communications, and productivity, and these improvements have had the effect (notably in Europe, the United States, Canada, Australia, and New Zealand, and later in Japan) of bringing a striking reduction in death-rates. The reduction in death-rates may be ascribed partly to greater regularity in food supplies, to the establishment of greater law and order, and to other fairly direct consequences of economic change. Other factors contributing to the decline – improvements in sanitation, the development of vaccines and other means of preventive medicine, and great and rapid strides in the treatment of disease – can themselves be considered as somewhat indirect consequences of economic change. Advances in medical knowledge can occur more readily in a secularized, less tradition-bound society that has resources available to support medical research. The means to build and the will to accept sanitary water supplies, sewage systems, and the like are more likely to exist in an industrial than in an agrarian society. For similar reasons, only in an advanced economy, with such characteristics as a high degree of division of labour and high levels of productivity, are there the means to construct large numbers of hospitals, to educate and train large numbers of doctors, and the like. It is often hard to determine in a given historical period whether general economic conditions or specific medical advances had the greater effect. In Europe even before 1800 there had been significant medical discoveries (including vaccination for small-pox with cowpox serum) that must have made *some* contribution to declining mortality. Nevertheless, the Population Division of the United Nations suggests that the reduction of mortality rates in the European cultural sphere in the eighteenth and the first part of the nineteenth centuries was due mostly to more or less direct effects of economic improvement, while in the latter part of the nineteenth and especially in the twentieth centuries the more direct factors at work have been improving medical knowledge and increasingly effective public health methods.[1] This conclusion must be considered highly conjectural.

The theory of the demographic transition asserts that the high birth-rates, as well as the death-rates, characteristic of an

[1] United Nations, Department of Social Affairs, Population Division, *The Determinants and Consequences of Population Trends*, Population Studies No. 17 (New York: United Nations, 1953), pp. 56–61.

agrarian low-income society are affected by economic develop-ment. The changing structure of production, with a declining importance of the family as a production unit, with the growth of impersonal systems for the allocation of jobs, and with the development of economic roles for women outside the home, tends to increase the possibility of economic mobility that can better be achieved with small families, and tends to decrease the economic advantages of a large family. One of the features of economic development is typically increasing urbanization, and children are usually more of a burden and less of an asset in an urban setting than in a rural. The whole process of economic change, moreover, weakens the force of traditional customs and beliefs. In most countries that have undergone the economic transition from an agrarian to an industrialized, market-oriented economy, the custom of the small family has started in the urban groups at the higher end of the socio-economic scale and has spread to smaller cities, lower-income groups, and eventually to rural areas.[1]

Just as early decline in the death-rate in the European cultural area preceded the development of modern medical innovations, the early decline in fertility preceded the develop-ment of modern techniques of birth control. In many areas a marked decline in fertility has depended only on techniques of contraception known in many societies for centuries. How-ever, both the extent and effectiveness of family limitation in industrialized countries have no doubt been facilitated by the development and manufacture of efficient contraceptive devices.

Although the events described by this theory can apparently be traced in every region where the economy has been subject to the evolution from an agrarian to a specialized market-dominated economy, the theory is not sufficiently quantitative and specific to tell how far and how fast the vital rates generally decline. It does, however, contain one further significant generalization, which is that the decline in the birth-rates typically occurs after a substantial time lag, in comparison with the decline in mortality rates. The slower response of the

[1] See F. W. Notestein, 'Economic Problems of Population Change', in *Proceedings of the Eighth International Conference of Agricultural Economists* (London: Oxford University Press, 1953).

birth-rate to economic change is attributed to the fact that a
fertility decline depends more strongly on the alteration of
long-established customs and institutions. Also, there is in
almost any society a general consensus in support of the reduction of suffering, illness, and death, while no such consensus
supports the desirability of small families and the patterns of
sex behaviour required to reduce the birth-rate. The historical
implications of the lag between the decline in the death-rate
and the decline in the birth-rate have been that the countries
affected have experienced a substantial growth in population
and a rapid one, at least by previous standards. Thus in the
period between 1750 and 1950 the 'area of European settlement' increased its population sixfold.[1] The population more
than doubled in the century from 1750 to 1850 and nearly
tripled in the interval 1850–1950.

In barest outline the sequence of events, according to the
theory of demographic transition, can be summarized as follows: the agrarian low-income economy is characterized by
high birth- and death-rates – the birth-rates relatively stable,
and the death-rates fluctuating in response to varying fortunes.
Then as the economy changes its form to a more interdepen-
dent and specialized market-dominated economy, the average
death-rate declines. It continues to decline under the impact of
better organization and improving medical knowledge and
care. Somewhat later the birth-rate begins to fall. The two rates
pursue a more or less parallel downward course, with the decline in the birth-rate lagging behind. Finally, as further
reductions in the death-rate become harder to attain, the birth-
rate again approaches equality with the death-rate and a more
gradual rate of growth is re-established, with, however, low
risks of mortality and small families as the typical pattern.
Mortality rates are now relatively stable from year to year, and
birth-rates – now responsive to voluntary decisions rather than
to deeply imbedded customs – may fluctuate from year to year.
This short description fits the experience of most countries
whose economies have undergone the kind of reorganization
we have been calling economic development. The part of the
description with the least certain applicability is the character-
ization of the final stage as a return to a condition of only

[1] United Nations, Population Division, op. cit., p. 11.

gradual growth. The populations of Canada, the United States, Australia, and New Zealand are growing at rates that would lead to a doubling approximately twice a century – a rate of growth well above the average rate in the area settled by northern and western Europeans during the period of the demographic transition itself. It remains uncertain how long this rather rapid growth in North America and Oceania will continue.

The theory of the demographic transition has been summarized here because it is the theory which seems to be the best available to describe the expected course of events in the low-income areas of the world today if their economies are developed. Shall we not expect that economic development in the contemporary low-income areas will bring with it a decline in death-rates followed by a decline in birth-rates, and will produce over an interim period an acceleration of population growth? A superficial survey of the demographic situation and apparent prospects in the low-income portions of the world gives reason for doubting the applicability of the demographic transition as an *exact* description of the likely course of events in these areas. The principal reason for doubting the precise applicability of the theory as to *death*-rates is that it appears feasible today to reduce death-rates markedly without a major reorganization of a peasant economy. Many low-income areas of the world today – for example, Ceylon, Malaya, some of the Caribbean islands, and much of Latin America – have, without abandoning their present agrarian structure, so reduced their death-rates, while birth-rates have remained essentially unchanged that their rate of natural increase exceeds any recorded in the course of the demographic transition in the areas inhabited by northern and western Europeans and their descendants.

In other words, *substantial economic improvement may be a sufficient condition for a decline in mortality, but it is not today a necessary condition.* The pace of recent improvement in mortality is indicated by the fact that for twenty-one countries where the crude death-rate was over 17 during the period 1935 through 1944, the average annual drop in crude death-rates from just before the Second World War until around 1950 was about seven-tenths of a point. (In other words, the death-rate was dropping at a pace that would reduce the crude death-rate by 7 per thousand population every ten years.[1]) This rate of improvement surpasses anything from the records of areas inhabited by northern and western Europeans. In many instances there is no evidence of major economic changes. The factors primarily responsible for the mortality declines in these areas are innovations in public health. These make possible drastic reductions in mortality at low cost – and in the absence of wholesale social reorganization. A somewhat similar reduction in mortality was achieved prior to the Second World War in low-income colonial areas where the influence of a more highly developed economy was strong. Colonial administrators frequently succeeded in introducing relatively low-cost programmes that had measurable effects on mortality. A notable case is that of Taiwan, where, under Japanese administration, the crude death-rate declined from an average of 33·4 per thousand in the years 1906–10 to 18·5 for the years 1941–3. Mortality declines have recently become widespread and precipitous, however, through the combined effects of the following factors:

(1) *The development of antibiotics and insecticides.* The incidence of malaria can in most environments be reduced to negligible proportions through the use of residual insecticides, especially DDT, at an annual cost of some 10–15 cents *per capita* of the population protected. Other serious diseases, such as yaws, syphilis, and perhaps eventually tuberculosis, respond to relatively inexpensive treatment with antibiotics.

(2) *The evolution of effective public health organizations in low-income areas.* This development has become possible, in some instances, through the establishment of public health training centres in low-income areas. In other instances public health workers from the low-income areas have been trained in European or American universities; and in still other instances expert demonstration teams operating under the

---

[1] These twenty-one areas were Taiwan, the Federation of Malaya, Malta and Gozo, the Maori population of New Zealand, Egypt, British Guiana, Chile, Costa Rica, El Salvador, Mexico, Puerto Rico, Ceylon, Mauritius, Venezuela, Guatemala, Barbados, Leeward Islands, British Honduras, Ecuador, Hong Kong, and Singapore.

auspices of the World Health Organization have helped to get programmes started.

(3) *The invention of suitable low-cost methods of sanitation* (such as inexpensive hand-flush latrines) and the discovery through public health experiments of effective techniques for introducing the use of such equipment and devices.

Experience in communication, persuasion, and leadership as well as in more directly medical aspects of public health in rural areas is accumulating rapidly. No doubt the lessons learned will make future public health work more effective.

Mortality experience in situations where economic development began in the eighteenth or nineteenth centuries provides a precedent possibly misleading on two scores as a guide to the likely course of death-rates in areas with current low incomes. First, the death-rate in many low-income areas either is already or may soon be going down more rapidly than it ever did in countries now enjoying high incomes; and second, this rapid drop in death-rates can occur with or without pronounced changes in economic structure.

Whether the pattern of fertility decline that has been observed in the industrializing areas of European settlement will be duplicated in the low-income areas of today is very uncertain. No published version of the theory of the demographic transition states precisely what conditions are essential for a fertility decline; much less is it possible to tell whether these conditions will be present in the areas in question during a specific interval. Perhaps the decline in mortality may in itself prove a sufficient cause for a substantial fertility reduction. Since much of the reduction in mortality typically occurs in childhood, it will be apparent that average family size is increasing as mortality rates decline; and the motives of ensuring family continuity and of obtaining support for old age can be satisfied with a smaller number of births. However, the record on this score is discouraging. In Taiwan, where the death-rate declined substantially under the Japanese colonial administration, birth-rates remained essentially unaltered. Similarly, in Ceylon between 1921 and the present, when death-rates declined consistently from around 30 per thousand to around

10 per thousand, there has been no important decline in fertility.[1]

The course of the birth-rate in Japan shows that the association between declining fertility and the rise of an urbanized industrial economy is not limited to Western European cultures. However, there are countries (notably Egypt and India) where the differential fertility between city and country is slight or even non-existent.[2] In short, urbanization alone is not always sufficient to cause a reduction in the birth-rate. Nor is it certain that small changes in economic organization or slight rises in *per capita* income will cause a reduction of fertility in low-income areas. It is questionable whether the economic and social change likely in the next two or three decades in many parts of the world will be enough to have an effect on fertility. The level of economic development in European countries (and in Japan) prevailing at the time that fertility began a significant decline might reasonably be regarded as representing the approximate 'threshold of decline'. It appears unlikely that this threshold will be crossed in the next two or three decades in, for example, Egypt, Pakistan, India, China, Malaya, or Indonesia.[3]

The demographic situation in areas in the incipient stages of economic development seems to differ from the pattern described by the theory of the demographic transition in the following ways: (1) The decline of death-rates from the high levels typical of peasant agrarian economies is occurring or is likely to occur more rapidly than it did in regions which industrialized earlier. Moreover, the decline is occurring in advance of (or in the absence of) profound changes in the economy and in *per capita* incomes. (2) The growth rates

[1] The registered birth-rate in Ceylon for 1954 was 36·2 per thousand compared to 39·4 for the preceding year. This is the first indication of a marked decline in the Ceylonese birth-rate. However, this decline may prove to be temporary or spurious. In the first place, the 1954 monthly figures show an incredibly low birth-rate for August. The likelihood that the low figure can be attributed to deficient registration is strengthened by the fact that there were serious civil disturbances in Ceylon during this month. Secondly, the 1955 rate shows a partial recovery to 37·9 per thousand.

[2] Cf. M. A. El-Badry, 'Some Aspects of Fertility in Egypt', *The Milbank Memorial Fund Quarterly*, Vol. XXXIV, No. 1 (January 1956), pp. 22–43; and Coale and Hoover, *Population Growth and Economic Development in Low-Income Countries*, pp. 47–8.

[3] Coale and Hoover, op. cit., pp. 57–9.

established, as mortality declines, are in excess of any observed in the records of areas industrializing earlier. (3) The prospect of rapid growth itself – particularly in areas where the current *per capita* incomes are very low – contributes to uncertainty about the likely course of fertility. The rapid growth rate may make it difficult to accomplish the economic and social changes that reduce fertility.

Innovations in the field of public health seem to have made it possible for death-rates to be substantially reduced in the absence of profound economic changes in low-income areas. However, the classic Malthusian argument makes it all too clear that low death-rates cannot be maintained long in the absence of profound changes either in the economy (so as to achieve a rapid rate of growth in output) or in the birth-rate (to keep the growth in population at moderate levels). A peasant agrarian economy is not usually characterized by a potential for rapid growth in output. The death-rates achievable at low cost by modern public health methods, combined with the birth-rate characteristic of such an economy, imply a doubling of the population every twenty to twenty-five years. If economic development does not *precede* the decline in mortality it must still occur eventually if the decline is to be maintained.

THE EFFECTS OF POPULATION GROWTH ON ECONOMIC DEVELOPMENT

In this chapter we shall list and briefly analyse the ways in which demographic factors can affect the level of *per capita* income. There will be no systematic attempt to review the various economic theories from the predecessors of Malthus to the neo-Keynesian stagnation theorists. The emphasis will be on relations relevant to low-income areas today.

There are three aspects of population growth that may be looked at separately in analysing the effects of population growth on the growth of *per capita* income. These are: (*a*) the size of a population; (*b*) its growth rate; and (*c*) its age distribution.

The relation between population size and *per capita* income is the subject to which optimum population theory has been addressed. The relationship of size to desired growth rate is straightforward. If optimum population theory indicates that a population is too large a negative growth or decline is advantageous, and any smaller positive growth rate is to be preferred to a larger. Optimum population theory is in essence an exercise in comparative economic statics. The principal point at issue is that of returns to scale, with two opposing forces at work – economies of scale favouring a rising *per capita* income, and diminishing returns a falling *per capita* income, with larger population size. The question is in effect one of the optimum relation of population to the other factors of production.

The question of whether a given population is larger than one yielding maximum *per capita* output is very difficult to answer in any concrete situation. One of the fundamental difficulties is that the shape of the curve relating output to labour force depends on the available techniques of production, which in turn depends on what skills the population possesses. Thus a population may be in a stage of sharply diminishing returns while it is utterly illiterate, whereas after a generation of education a population of the same size might be of optimum or even sub-optimum size. Moreover, the whole question of increasing and decreasing returns with respect to the size of the labour force depends upon the availability of other factors of production. Indeed, the idea of diminishing returns is simply another way of picturing the consequences of the limited availability of some factor of production. One of the factors most likely to lead to diminishing returns, especially in the low-income areas of the world, is the limited quantity of capital available. With larger quantities of capital, larger-scale techniques at high levels of efficiency might become feasible. Here, again, the locus of the point at which diminishing returns sets in can shift with the passage of time.

The classic example of the factor in fixed supply that causes diminishing returns in other factors is *land* or, more generally, natural resources. When the availability of capital changes, however, the point of diminishing returns to labour with a fixed supply of land may vary. In any event, the effective supply of land or of useful natural resources is in actual fact partly a function of technical knowledge and skills. Hence judgements that a population has too large a size on the criterion of average income should be provisional, and may prove to be obsolete, even if originally correct.

The basic defect in analysing the effects of population growth by considering alternative sizes alone is that such a scheme of analysis ignores the dynamic effect of the *change* in population size or the growth rate of population. The alternative population developments which may in fact be available at any time are usually a range, perhaps a narrow one, of alternative rates of population growth arising through either alternative possible death-rates or alternative possible birth-rates, or both. It makes a big difference which of these growth rates is selected, quite aside from the question of whether the population with given resources (including the initial stock of capital) and given techniques is too large or too small.

This brings us to the second factor that may be considered in analysing the effect of population growth on economic development, namely, the rate of growth itself. The significant feature of population *growth* as such is that a *higher rate* of population growth implies a *higher level* of needed investment to achieve a given *per capita* output, while there is nothing about faster growth that generates a greater *supply* of investible resources. This point may be clarified by a simple example. Assume that technical change is negligible over the short run and that capital and labour force are the only ingredients of output. Then an increase of x per cent per annum in population and of x per cent per annum in accumulated capital will produce an increase of x per cent per annum in output – or an unaltered *per capita* output. Now consider two populations equal, at a given moment, in size, in accumulated capital, and in output. Assume that population A is growing at a rate of 1 per cent per annum, and population B at 3 per cent. If the ratio of capital stock to current annual output is 3 to 1 population A must invest 3 per cent of current output to maintain its *per capita* income, while population B must invest 9 per cent of current output. But under ordinary circumstances the supply of new capital will be no greater in B than in A. There is nothing about faster growth *per se* to lower consumption and raise savings – certainly not by such a large margin.

In low-income areas it is especially difficult to attain adequate levels of investment, and there is no visible way in such areas by which more rapid population growth can evoke a significantly greater flow of invested resources. When the supply of capital is inelastic a higher rate of population growth forces the diversion of investment to duplicate existing facilities, preventing an increase in the capital available for each worker.

Seen from another point of view, the relationship between population growth and investment has served as one of the principal underpinnings for the theory of stagnation that was popular in the 1930s. Here the point was that economic stagnation is caused by an inadequate level of new investment, and that new investment is sometimes deficient in part because of the slow growth of population. However, this reasoning applies only when the barrier to greater investment is the absence of a motive to invest (low marginal efficiency of capital, in Keynesian terms) rather than a poor supply of investible resources.

In periods of depression in highly industrialized economies any rise in the prospective profitability of investment should tend to increase the employment of labour and capital that would otherwise be idle, and to raise *per capita* product. If, in

B

the face of an elastic supply of capital, the greater *need* for capital (to maintain a given level of *per capita* output) caused by more rapid growth is translated into higher or more certain prospects of profit, population growth serves as an important stimulant to higher investment levels.[1]

We may picture two extreme situations with respect to the effect of population growth rates on the growth of *per capita* income. One picture is that of a relatively high-income economy where the chronic problem is that of assuring a full utilization of the resources available – to avoid unemployment both of the labour force and of capital goods. Keynesian analysis shows that under these circumstances a rise in the demand for capital goods (a rise in the marginal efficiency of capital) will have a stimulating effect on the whole economy, and will tend towards generally higher incomes. It can well be argued that a possible source of such stimulus to demand is a faster rather than a slower population growth rate. In the other extreme is an economy which suffers from a deficiency not of effective demand primarily but of a supply of capital. In such an economy a higher schedule of saving rather than of consumption would help to generate higher incomes in the future by making possible a more rapid rate of investment. Similarly, a reduced need for investment merely to duplicate facilities would permit a greater increase in the amount of capital per worker, higher *per capita* output, and higher *per capita* income.

There may be some basis for the belief that in fact deficiencies of effective demand are often a problem in low-income economies as well as in high-income economies. It might sometimes be the case that government deficits or increased spending by upper-income groups would serve as a real stimulus to increased output. But even if deficiencies of effective demand as a barrier to economic growth are accepted as a possibility in low-income economies, it does not follow that more rapid population growth will under these circumstances serve as a major stimulus, since there is no apparent way in a low-income economy for greater numbers to be translated into very much

---

[1] The existence of a greater *need* for investment does not necessarily imply a greater *demand* for investment. Labour force growth could merely add to the unemployed, while profit prospects remained gloomy and investment remained low.

higher consumption expenditures or higher prospective returns to capital. Most families will not have the capability for enlarging their consumption, but must spread meagre income over a larger number. In other words, faster growth may have little effect in low-income economies on either the consumption function or the 'marginal efficiency of capital'.

To summarize, if we assume away the problem of effective demand (i.e. assume it either non-existent or adequately solved through government action in a low-income agrarian economy), rapid growth *does* tend to diminish the amount of capital available for increasing the average productivity of the work force and increasing the average *per capita* income.

The third factor which enters in an analysis of the effect of population growth on economic development is the distribution of population by age, which turns out to be strongly influenced by the same elements that determine the rate of population growth. We will have to digress before discussing the effect of age distributions on economic growth to discuss briefly the factors determining the shape of an age distribution. If one deals with a closed population (namely, one in which gains or losses by migration are negligible), the principal determinant of the age distribution is the course of fertility. Persistent high levels of fertility give a broad-based distribution that tapers rapidly with age; persistent low levels of fertility give a narrow-based age distribution. If fertility is low enough the age distribution may be broader in the shoulder than at the base. Even irregularities such as gaps and humps in an age distribution are usually the result of variations in fertility.

Conversely, mortality changes of a sort that usually occur have only a slight effect on the age distribution.[1] The net consequence of these facts is that a change in the growth rate caused by a change in fertility will generally have associated with it a large change in the percentage distribution. On the other hand, a change in the growth rate brought about by a change in mortality will generally be accompanied by only a slight effect on the percentage distribution. A further implication is that all low-income agrarian areas, which without exception have relatively high birth-rates, have, no matter what their

[1] The chief exception is war casualties, which have their own peculiar incidence by age and sex.

mortality levels, a broadly based and sharply tapering age distribution, with a large fraction of the population under 15. Of course, low birth-rates ultimately lead to higher proportions over age 65, but the decrease in the proportion under 15 outweighs this increase.

The fact is, then, that the burden of dependency, or the ratio of persons who are in a dependent status because of their age (too young or too old to work) to persons at ages making them eligible for productive work, is relatively high in areas characterized by persistent high birth-rates, and is low in areas with low birth-rates.

The reduction of mortality, particularly among children, is an inestimable gain for its own sake. As social goals, reduced pain, suffering, and grief rank at least as high as reduced poverty. Moreover, the public health measures that yield lower death-rates also raise productivity and morale by reducing absenteeism, weakness, fatigue, lassitude, and disability. But it is *not* true, as is commonly believed, that mortality reduction reduces the so-called 'burden of dependency'. The argument offered in support of this belief is that when childhood mortality rates are high (and childhood mortality rates are typically high when the general level of mortality is high) the economy must support a large number of children during the part of their lives when they consume only and do not produce; moreover, the economy does not benefit from production by these children during the interval of their working ages, when they might produce more than they would consume. Therefore – so the argument runs – if an improvement in mortality would permit more children to reach adult ages this waste would be avoided and the burden of dependency would be reduced.

This argument as just summarized makes no explicit assumptions about levels of fertility. If now it is assumed that during the sequence just described levels of fertility are unchanged, the argument proves fallacious. The source of the fallacy is that if more children are enabled to survive to their adult years there will be not only more workers but also more parents; the larger number of parents, if fertility rates remain unchanged, will produce more children. Analysis shows that the rise in the number of children is indeed somewhat greater than the rise in the number of workers.[1] So while it is true that a decrease in childhood mortality will yield a larger population at the working ages than would otherwise have resulted, it produces an even greater rise in the number of children whom the people of working ages must support.

High childhood mortality rates *do* cause expenditures on children who because they die make no contribution at a later time to the economy. The relevant consideration, however, is the non-productive expenditures at any moment in support of non-productive persons. Since the proportion of children *rises* slightly with typical mortality improvements, the economy must 'waste' *more* (not less) of its substance on non-productive persons. A reduction in mortality 'saves' more people for the labour force ages, but it also saves them for parenthood, and 'wasteful' expenditure is expanded more than the labour force itself. In short, the 'waste' of always supporting a much larger next generation (the waste of very rapid growth) replaces the waste of spending on persons who later die. A change in the mortality rate operates primarily on the growth rate of the population – it produces more people in the working age but also produces more people in the dependent ages. On the other hand, a decline in birth-rates yields a smaller number of children without immediately affecting numbers at older ages. The effect on the age distribution in the short and long run is a smaller fraction of dependent children.

We shall, in what follows, neglect as relatively minor age-distribution effects of mortality changes, and discuss only the effect of changes of *fertility* on the age distribution. Consider two populations of the same size, one characterized by a history of high birth-rates, the other characterized by low birth-rates at least over an interval of fifteen to twenty years prior to the date in question. The population with the high birth-rates may have some 55–60 per cent of its numbers in the ages from 15–65, whereas the population with the low birth-rates may have some 65–70 per cent of its population in the productive ages. With the same resources and capital available the lower

[1] A. J. Coale, 'The Effects of Changes in Mortality and Fertility on Age Composition', *The Milbank Memorial Fund Quarterly*, Vol. XXXIV, No. 1 (January 1956), pp. 79–114; and 'The Effect of Declines in Mortality on Age Distribution', *Trends and Differentials in Mortality*, Milbank Memorial Fund (New York, 1956), pp. 125–32.

birth-rate population should have higher *per capita* output and higher *per capita* income as a direct result of having a higher fraction of its population eligible on account of age for productive work.

Another instructive comparison is between two populations again differing only through the history of their birth-rates, which are equal now not in terms of their total size but in terms of the size of their labour force. In this case the labour force in the economy characterized by high birth-rates would have to support substantially larger numbers of children. This necessity would have a two-edged effect on the availability of capital for the possible expansion of output. First of all, the supply of capital would tend to be reduced because the larger number of consumers implied by the past history of higher birth-rates would exert a depressing force on the level of savings. A family with the same total income but with a larger number of children would surely tend to consume more and save less, other things being equal. Also, an economy that had been characterized by high birth-rates would tend to have a more rapidly rising number of children, which in turn would tend to divert some of the capital accumulated each year into expenditures such as for school and child-welfare programmes. These expenditures would reduce the availability of capital for directly adding to the productivity of the labour force.[1]

The three demographic factors identified as basic in an analysis of the effects of population growth on economic development are population size, rate of population growth, and age-distribution effects. Actually, of course, these three factors are never independent. A continuation of a more rapid population growth inevitably produces, in a closed population, larger numbers. A slower rate of population growth brought about by a reduction in birth-rates inevitably has age-distribution effects.

Our study of demographic and economic prospects in India over the next twenty-five or thirty years will take implicit or

[1] In an economy where the level of effective demand is an important barrier to the employment of available resources there are further important and quite different economic effects of age-distribution differences. If effective demand is deficient a high burden of dependency – a large number of children as opposed to a small number – should serve as a stimulant to higher consumption and should create a demand for capital investment.

explicit account of all these factors. All turn out to be important. The device of population projection, through which the likely evolution of death-rates and possible variations in birth-rates in India can be translated into estimated future populations of India by age and sex, enables us to bracket, we think, the likely variations in potential size, growth rates, and age-distributions for India over the next twenty-five to thirty years. A consideration of the Indian economy at the end of the First Five Year Plan, plus a consideration of the nature of the next Five Year Plan, enables us to take account of the actual objectives of Indian economic development and the institutional framework within which that development will likely proceed, and gives us more realistic and detailed ways of appraising the consequences of alternative courses of population growth.

2 Some Unsettled Problems in English and Irish Population History, 1750–1845

K. H. CONNELL

[This article was first published in *Irish Historical Studies*, Vol. VII, No. 28 (Dublin, 1951).]

So far as is known there was no precedent in the experience of England and Ireland for population increase as rapid or as sustained as that which appears to have begun in England in the 1750s and in Ireland some thirty years later. If the available figures can be trusted the number of Englishmen (and Welshmen) more than doubled between 1750 and 1831 and the number of Irish living in Ireland doubled between 1780 and 1841. In England the rapid growth of population provides an essential part of the explanation of the coming of the Industrial Revolution. In Ireland it did even more than largely determine the magnitude of the catastrophe of the Famine. It was unbridled population growth, succeeded by famine, which incised on the minds of the Irish and their rulers unforgettable lessons which guided their conduct in the following century and ensured that Irish economic and social development, moulded by the exigencies of a declining population, should provide a unique model for the historian – and one which he has examined all too little.

It is tantalizing that the elucidation of the dimensions and the structure of a problem of such overriding importance should be so elusive. The elusiveness, of course, must largely be attributed to the non-existence or the inadequacy of the appropriate statistics. It was not until half a century after the growth of population had begun that parliament at last insisted that the people be counted regularly. While we must be critical of the figures the early census volumes offer us for overall population, our main complaint against them is that (with the exception of the remarkable Irish census of 1841) they give no data of any value to an attempt to determine whether the main reason for the rapid rate of population increase was unusually low mortality or unusually high fertility. With the foundation of statistics suspect or absent, surmise must oust certainty in historical demography. The historian can merely construct a logical framework showing the possible causes of variations in fertility and mortality and, from his knowledge of the social and economic history of the period he is reviewing, try to find which of these causes were in fact operative. With so much left to the historian's judgement it is not surprising that there is no agreed explanation of the population problems of the age of Malthus.

It is remarkable, to the economic historian at any rate, that population in two countries whose economic structures were widely disparate should have begun to leap upwards at about the same time and with something like the same force. The coincidence, however, is tacitly accepted, though seldom proclaimed. Independent explanations of the growth of population in each country hold the ground.

For England the current explanation[1] is that a rising birthrate was of subsidiary importance: the main contribution is said to have come from rapidly falling mortality. Several threads, not all of any great firmness, are woven into the explanation of this phenomenon. Legislative control of the sale of spirits lowered infantile and general mortality. The towns became safer places in which to live as water supply and sanitation were improved and as Georgian architects added to the health as well as the elegance of their society. There were advances in the theory and practice of medicine: anatomy, surgery, and midwifery were systematically taught and systematically practised in hospitals and homes. Smallpox was curbed, first by inoculation, then by vaccination. While the medical value of cleanliness was becoming increasingly appreciated, the opportunity to be clean was correspondingly enlarged by the introduction of cheap and easily washed cotton clothes and by the extending use of soap. As a result, mortality from fevers and other diseases fostered by dirt dwindled. In

[1] See, in particular, G. T. Griffith, *Population Problems of the Age of Malthus* (Cambridge, 1926) and M. C. Buer, *Health, Wealth, and Population in the Early Days of the Industrial Revolution* (1926).

agriculture the introduction of roots provided a winter food for livestock: this gave the breeders an opportunity they were not slow to seize for developing animals of greater value to the butcher and the dairyman. Developments in stock-farming reacted on arable farming by providing more manure, and there was much independent advance as fallow was eliminated and waste reclaimed, as new crops and new crop-rotations were introduced, and as the land was better fertilized, drained, and cleaned. The upshot of it all was an improvement in the quantity, quality, and variety of food supply. As diet became more satisfactory, so mortality, and especially infant mortality fell away.

Few points in this explanation of the growth of population in England find their way into the interpretation of the contemporary growth in Ireland.[1] Vaccination was practised there early in the nineteenth century, but in the following decades its advance was more restrained than in England. Hospitals were built and there were improvements in medical training, but neither development appears to have lengthened the lives of more than a small proportion of the Irish people. The sharp increase in their number is attributed rather to the fact that more were being born. This, in turn, is explained largely in terms of earlier marriage. Wretched, hopeless living conditions, and the temperamental recklessness which they induced, had long isolated the peasants' children from the economic and social considerations which in other societies have led to a not unwilling postponement of marriage. The traditional obstacle to very early marriage in the Irish countryside had been the difficulty of finding a 'settlement' on which the marriage and its children might be sustained. Pastoral farming was dominant, its intensity does not seem to have increased nor was the area on which it was practised considerably enlarged. Much as in rural Ireland today, a son could hope to marry only when he could step into his father's shoes. And by the time the father died the son was no longer a stripling. What was changing by the 1780s, when the upward turn in the population curve seems to have begun, was that 'settlements', for the first time, were available almost for all. By then, because of the growth of England's own population she was no longer an exporter of

[1] See K. H. Connell, *The Population of Ireland, 1750–1845* (Oxford, 1950).

corn and she could look with less jealousy upon its production in Ireland. The Irish parliament now found itself free to encourage corn-growing. Within a few years the food scares of the French wars and their reflection in grain prices gave further incentive to the extension of arable. More arable farming presupposed smaller-scale farming, because there was no class of men with the capital and the skill to manage large tillage farms. The subdivision of holdings, thus begun, drew added strength from the Irishman's dependence on the potato, the most prolific of temperate food crops, and therefore one that allowed him to reduce the size of his farm without necessarily going short of food. The movement continued, its force hardly abated, until the Famine taught the peasants its folly and enabled the landlords to give effect to their own belated realization that an agrarian policy which multiplied the people on their estates was unlikely also to multiply the rents that could be paid. Extensive reclamation of waste land, at least during the French wars, and in the dozen or more years preceding the Famine, added to the impetus which subdivision gave to the growth of population. Both movements allowed men, at however youthful an age, to occupy the holding on which they might marry and establish a family. They married, it seems, women no less youthful than themselves. The more of her childbearing years a woman spent in the state of marriage, the more children she was likely to have.[1]

Here, then, with omissions and simplifications, are the

---

[1] Mr M. E. Ogborn, joint editor of the *Journal of the Institute of Actuaries*, has pointed out in a review in that journal (LXXVI (1950), 304) that earlier marriage tended also towards the growth of population in so far as it meant that the generations succeeded one another with greater frequency.

I should like here to draw attention to two errors which reviewers have detected in the statistical tables of my *Population of Ireland*. (1) Mr Ogborn has shown, in the review referred to above, that the figures in Table 14, p. 39, which purport to show the number of marriages in England and Wales in 1847, relate in fact to the minority of marriages in that year for which the Registrar-General had precise information on the ages of both partners. (2) Dr R. C. Geary, in a review in *Studies* (Dublin) for December 1950 (p. 473), has shown that the figures which I give in Table 6, p. 30, for the number of children under 1 and under 5 in Ireland in 1841 relate to the number under 2 and under 6. The census data, as Dr Geary points out, show that the number of children under 5 per 1,000 women aged 15–44 was 532, not as I have said 644. As the comparable figure for England and Wales is 552, the corrected table, in so far as the data on which it is based are reliable, no longer supports the conclusion that fertility was remarkably higher in Ireland than in England.

current explanations of a contemporaneous and quantitatively not dissimilar growth of population in the two countries. Each approaches the problem from a different direction; neither draws considerably from the armoury of the other. Are these explanations in fact satisfactory? Must we conclude that, quite fortuitously, fertility happened to increase in Ireland at about the same time as mortality diminished in England, and that in so far as social and economic factors bear on the growth of population, these influences were of different categories in the two countries?

Neither explanation is wholly convincing, nor, in the absence of appropriate statistics, is conviction ever likely to be attained. First, as far as England is concerned, it is by no means certain that people were becoming cleaner, and therefore less susceptible to disease. The increasing revenue from the excise on soap is treacherous evidence in a period when more industries than one were being transferred from the privacy of the home to the workshop or factory where the revenue collector could discharge his duties more satisfactorily. Moreover, when peasants were becoming labourers and labourers also were losing their self-respect, when the real wages of many were falling and when pressure on house space was becoming more acute, it strains our sense of credulity to try to believe that, by and large, people were washing more frequently.

Second, that in England the overall production of foodstuffs substantially increased in the decades of the Industrial Revolution cannot be denied. Indeed, to do so would be to contest the core of the Malthusian argument, and it is seldom wise for the historian to dispute what seemed common sense to contemporaries. The growth of population had traditionally been limited by the supply of food: for population in the eighteenth century to have grown there must have been a parallel expansion in the supply of nutrition. But this is not to say that the increased production of food meant that people were better fed and therefore lived longer. Theoretically the influence of a more favourable food supply would have been equally effective had it been brought to bear through allowing people whose lives had been saved by other agencies to go on living, or through permitting the survival of an additional number of infants born. And when we examine the social history of the

Industrial Revolution the aptness of this alternative explanation becomes apparent. Neither the evidence of such family dietaries as survive nor our knowledge of the impact of the forces which were reshaping both agriculture and industry can persuade us that there was a general improvement in standards of nutrition.

But there is a third and more formidable obstacle to our acceptance of the English explanation. Much of the fall in mortality which it posits is attributed to two factors: first, the greater skill of the doctors and the wider and more suitable field for its practice which followed the work of the hospital-builders; and, second, the improvements in water supply and drainage. Any developments there may have been in either of these spheres affected chiefly, if not exclusively, those who lived in the towns, not those who lived in the country. Such drains and water-pipes as were laid added to the amenities of urban life. It is unlikely that the most capable doctors had country practices. It was in the towns, too, that most of the hospitals were situated: it was seldom that they had enough beds for all of the townsmen who needed their services, and, in any case, the sick countryman was normally isolated from their facilities by the difficulty of transport. In so far as lives were prolonged, it was therefore the lives of town-dwellers. Yet continuously during the period of the Industrial Revolution only a minority of the population lived in towns. For developments affecting them almost exclusively to have had so great an impact on the overall population they must indeed have been potent. Yet we are forced to doubt their potency when we read the reports of the 1830s on urban sanitary conditions and when we learn, from such figures as are available for the same period, that the expectation of life in the towns was briefer than in the country. We are left to wonder how the towns of the eighteenth century could possibly have shortened life more effectively than those of the 1830s. During the Industrial Revolution the towns were undoubtedly growing rapidly; but their growth was largely the result of an influx from the healthier countryside.

Turning now to the explanation of the growth of the Irish population, its weakest point appears to be that, at best, it is no more than a hypothesis. Because there are no adequate fertility and mortality statistics, this is a matter in which certainty can never be attained. But there is more than the inevitable degree of uncertainty. The crux of the whole explanation is that in the 1780s people were marrying earlier than had been their custom in former generations. Yet Petty, in the seventeenth century, noticed that the Irish commonly married 'upon the first capacity'.[1] If he reported fairly, and if such early marriage persisted generally for another hundred years, then indeed we are astray in attributing the new buoyancy of population growth in the 1780s to earlier marriage.

Second, even granted earlier marriage, would this normally be followed by higher fertility? And, if so, could any likely increase of fertility have largely accounted for the rapid growth of population? These are problems, the one for the physiologist and pathologist, and the other for the statistician: there is little of any value that can be said about them here.

We cannot, then, accept with full confidence either of the current explanations of the population problems of the age of Malthus. We cannot be sure that the population of England increased chiefly in consequence of the work of the doctors, the hospital builders, and the sanitary engineers, nor that the population of Ireland increased largely because of the earlier marriage made possible by subdivision of holdings and the reclamation of waste land. If either explanation should ever be refuted, in what directions could we look for alternative hypotheses?

In the first place the dimensions of the problem might be reduced if the historical statisticians could produce more accurate figures for the size of population at various dates. There is some reason for believing that the estimates for the eighteenth century are more deficient than the early census figures and that there are more omissions from these than from the mid-century census returns. The whole run of estimates, therefore, may tend to make the problem to be explained appear more formidable than it is.

We should also bear in mind that a population increase arising from any cause other than the prolongation of lives of those in the upper age-groups bears within itself at least a

---

[1] W. Petty, *Treatise of Ireland, 1687*, reprinted in *The Economic Writings of Sir William Petty*, ed. C. H. Hull (Cambridge, 1899), II, 608.

partial explanation of its continuance. If the lives of young people are saved, or if fertility rises, then immediately, or after the lapse of some years, the proportion of the population in the age groups in which marriage is customary increases and a new upward movement in fertility is likely to follow.

But it is out of the question that the statisticians can explain away the problems that have concerned us. If the interpretations which have been outlined are effectively questioned, then some new hypotheses must be raised in their place. It is not at all improbable that a weightier contribution is called for from the medical historians than any which they seem to have made. Several diseases appear to have cycles of virulence independent of changes in man's resistance to them. It is not impossible, for instance, that the various fevers, the incidence of which is said to have been reduced in England by greater cleanliness, did in fact diminish, but that the diminution was due to a change in the habits of lice, not of men. If such a theory should appear plausible, then the economic historian could explain an ensuing growth in population largely in terms of developments which allowed the production of the food and the houses and so forth needed for a denser population.

Leaving aside the help he may be given from workers in neighbouring fields, the most promising area of advance for the economic historian would seem to lie in some fusion, or at least some mutual aid, between the interpretations at present advanced in isolation in explanation of not dissimilar phenomena in England and Ireland. Those who believe that falling mortality was the efficient cause in England appear to have arranged in their show-case all the possible causes of longer life – and to have displayed some of them with such advantage that they appear larger than life size. Similarly, the Irish explanation seems to have exhausted the possible causes of an increase in fertility. If, then, there is to be revision the English historians must look to the birth-rate, and the Irish to the death-rate. Perhaps the English could test the hypothesis that for certain groups of the population wretched and hopeless living standards led to a lowering of the age at marriage. Perhaps, also, to a greater extent than has been realized, classes of people who hitherto had normally remained celibate were marrying more generally: perhaps, too, the greater mobility of the people, by widening the area from which husband or wife could be drawn, may have lessened the involuntary infertility of marriage.

As for Ireland, if we are to renew interest in the causes of a possible fall in mortality it would be worth while, at the outset, to see if sufficient weight has been given to one of the most startling of the many paradoxes in Irish social history – the fact that a people whose wretchedness was said seldom to have been exceeded, seem, nevertheless, to have enjoyed for many years a standard of nutrition which to the biochemist, if not to the gourmet, was almost perfect. Up to the present the dietetic influence of the potato has been discounted, because there does not appear to have been a marked change in food habits at the time when the upward bound in the population figures is thought to have begun. The influence of the potato is therefore allied with that of rising fertility: it allowed the survival of an increasing number of children. But this judgement may err in placing the Irishman's dependence on the potato in too early a period. It is by no means impossible that standards of nutrition did improve in the 1780s, and did lead to a marked lengthening of life, notably, perhaps, through the saving of infant life. More probably the error, if error there be, lies in accepting the indication of insecure statistics that the great increase in population began in the 1780s, not, say, twenty or thirty years earlier, when it may well have followed hard upon the generalization of a potato dietary.

The coincidence, then, between the growth of population in England and Ireland may, perhaps, be detected also in not altogether dissimilar movements in fertility and mortality. Whether, in fact, it was quite fortuitous that the population of Ireland began to climb upwards at about the same time as did that of England is yet another problem that merits further inquiry. Some links, at least, between the two movements may be detected. The growth of population in England increased the profits of arable farming in Ireland and therefore gave momentum to both the subdivision of holdings and the reclamation of waste land: and whatever interpretation of Ireland's population growth we may adopt, it is unlikely that these developments will be reduced to a negligible role. Conversely, the growth of the population of Ireland was not without its impact on England. Ireland's growing population allowed her to send to England mounting streams of men, rent-payments, and grain. This largely unrequited impact of labour, capital, and food was of no small consequence in allowing the progress of the industrial and agrarian revolutions – in allowing, that is, the growth of England's own population.

3 Medical Evidence Related to English Population Changes in the Eighteenth Century

THOMAS McKEOWN and R. G. BROWN

[This article was first published in *Population Studies*, Vol. IX, (London, 1955).]

In a recent communication[1] Professor Habakkuk has raised doubts about the acceptability of the traditional view which attributes the increase in the population of England during the eighteenth century to a fall in the death-rate. He is unable to accept Griffith's[2] suggestion that medical measures introduced during that century had a substantial effect on the death-rate, and considers the statistical evidence that mortality declined unreliable. These conclusions led Habakkuk to re-examine the possibility that an increase in the birth-rate was the more important cause of the rise in population, and he suggests that 'the acceleration of population growth in the late eighteenth century was to a very large extent the result of a high birth-rate, and that in turn was the result of the economic developments'.[3] His reason for preferring this interpretation is not merely that the traditional view is unacceptable; he is also impressed by evidence of the significance of the birth-rate in the growth of population in certain pre-industrial societies (such as eighteenth-century France and colonial America), as well as by opinions expressed by eighteenth-century writers about the effect of economic conditions, in particular the demand for labour, on the birth-rate.

These views are influenced by recent work on population problems. But in the period since Griffith's book was published

---

[1] H. J. Habakkuk, 'English Population in the Eighteenth Century', *The Economic History Review*, 2nd Series, VI (1953), 117–33.

[2] G. T. Griffith, *Population Problems of the Age of Malthus* (Cambridge, 1926).

[3] Habakkuk, op. cit., p. 130.

there has also been a considerable advance in medical knowledge of matters which have a bearing on the interpretation of population trends. For example, we are now able to assess more accurately the contribution of medical measures to reduction of the death-rate during the eighteenth century. We can also express a more confident opinion about the probable effect of environmental change on the common causes of mortality. Finally, and perhaps most important in this context, we can form a judgement about the relative difficulty of (*a*) increasing the birth-rate, and (*b*) reducing the death-rate, in a period when both rates were undoubtedly high.

The discussion which follows is mainly concerned with a review of the medical evidence. This evidence supports the conclusion that specific medical measures introduced during the eighteenth century are unlikely to have contributed substantially to a reduction in the death-rate, but seems to us to suggest that a decline in mortality is, nevertheless, a more plausible explanation of the increase in population than a rise in the birth-rate. We begin by inquiring to what extent medical effort contributed to reduction of the death-rate. The traditional interpretation of the rise in population has rested on Griffith's answer to this question.

(I) EFFECTIVENESS OF MEDICAL MEASURES DURING THE EIGHTEENTH CENTURY

At first sight a list of developments in medicine during the eighteenth century seems impressive. It includes expansion of hospital, dispensary, and midwifery services; notable changes in medical education; advances in understanding of physiology and morbid anatomy; and introduction of the first example of effective protective therapy (inoculation against smallpox). It is scarcely surprising that Griffith, like most other writers, should have concluded that these changes contributed materially to the health of the people. This conclusion derives from failure to distinguish clearly between the interests of the doctor and the interests of the patient, a common error in the interpretation of medical history. From the point of view of a student or practitioner of medicine, increased knowledge of anatomy, physiology, and morbid anatomy are naturally regarded as important professional advances, as indeed they are. But from the point of view of the patient, none of these changes has any practical significance until such time as they contribute to preservation of health or recovery from illness. It is because there is often a substantial interval of time between acquisition of new knowledge and the possibility of any demonstrable benefit to the patient that we cannot accept changes in medical education and institutions as evidence of the immediate effectiveness of medical effort. To arrive at a reliable opinion we must look closely at the work of doctors during the eighteenth century, and inquire whether in the light of modern knowledge it seems likely to have contributed to the health of their patients.

(a) SURGERY

There is little difficulty in coming to a conclusion about the value of eighteenth-century surgery. Before the introduction of anaesthesia, operations were almost restricted to the following: amputation, lithotomy, trephining of the skull, incision of abscess, and operation for cataract. For a modern reader the circumstances in which these procedures were carried out are almost unbelievable. The discovery of the anaesthetic properties of nitrous oxide in 1800, and a practical demonstration of the use of ether in 1846, greatly extended the scope of surgery. It did not increase its safety, and as recently as the last quarter of the nineteenth century results of the common operations were, by any standards, appalling. In 1874 the senior surgeon to University College Hospital reviewed thirty years' experience in surgery,[1] and concluded that 'skill in the performances has far outstripped the success in the result'. He showed that mortality following all forms of amputation was between 35 and 50 per cent, and following certain forms it was as high as 90 per cent. These figures were based on the work of the most expert surgeons, working in the largest hospitals, and are probably no worse than would have been obtained elsewhere; indeed, in continental hospitals at the same period mortality was even higher. Results of other types of operation were equally bad; it was not until the introduction of antiseptic

[1] J. E. Ericksen, *On Hospitalism and the Causes of Death after Operations* (London 1874).

procedures that surgery became relatively safe. Ericksen's observations were based upon the third quarter of the nineteenth century; there is certainly no reason to suppose that earlier results were better, and Singer is unquestionably correct in his judgement that 'surgery had an almost inappreciable effect on vital statistics until the advent of Anaesthesia and Antiseptics'.[1] Indeed, from the point of view of the surgeon this is a generous judgement.

(*b*) MIDWIFERY

To assess the influence of midwifery on mortality we must consider two important changes in obstetric practice during the eighteenth century. These were the introduction on a substantial scale of institutional delivery and a change in obstetric technique and management which possibly had its main impact on domiciliary practice.

Before 1749, when the first lying-in hospital was founded in London, institutional delivery was very uncommon. A considerable number of lying-in hospitals were established during the second half of the eighteenth century, and Griffith included them among 'notable improvements during the period'.[2] It is very easy to satisfy oneself that when first introduced, and for many years after, the practice of institutional confinement had an adverse effect on mortality. We shall first examine statistics for the nineteenth century, which are more reliable and complete than those for the earlier period.

During the thirteen years 1855–67 there were 4·83 maternal deaths per thousand deliveries in England.[3] But results of institutional and domiciliary delivery were quite different. Lefort[4] estimated mortality in a large number of confinements in all parts of Europe as 34 and 4·7 per thousand deliveries for institutional and domiciliary deliveries respectively; contemporary English estimates[5] were consistent with these figures. There were substantial variations in the rates from one hospital to another, and in the same hospital from year to year, but with few exceptions hospital death-rates were many times

[1] C. Singer, *A Short History of Medicine* (Oxford, 1928), p. 162.
[2] Griffith, op. cit., p. 238.
[3] *30th Annual Report of the Registrar General* (1867), p. 223.
[4] L. Lefort, *Des Maternités* (Paris, 1866).
[5] F. Nightingale, *Introductory Notes on Lying-in Hospitals* (London, 1871).

greater than those for related home deliveries. Indeed, the
difference was so conspicuous that it was obvious to contemporary observers, and Ericksen noted that 'a woman has a
better chance of recovery after delivery in the meanest,
poorest hovel, than in the best-conducted general hospital,
furnished with every appliance that can add to her comfort,
and with the best skill that a metropolis can afford'.[1] There is,
of course, no mystery about the reason for the high death-
rates; in most cases death was due to puerperal infection.

The figures quoted are from the mid-nineteenth century, and
it may be asked whether results of institutional delivery at the
earlier period were equally bad. There is reason to believe
that they were worse. National statistics are not, of course,
available, but from records of individual hospitals[2] it seems
probable that results were slightly better in the nineteenth
century than in the last quarter of the eighteenth. There can be
no doubt that the effect of institutional confinement on maternal
mortality was wholly bad, and indeed had the proportion of
deliveries conducted in hospitals approached that in some
modern communities the results would very rapidly have been
reflected in national statistics.

We must now inquire whether changes in obstetric technique and management contributed to a reduction of mortality.
During the second half of the century delivery by forceps and
other artificial means became more common, and the formidable instruments in earlier use had been modified to some
extent. Data quoted by Simpson and others[3] show that even in
hospital practice delivery by forceps was unusual (a few cases
in every thousand deliveries), and results on the mortality of
mother and child were extremely bad. For example, in a Dublin
series the proportion of deaths after operative or artificial
delivery was approximately 3 in 4 for children and 1 in 4 for

[1] Ericksen, op. cit., p. 43.
[2] R. Bland, 'Some Calculations . . . from the Midwifery Reports of The West-
minster General Dispensary', *Transactions of the Royal Society*, LXXI (1781), 355;
J. Clarke, 'Observations on Some Causes of the Excess of the Mortality of Males
above that of Females', *Transactions of the Royal Society*, LXXVI (1786), 349; R.
Collins, *A Practical Treatise on Midwifery* (London, 1835); H. Graham, *Eternal
Eve* (London, 1950), p. 369.
[3] Bland, op. cit., p. 360; F. B. Hawkins, *Elements of Medical Statistics* (London,
1829), p. 123; J. Y. Simpson, *Obstetric Memoirs and Contributions*, Vol. 1 (Edinburgh, 1855), pp. 626, 855.

mothers.[1] Even if artificial delivery were relatively more common in home confinements, as is unlikely,[2] and if results were much better than in hospital, as is quite possible, it seems inconceivable that the use of instruments had any substantial effect on results of obstetric practice.

A far more significant influence was a change in the conditions under which deliveries were conducted. This was not so much a change in obstetric technique as an improvement of hygiene in the labour room. White,[3] for example, recommended cleanliness and adequate ventilation, and claimed that by having regard to these essentials he had lost no patients because of puerperal infection. We do not know how widely such practices were followed in domiciliary obstetrics in the late eighteenth century, and it must be remembered that many years later it was by no means generally accepted, even by medical men, that the environment contributed to ill-health. Nevertheless, there is reason to believe that maternal mortality fell during the eighteenth century,[4] and the simple hygienic measures practised by White and others are undoubtedly the most important contribution which doctors made to this improvement.

We have so far been examining the influence of midwifery on maternal mortality. Today in most western countries maternal mortality is so low that the mortality of the foetus or newborn infant provides a more sensitive index of the effectiveness of an obstetric service. But in the eighteenth and nineteenth centuries high infant death-rates were generally regarded as inevitable, and infant mortality rates were not given in national statistics until 1841, and stillbirth rates until 1927. Nevertheless, there seems no reason to doubt that the conclusions which

[1] Simpson, op. cit., Vol. 1, p. 626.
[2] In respect of use of forceps Collins stated: 'Most physicians, in private practice, would require to use them but seldom; as, supposing an individual to attend 4,000 cases in the course of his life, which is a greater number than falls to the lot of most men, the forceps or lever would be necessary in little more than six cases', op. cit., p. 10.
[3] C. White, *A Treatise on the Management of Pregnant and Lying-in Women* (1773). Cited by F. H. Garrison, *An Introduction to the History of Medicine*, 3rd edn. (Philadelphia, 1924), p. 347.
[4] Estimates from the London Bills of Mortality suggest that maternal mortality was halved in the period 1700–1800. Merriman, *A Synopsis of Difficult Parturition*, p. 343. Cited by Simpson, op. cit., Vol. II, p. 544.

emerge from consideration of maternal mortality would be confirmed if statistics on foetal and infant mortality were available. These conclusions are:

(*a*) That the introduction of institutional confinement had an adverse effect on mortality. New-born infants are even more vulnerable than their mothers to infectious disease. It should be noted that the point is not that there was no improvement in mortality among children delivered in hospital during the second half of the eighteenth century[1] but that mortality rates in hospital were consistently much higher than in domiciliary practice.

(*b*) That the only change in obstetric practice likely to have contributed to a reduction of maternal or infant mortality was an improvement in the hygiene of the labour room.

(*c*) MEDICINES

The number of drugs available for treatment of disease during the eighteenth century was very large. Fortunately, in the present context we are not required to assess the pharmacological properties of these remedies, but need only inquire whether there were improvements in therapy, either by introduction of new drugs or from more efficient use of existing ones, which are likely to have contributed to a reduction of mortality.

According to Singer,[2] the only important drugs introduced between Hippocratic times and the beginning of the nineteenth century were laudanum, liver extract, mercury, cinchona, ipecacuanha, and digitalis. Laudanum, liver extract (in the circumstances in which it was then used), and ipecacuanha cannot be regarded as life-saving remedies, and we need only consider more fully the claims of mercury, digitalis, and cinchona.

The use of mercury in the treatment of syphilis was introduced during the late fifteenth century, largely abandoned

[1] It is possible that there was some improvement in mortality rates in lying-in hospitals during the second half of the eighteenth century, although from present knowledge of the incidence of deaths from causes other than infection, the figures given by Heberden for mortality in the British Lying-in Hospital (in 1799–1800: 1 in 938 for mothers and 1 in 118 for children) are frankly incredible. Cited by Griffith, op. cit., p. 241.

[2] C. Singer, *British Medical Journal*, 1951, I, p. 569.

during the sixteenth and seventeenth centuries, and re-introduced during the eighteenth. This drug is no longer used by itself, although until recently it was valued as a therapeutic agent in syphilis. But while mercury may have had some effect upon the course of the disease in individual cases, it is hard to believe that its influence can have been reflected in national mortality rates.

Even today, when used correctly, digitalis adds no more than a few years to the life-expectation of well-chosen patients. The drug was included in the London Pharmacopeia of 1650,[1] but was certainly used incorrectly before 1785, when Withering published his *Account of the Foxglove*, and can have had very little value before the nineteenth century, when Bright distinguished between dropsy of cardiac and renal origin. It is inconceivable that digitalis made any substantial contribution to treatment of heart disease during the eighteenth century, much less that it had any effect on mortality trends.

Cinchona was known in England from about 1655 and was listed in the London Pharmacopeia in 1677.[2] It is undoubtedly effective in the treatment of malaria, and in some modern communities (for example, in Cyprus) control of this disease has very rapidly influenced both the death-rate and growth of population. During most of the eighteenth century cinchona was given in doses which were too small to be really effective,[3] until Lind demonstrated in 1786 that large doses were essential; it was also used indiscriminately, since malaria was not clearly identified from other fevers. Moreover, the number of deaths attributed to ague was insignificant in relation to the total death-rate; according to Blane,[4] there were 44 deaths in the Bills of Mortality 1728, and only 16 in 1730.[5]

[1] F. A. Flückiger and D. Hanbury, *Pharmacographia* (London, 1874), p. 422.

[2] Flückiger and Hanbury, op. cit., p. 304.

[3] G. M. Findlay, *Recent Advances in Chemotherapy*, 3rd edn., Vol. II (London, 1951), p. 271.

[4] G. Blane, 'Observations on the Comparative Prevalence, Mortality and Treatment of Different Diseases', *Medico-Chirurgical Transactions*, IV (1813), 94.

[5] Not all epidemiologists are agreed that endemic malaria ever existed in Great Britain. Professor Shrewsbury believes that the common ague was not malaria, on the grounds that: (*a*) the clinical descriptions of individual cases of 'ague' recorded in medical and lay writings during the sixteenth and seventeenth centuries show that any febrile state, which was not accompanied by an identifiable eruption, was classed as 'ague'; (*b*) ague was common in districts where anopheline mosquitoes are relatively scarce today; (*c*) when, as at the end of war,

We have been discussing drugs introduced during or shortly before the eighteenth century. Among the large number used in ancient medicine were a good many which are still included in modern pharmacopeias. A few of these older remedies were of some value, but perhaps the only one which might now be regarded as of life-saving character is iron. It was not greatly valued by Greek and Arabic physicians, but was widely used in the seventeenth and eighteenth centuries. Sydenham and other physicians employed it as a tonic, and gave it in a variety of conditions which appear to have included some iron-deficiency anaemias. It is impossible to express a confident opinion about what this treatment achieved, but it can safely be asserted that it could have had no appreciable influence on the national death rate.

(d) HOSPITALS AND DISPENSARIES

Great significance has always been attached to the rapid growth of hospitals during the eighteenth century. In 1700 there were two hospitals in London (St Bartholomew's and St Thomas's), and only five in the whole of England; by 1800 there were at least fifty hospitals in England and, according to Griffith,[1] accommodation available in London was nothing to be ashamed of, even when judged by modern standards. But in assessing the contribution of hospitals to reduction of mortality we are less concerned with the number of beds than with the results of treatment of the patients who occupied them. On this matter the evidence is far from reassuring.

Griffith assumed that the growth of hospital accommodation was largely responsible for the steady drop in the death-rate during the late nineteenth and early twentieth centuries, and concluded that hospitals must also have contributed materially to reduction of mortality in the eighteenth century. On present evidence it seems most unlikely that either the assumption or the conclusion based on it is correct. The decline of the death-

---

malaria is introduced from abroad no new cases are found after the first winter; (d) there is no evidence that the climate of Britain during the last thousand years has been more favourable for the overwintering of the malarial plasmodium than during the years immediately succeeding the last two world wars (personal communication).

[1] Griffith, op. cit., p. 219.

rate during the nineteenth century was almost wholly attributable to environmental change, and owed little to specific
therapy, preventive or curative. (A reservation must be added
in respect of vaccination against smallpox.) Perhaps the only
useful contribution made by hospitals was in the isolation of
infectious patients, first in separate wards of general hospitals
and later in fever hospitals (mainly after the passage of the 1875
Public Health Act). But during the eighteenth and early nineteenth centuries the importance of segregating infectious
patients was not appreciated. It was believed that infectious and
non-infectious cases could be mixed in the ratio of one to
six, and as recently as 1854 persons infected with cholera
were admitted to the general wards of St Bartholomew's
Hospital.[1]

Indeed, the chief indictment of hospital work at this period is
not that it did no good but that it positively did harm. Contemporary accounts of the unsatisfactory conditions in eighteenth-century hospitals are available in the writings of
Percival, Howard, and others,[2] and we have already referred to
the very bad results of surgery and institutional midwifery.
The common cause of death was infectious disease; any patient
admitted to hospital faced the risk of contracting a mortal
infection. This risk existed until the second half of the nineteenth century, when Florence Nightingale found civil hospitals
'just as bad or worse' than military hospitals, and introduced
her *Notes on Hospitals* with the well-known observation that the
first requirement in a hospital is 'that it should do the sick no
harm'. This objective was certainly not realized during the
eighteenth century; it was not until much later that hospital
patients could be reasonably certain of dying from the disease
with which they were admitted.

It is somewhat more difficult to assess the influence of the
dispensary movement in the second half of the eighteenth
century. The first London dispensary was founded in 1769, and
sixteen more were added before 1800. Unquestionably they
brought treatment within the reach of a greater number of poor

---

[1] W. M. Frazer, *A History of English Public Health, 1834–1939* (London, 1950),
p. 152.
[2] For a description of the poor conditions in French hospitals see Tenon,
Mémoires sur les hôpitaux de Paris (Paris, 1788).

people, but whether the treatment was of any value is another matter. We have already seen that few of the medicines available in the eighteenth century would now be judged to be of value. Moreover, their usefulness was restricted by inability to identify the conditions in which they should be given and by lack of knowledge of methods of administration. It is evident that the therapy administered from dispensaries was no better, even if no worse, than that available in hospitals and private practice.

Yet it is possible that dispensaries made a more important, if less specific, contribution to health. According to Lettsom,[1] they had a substantial effect upon sanitary standards, by teaching the importance of cleanliness and ventilation. Their contribution is comparable to that of obstetricians who added nothing to the safety of the act of delivery, but justified their presence in the labour room by recommending improved standards of hygiene.

(e) PREVENTIVE THERAPY

The only disease upon which specific preventive therapy could conceivably have had a substantial effect during the eighteenth century was smallpox. Throughout the century about 10 per cent of the deaths recorded in the London Bills of Mortality were attributed to smallpox, and a marked reduction in its incidence would undoubtedly have been reflected in national mortality trends.

Vaccination was not introduced until the beginning of the nineteenth century, the procedure used earlier being inoculation with infected material obtained from patients with smallpox. This was practised on a modest scale between 1721 and 1728, rarely used during the next twelve years, and revived in 1740. Inoculation was an expensive as well as a dangerous practice, and after preliminary trials on convicts it was at first mainly restricted to the upper classes. But in the later years of the eighteenth century charitable funds made it possible for large numbers of persons of all classes to be inoculated.

In Creighton's opinion inoculation was not a success. He stated that 'the ordinary course of smallpox in Britain was little

---

[1] J. C. Lettsom, *On the Improvement of Medicine in London on the Basis of Public Good*, 2nd edn. (London, 1775), p. 51.

touched by inoculation'.[1] Not all historians of infectious disease agree with this view.[2] But in the present context it will suffice to note that in the London Bills of Mortality both (*a*) the number of deaths attributed to smallpox and (*b*) the proportion of all deaths attributed to smallpox remained fairly constant throughout the eighteenth century.[3] These observations are, of course, consistent with a reduction in incidence if the population was increasing and the death-rate from all causes decreasing. But with due regard for the unreliability of death registration, and for the unrepresentative character of the London Bills of Mortality, it is hard to believe that inoculation can have been responsible for a reduction in the incidence of smallpox large enough to have had a substantial effect on national mortality trends.

(*f*) CONTROL OF THE ENVIRONMENT

We have concluded that the therapeutic measures employed by doctors, whether in the field of preventive or curative medicine, could have had no appreciable effect on eighteenth-century mortality trends. Indeed, it might safely be said that specific medical treatment had no useful effects at all, were it not for some doubts about the results of the use of mercury in syphilis, iron in anaemia, cinchona in malaria, and inoculation against smallpox. But during the century doctors began to interest themselves in a far more significant if less spectacular field: they started to explore the association between environment and disease. The most important contributions are too well known to require detailed comment, but the dates of publication are of interest: Mead's *Short Discourse concerning Pestilential Contagion, and the Methods to be used to Prevent it*, 1720; Pringle's *Observations on the Diseases of the Army*, 1752; Lind's *Treatise on Scurvy*, 1753; Baker's *An Essay concerning the cause of the Endemial Colic of Devonshire*, 1767; Blane's *Observations on the Diseases of Seamen*, 1785.

---

[1] C. Creighton, *A History of Epidemics in Britain*, Vol. II (Cambridge, 1894), p. 516.

[2] Professor Shrewsbury, for example, believes that inoculation influenced smallpox mortality (personal communication).

[3] G. Blane, *A Statement of Facts Tending to Establish an Estimate of the True Value and Present State of Vaccination* (London, 1820), p. 17.

Each of these works was important; collectively they represented an immense advance in understanding of the influence of the environment on disease, particularly infectious disease. It was not, of course, an understanding based on knowledge of the mechanism of infection; it was derived empirically by noting the association between sickness and bad living conditions. But some of the simple measures prescribed by Mead as early as 1720 – better housing, cleanliness, ventilation, disinfection, control of nuisances – were those applied extensively during the nineteenth century, for whose effectiveness the science of bacteriology finally provided a rational explanation.

There is thus no doubt that early in the eighteenth century a few doctors were alive to the significance of the environment in relation to health. What interests us in the present context is whether their teaching made any immediate impact on hygienic practices. We propose to leave the question open at this point, and to return to it in Section V. For the present we conclude that specific medical treatment had no effect on population trends during the eighteenth century, and any influence exerted by doctors resulted from their contribution to improved living conditions.

(2) RELATIVE INFLUENCE OF THE BIRTH-RATE AND
DEATH-RATE ON POPULATION ACCORDING TO
THE LEVELS OF THE TWO RATES

It would probably be generally agreed that no statistics are available which put the relative importance of the birth-rate and death-rate during the eighteenth century beyond dispute. In these circumstances interpretation of the existing evidence is inevitably influenced by the point of view from which it is approached. Griffith, for example, approached the matter with the conviction that medical effort had had a substantial effect on the death-rate. Habakkuk, on the other hand, was not persuaded that medical measures were important, but was impressed by the apparent significance of the birth-rate in certain pre-industrial societies. Before considering once again the uncertainties of the statistical evidence, it seems worth while to inquire in what circumstances an increase in the birth-rate or a decrease in the death-rate is the more likely primary cause of a rise in population.

At the outset we should recognize that the probable influence of the two rates is mainly determined by their levels. When both rates are high it is very much easier to increase the population by reducing the death-rate than by increasing the birth-rate; when the rates are low the reverse is true.

(*a*) WHEN THE BIRTH-RATE AND DEATH-RATE ARE HIGH

The relatively high death-rates in some countries today, and in all countries in the recent past, are chiefly attributable to a high incidence of infectious diseases. The incidence of infection is largely determined by environmental conditions, and when it is high even modest improvements in the environment are very rapidly reflected in a reduced death-rate. This reduction mainly affects young children and infants: unless offset by a decline in fertility, it results, first, in an increase in population; second, in a temporary reduction in the birth-rate (because the number of persons alive is increased, but not at once, proportionately, the number of births); and third, in a rise in the birth-rate, as young people who have survived reach reproductive age.[1] Hence when the death-rate is high relatively small improvements in environmental conditions will be reflected immediately in an increase of population, and later in a rise in the birth-rate.[2]

It is much more difficult to effect an increase in population by a primary increase in the birth-rate when that rate is already high. Natural fertility sets limits to the number of children

---

[1] These conclusions are consistent with Lorimer's projection of populations having initially high mortality and fertility rates. He examined a transition from Indian to Japanese levels of mortality, on the assumption that the birth-rate at each age remained constant, while the death-rate at each age declined to reach, at the end of thirty years, the level of the Japanese life table for 1926–30: there were large decreases in death-rates over a wide range of ages, and especially in the ages of infancy and early childhood. The saving of lives at the early ages had a strong influence in accelerating the rate of population growth, and the proportion of children under 15 rose slightly. F. Lorimer, 'Dynamics of Age Structure in a Population with initially high Fertility and Mortality', in United Nations: *Population Bulletin* No. 1, 1951, p. 31.

[2] This seems to us the most acceptable explanation of Yule's observation that in several European countries a falling death-rate was associated with a rising birth-rate. G. U. Yule, 'The Growth of Population and the Factors which Control It', *Journal of the Royal Statistical Society*, LXXXVIII (1925), 1.

born, and unless the rate of reproduction has previously been artificially restricted (for example, by contraception, or by changes in frequency or age of marriage) it cannot be much increased. That is to say when the birth-rate is very high it can scarcely increase much except in consequence of a shift in the age distribution of the population (secondary to reduced mortality, as suggested above).

(*b*) WHEN THE BIRTH-RATE AND DEATH-RATE ARE LOW

When both rates are low it is evidently easier to influence population by increasing the birth-rate than by lowering mortality. The low birth-rate is voluntarily restricted, and could be increased voluntarily, for example in response to improved economic conditions. But lack of medical knowledge sets limits to the extent to which mortality can be reduced, even among individuals in the most favourable environmental circumstances. For example, inspection of the common causes of infant deaths indicates that without new knowledge infant mortality is unlikely to be reduced much below about 15 (per 1,000 live births); nor can we yet add appreciably to expectation of life of persons in the older age groups.

Finally, we must consider the situation when the death-rate is high and the birth-rate is not. (For although no one is likely to question that mortality was high throughout the eighteenth century, it is evidently not generally accepted that the birth-rate was also. Habakkuk's conclusion that economic conditions influenced the birth-rate presupposes that it was restricted at certain periods.) Even in these circumstances there are reasons for believing that an increase in the rate would be unlikely to have much influence on population so long as mortality rates remain high. In the first place the deaths of a considerable proportion of children within a few years of birth substantially reduce the effect on population. Secondly, because mortality in infancy is sharply related to family size, the increasing birth-rate would be still further compensated by an increase in mortality due to increasing family size. This is true of the relatively small families and low mortality rates of today.[1] The

---

[1] For example, in Birmingham in 1947 infant mortality was generally more than twice as great among fourth and later children than among first born, and about eight times as great in the case of children in the poorest environment.

effect must have been much more marked in the eighteenth century when families were larger and mortality greater. The increase in mortality would be expected unless the change in the birth-rate were mainly due to an increase in the number of one-child families. This would require a substantial increase in the proportion of women who marry, which we later suggest did not change much.[1]

To sum up. The relative difficulty of effecting an increase in population by reducing the death-rate or increasing the birth-rate is determined by the levels of the two rates. High mortality rates are mainly due to a high incidence of infectious disease, and are very sensitive to improvements in the environment. Reduction of mortality from infection has an immediate effect on population, and since it mainly affects infants and young children, may also have a delayed effect from a secondary rise in the birth-rate. So long as mortality remains high, an increase in the birth-rate can have relatively little influence on population growth, first, because a high proportion of children die shortly after birth, and second, because the proportion who die increases as the birth-rate increases. These considerations lead us to conclude that when mortality is high a reduction in mortality is inherently a more plausible explanation of population growth than is a rise in the birth-rate.

(3) THE BIRTH-RATE

We now examine the possibility that a rise in the birth-rate was the primary cause of the increase in population during the second half of the eighteenth century. The birth-rate in a given year is determined by: (1) the proportion of the population which consists of women of child-bearing age, and (2) the

---

The higher death-rates experienced by late-born children were almost entirely due to infectious disease. J. R. Gibson and T. McKeown, 'Observations on All Births (23,970) in Birmingham, 1947, VII. The Effect of Changing Family Size on Infant Mortality', *British Journal of Social Medicine*, VI (1952), 183.

[1] The high level of fertility observed among women who married late during the nineteenth century makes it unlikely that changes in age at marriage would have much influence on the proportion of one-child families. England and Wales, *Census 1911, Vol. 13. 'Fertility of Marriage, Part 2'*, Table XLIV, p. xcvii.

C

number of live children born during the year to women of child-bearing age.

(1) The proportion of the female population[1] which consists of women of child-bearing age may increase as a result of: (*a*) an increase in the birth-rate, or (*b*) a change (increase or decrease) in mortality rates which favours females in or below the reproductive age groups more than those in older age groups. It follows from what has been said above that because of high early mortality and the marked association between mortality rates and family size, an increase in the birth-rate would need to be very substantial to have much influence on the age distribution of the female population when mortality from infection is high, unless accompanied by a reduction in mortality rates. If this is true a substantial increase in the proportion of females in reproductive age groups is unlikely to have occurred except as a secondary effect of a change in mortality.

(2) If we ignore variations in the incidence of illegitimacy the number of children born to women of child-bearing age is determined by: (*a*) the proportion of women who marry; (*b*) mean age of women at marriage; (*c*) reproductive capacity[2] of married women; and (*d*) the extent of deliberate limitation of family size.

(*a*) It is recognized that there is an association between economic circumstances and marriage rates. Data for England and Wales examined by Glass show a high correlation ($r = 0 \cdot 706 \pm 0 \cdot 065$) between marriage rate and an index of real wages during the period 1856–1932.[3] But the correlation is mainly determined by changes in age at marriage, rather than by variation in the proportion of women who ultimately marry. This is suggested by the fact that between 1851 and 1911 the

---

[1] Although the incidence of some causes of death, including some infectious diseases, is different in the two sexes, it seems to us permissible in this context to consider only changes in the age composition of the female population. That is to say we are assuming that the sex ratio of the total population did not change very much.

[2] 'Reproductive capacity' is used in the sense in which it was employed by the Royal Commission on Population (1949), in preference to the more ambiguous terms: fertility and fecundity.

[3] D. V. Glass, 'Marriage Frequency and Economic Fluctuations in England and Wales, 1851 to 1934', in L. Hogben (ed.), *Political Arithmetic* (London, 1938), p. 266.

percentage of persons married varied between 19 (1911) and 28 per cent (1871) for ages 20–24, but remained fairly constant at 86–88 per cent for ages 50–54.[1] From 1851, from which time data are fairly complete, a woman's chance of getting married before the age of 50 fluctuated between 82 (in 1910–12) and 96 per cent (in 1940).[2] Since the proportion of women who can marry is considerably below 100 per cent (it is well below 96 per cent for any prolonged period) – because of the greater proportion of women than of men in the adult population – it is clear that at no time since 1851 has there been scope for a substantial increase. There is no evidence that frequency of marriage was substantially lower in the eighteenth century.[3] Data examined by Griffith[4] and Marshall[5] show no considerable increase in English marriage rates during the second half of the century; reliable statistics are not available for the first half.

(*b*) It seems to us that we should require very strong evidence before accepting the view that changes in age at marriage had a substantial influence on the mean number of children born to women of child-bearing age during the eighteenth century. As suggested above, the correlation between marriage rates and economic conditions is almost certainly attributable to variation in age at marriage, rather than to changes in the proportions who ultimately marry. But it does not follow that variation in age at marriage was substantial, for the high correlations are quite compatible with relatively small changes in mean age. For example, in England and Wales for the years 1890–1907 and 1926–32 correlations between marriage rate and an index of real wages were 0·603 and 0·677 respectively;

[1] *Report of the Royal Commission on Population*, Table XIII, p. 22 (London, 1949).

[2] PEP. *Population Policy in Great Britain* (London, 1948), p. 1.

[3] According to Swedish estimates, in 1750 only 74·6 per cent of women aged 45–49 were married. But the proportion of men married in 1750 at the same age was 91 per cent and the proportions of women aged 45–49 married in 1900 and 1940 were 71·2 per cent and 69·3 per cent respectively. This suggests that the relatively low proportion of women married in 1750 was determined by the low proportion of men in the adult population. H. Gille, 'The Demographic History of the Northern European Countries in the Eighteenth Century', *Population Studies*, Vol. III, 1949–50, p. 27.

[4] Griffith, op. cit., p. 34.

[5] T. H. Marshall, 'The Population Problem during the Industrial Revolution', *Economic Journal*, 1929, p. 444.

yet changes in mean age at marriage of women during the period 1896–1951 were trivial.[1]

Moreover, there are reasons for believing that postponement of marriage would have less influence on the number of live births than is commonly supposed. In the first place there is no evidence that within fairly wide limits age of husband has any biological influence on reproductive capacity, and when they postpone marriage men frequently marry women younger than themselves. In England and Wales in 1911, when postponement is believed to have been common,[2] men at all ages over 21 married wives younger than themselves, and the difference in mean age increased as age at marriage increased: mean ages of wives of men aged 22 and 35–39 were 21·98 and 31·97 respectively.[3] In Ireland, where postponement of marriage is common, it is also more marked among men than among women: in 1936 proportions unmarried in the age group 35–39 were 48·4 and 32·8 per cent for males and females respectively.[4] Secondly, in the absence of widespread birth control a moderate increase in mean age at marriage does not have a very marked effect on fertility. For women married 30–35 years in rural Ireland in 1911, whose ages at marriage were under 20, 20–24, 25–29, and 30–34, mean numbers of live births were 8·81, 8·04, 6·79, and 5·57 respectively.[5] The impression that fertility drops sharply with increasing age derives from consideration of the general population of women who marry relatively early. In these circumstances mothers who have a first child late have smaller families than those who have a first child early, partly because the remaining reproductive period is shorter, and partly because the birth of a first child at a late age means that on the average they are less fertile. The comparison provides no reliable information about the number of children to be expected when women of normal fertility postpone reproduction. The best indication of the effect of

[1] Glass, loc. cit.; *74th Annual Report of the Registrar-General*, 1911, Table VII, p. xvii; General Register Office, *Statistical Review, Tables, Part II, Civil, 1951*, Table 1, p. 71 (London, 1953).

[2] *Report of the Royal Commission on Population*, p. 22.

[3] From data in *74th Annual Report of the Registrar-General*, p. 132.

[4] Ireland. *Census of Population* (1936), Vol. V, Part 1, p. 217.

[5] D. V. Glass and E. Grebenik, *The Trend and Pattern of Fertility in Great Britain*, Part 1, p. 271 (London, 1954).

postponement of childbirth among normal women is obtained by relating mean numbers of liveborn children to age at marriage (as above), or by examining the proportion of women who were childless according to age at marriage.[1]

In short, if we may accept the Irish data as a rough guide to the effect of postponement of marriage on the number of live-born children in families whose size is not intentionally restricted it appears that an advance in mean age of wives at marriage of about five years would be needed to reduce the mean number of live births by one. Since 1896 mean age of women at marriage in England and Wales has varied by little more than a fraction of a year (range: 25·66–27·14).[2] Unless we are prepared to believe that changes in age at marriage in the eighteenth century were of quite a different order, it seems unlikely that they can have had a very marked influence on the mean number of live births per family.

(*c*) A third influence affecting the mean number of children born to women of child-bearing age is reproductive capacity, and it has been suggested that it may have fluctuated during the eighteenth century as a result of disease, changes of diet, and other environmental influences. This possibility cannot be excluded. But the effect of such influences on reproductive capacity – defined as the ability to conceive and give birth to living children – must have been small as compared with their effect on mortality in infancy. Post-natal mortality is incomparably more sensitive to change in the environment than is either the conception rate or pre-natal mortality.[3]

(*d*) The only methods of limiting family size which could conceivably have been effective during the eighteenth century were abstinence, abortion, and *coitus interruptus*. Needless to say,

---

[1] D. V. Glass and E. Grebenik, *The Trend and Pattern of Fertility in Great Britain*, Part I, p. 96 (London, 1954).

[2] *74th Annual Report of the Registrar-General*, p. xvii; General Register Office, 1953, op. cit., p. 71.

[3] It is well recognized that of the four relevant rates – conception rate, abortion rate, stillbirth rate, and infant mortality rate – the fourth has responded much more sharply than the other three to improvements in the environment since 1900. This difference must have been even more conspicuous during the eighteenth century, when mortality from infection was much higher. In Sweden the stillbirth rate has not altered to any appreciable extent since 1751: Gille reported stillbirth rates of 24·8 (per 1,000 total births) in 1751–60 and 27·9 in 1936–40, op. cit., p. 32.

we have no worthwhile information about them. Abstinence was recommended by Malthus and others as the only acceptable means of avoiding pregnancy, but it is doubtful whether it has ever had much influence on population trends. It is agreed that abortion is now very common:[1] but the two effective methods – insertion of a foreign body into the cervix of the uterus and interference by a professional abortionist – cannot have been either common or safe until recent times. Again, the probability of death of the child after birth must have made termination of unwanted pregnancies less urgent than it is today,[2] and it is believed that the incidence of abortion increased during the second half of the nineteenth century.[3] *Coitus interruptus* is among the oldest forms of contraception; it is less reliable than the alternative methods now available, and to be effective requires more self-control than is usually credited to the majority of people. Nevertheless, the early fall in the French birth-rate is usually attributed to withdrawal.[4] Kuczynski,[5] however, found little evidence of the practice of birth control in the English demographic literature of the century preceding the Industrial Revolution, and there is no reason to believe that it was common during the later years of the eighteenth century. Recent experience of countries such as Puerto Rico[6] and Japan[7] indicates that even when effective methods of contraception are readily available, an appreciable reduction in fertility cannot be rapidly effected.

This examination of possible causes of a change in the birth-rate leads us to conclude that a substantial increase is unlikely to have occurred during the eighteenth century, except as a

[1] The literature is reviewed in the 'Report of the Biological and Medical Committee on Reproductive Wastage', *Papers of the Royal Commission on Population*, Vol. 4 (London, 1950).

[2] If the average risk of death of children was anything like so high as suggested by Garnett and others (cited by Griffith, op. cit., p. 242) the probability of death of an unwanted child must have been very high indeed.

[3] *Report of the Royal Commission on Population*, p. 33; United Nations, *The Determinants and Consequences of Population Trends* (1953), p. 76.

[4] *Report of the Royal Commission on Population*, p. 37.

[5] R. R. Kuczynski, 'British Demographers' Opinions on Fertility 1600–1760', in L. Hogben (ed.), *Political Arithmetic* (London, 1938), p. 283.

[6] J. L. Janer, World Population Conference, Rome, 1954.

[7] T. Honda, World Population Conference, Rome, 1954; I. B. Tacuber and E. G. Beal, 'The Dynamics of Population in Japan', in *Demographic Studies of Selected Areas of Rapid Growth* (New York, 1944), Milbank Memorial Fund.

secondary result of a reduction of mortality. Moreover, the effect of an increase in the birth-rate on population would be seriously reduced by post-natal mortality. Infant mortality (deaths in the first year of life) cannot have been less than 200 per 1,000 live births (the rate was 150 in 1900), and was probably considerably more. The extent of mortality in childhood is exhibited in a table prepared from data reported by Bland,[1] who gave numbers of previous live births and surviving children for 1,389 pregnant women attending the Westminster Dispensary between 1774 and 1781. However large the number of previous live births, the mean number of surviving children is in no case higher than 3·38.

Mortality according to parity. (From data for the West-minster General Dispensary, 1774–81, reported by Bland, 1781.)

Parity (number of previous children)	Number of women (a)	Total number of children born (b)	Total number of children living (c)	Proportion of children surviving $\left(\dfrac{c}{b}\right)$	Mean number of children surviving $\left(\dfrac{c}{a}\right)$
1–2	553	807	430	0·53	0·78
3–4	377	1,300	592	0·46	1·57
5–6	227	1,224	502	0·41	2·21
7–8	130	966	364	0·38	2·80
9–10	55	517	177	0·34	3·22
11–24	47	605	159	0·26	3·38
Total	1,389	5,419	2,224	0·41	1·60

The data also exhibit an association between the proportion of surviving children and parity, and while this association is, of course, considerably influenced by the different periods at risk (children in nine-child families had a much longer period at risk than children in one-child families) mortality was evidently affected by family size. For example, in families with nine to ten previous children two in three died within a few years of birth. It can scarcely be doubted that this death-rate was much higher than the average for all children. If this is true, the influence of a rise in the birth-rate on population would have been largely offset by a secondary rise in mortality (because children would mainly be added to existing families).

[1] Bland, op. cit., p. 366.

To sum up: Of the possible causes of an increase in the birth-rate during the eighteenth century the only one which seems to us to merit serious attention is a decrease in age at marriage. It is suggested that so long as mortality rates remained high a change in age at marriage is unlikely to have had a substantial influence on growth of population. This conclusion is based on the following considerations:

(*a*) Within wide limits, age of husband has no biological influence on fertility, and postponement of age of marriage is less marked in the case of women than of men.

(*b*) Unless eighteenth-century changes in age at marriage were very much more marked than those recorded in the nineteenth and twentieth centuries, their effect on the birth-rate is unlikely to have been large.

(*c*) An increase in the birth-rate would have been due chiefly to addition of children to existing families, rather than to an increase in the number of one-child families. Since mortality from infectious disease in infancy and child-hood increases sharply with increasing family size, any increase in the birth-rate would have been largely offset by an increase in post-natal mortality.

(4) THE DEATH-RATE

We have already suggested reasons for believing that the primary cause of the rise in population was not an increase in the birth-rate, and now inquire whether from a medical viewpoint it seems more reasonable to attribute it to a change in mortality rates. So far as we are aware, the statement that mortality declined during the later years of the eighteenth century has not been seriously questioned: it was accepted by contemporary writers, and supported by statistical evidence examined by Rickman, Farr, Brownlee, Griffith, and others. What has been questioned is the view that a decrease in mortality was the primary cause of the increase in population, rather than a secondary 'result of changes in the age composition of the population brought about by the rising birth-rate of earlier decades'.[1]

[1] Habakkuk, op. cit., p. 127.

Griffith's interpretation has been so widely accepted that its rejection may be thought seriously to weaken the evidence for the significance of mortality. But medical effort is only one of the possible causes of a reduction of mortality, and the conclusion that it had no substantial influence merely leaves the relative importance of the birth-rate and the death-rate an open question.

There is little doubt about two important points concerning interpretation of mortality trends during the second half of the eighteenth century. Firstly, death-rates were consistently much higher than modern rates for England and Wales. Mortality rates prepared by Brownlee and Griffith[1] for the third quarter of the century are all above 25 (per 1,000 population). Secondly, with due regard for the unreliability of medical diagnosis, there can be no doubt that the high mortality was chiefly attributable to infectious disease,[2] whose incidence was much greater in infancy and childhood than in adult life. Brownlee[3] estimated mortality in London during the first two years of life to be 300–400 (per 1,000 live births) and according to Edmonds,[4] 51·5 per cent of infants baptized in London in the period 1770–89 were dead before the age of 5. The association between mortality and age was shown by Bland[5] from information given by pregnant women attending the Westminster Dispensary between 1774 and 1781; he concluded that 5 of 12 children born were dead before the age of 2, and 7 of 10 before the age of 26. His estimate was based on the erroneous premise that mortality and frequency of births are unrelated to family size, but in spite of this error, it is certain that mortality was highest shortly after birth. The same conclusion emerges from Brownlee's data.

We must now consider the central question: if we accept the view that medicine made no specific contribution, is it likely

[1] J. R. Brownlee, 'The History of the Birth and Death Rates in England and Wales taken as a Whole, from 1750 to the Present Time', *Public Health*, XIX (1916), 211, 228. Griffith, op. cit., p. 35.

[2] Creighton, op. cit., *passim*. J. R. McCulloch, *Descriptive and Statistical Account of the British Empire* (London, 1854), vol. II, p. 610.

[3] J. R. Brownlee, 'The Health of London in the 18th Century', *Proceedings of the Royal Society of Medicine*, XVIII (1925), 75.

[4] T. R. Edmonds, 'On the Mortality of Infants in England', *The Lancet*, 1835, i, p. 692.

[5] Bland, op. cit., p. 369.

that the observed decline in mortality was anything more than a secondary phenomenon? To answer this question we must turn once again to evidence from the nineteenth century, when a decline in mortality was brought about by a reduction in the incidence of infectious disease, and was almost wholly independent of specific therapy. (The only medical procedure which can be accepted as having made a substantial contribution earlier than the twentieth century was vaccination, and its influence was limited to a single disease.) As stated previously, Griffith and others who considered this matter were completely mistaken in attaching great significance to growth of hospitals and other medical institutions.

It may be asked whether we are entitled to draw conclusions about what may have happened in the late eighteenth century from what we believe happened in the late nineteenth. Between 1775 and 1850 there had undoubtedly been a considerable reduction of mortality, and some change in the relative importance of different infectious diseases as causes of death. Nevertheless, in respect of the two matters referred to above which affect the interpretation of mortality trends (the predominant position of the infectious diseases and the very high death-rates in infancy and early childhood) the position was virtually unchanged. We conclude that the decline in mortality in the second half of the eighteenth century could have been independent of a rise in the birth-rate.

Because it is based on a nineteenth-century analogy, the last conclusion has been stated cautiously. But it gains considerable support from the fact that the alternative explanation which ascribes the fall in the death-rate to a secondary effect of a rising birth-rate is unacceptable. It is evident that a reduction in mortality which was most marked at early ages would probably, though not certainly, be followed by a secondary rise in the birth-rate. But as suggested previously, at a time when mortality from infection was high a rising birth-rate would inevitably be followed by a substantial increase in mortality: (a) because new births added to the population enter the most vulnerable age groups, and (b) because mortality in the vulnerable age groups would probably increase, since expansion of the population would mainly be due to an increase in size of existing families.

Moreover, unlike a rising birth-rate, which we have suggested would have relatively little effect on population when mortality is high, a declining death-rate would be very effective. Every death prevented makes an immediate addition to the population; the addition is most commonly in the younger age groups, where expectation of life is longest once the hazards of the first few years are passed; and a rise in the birth-rate is a probable secondary result of the decline in mortality.

Professor Habakkuk concluded that the birth-rate was more important than the death-rate, and that 'the most likely causes of differences in the birth-rate were the age at and frequency of marriage'.[1] In coming to this conclusion he was influenced by views expressed by other writers about certain pre-industrial societies.

(i) The slow growth of population in France in the late eighteenth century, for example, was attributed to a low birth-rate, largely on the grounds that 'there is no reason to suppose that the French death-rate was unusually high'. It is generally believed that the French birth-rate declined during the last years of the century,[2] but the statistics are certainly no more reliable than English data for the same period, and scarcely permit a confident assessment of the relative importance of the birth-rate and death-rate. For what they are worth, the mortality rates quoted by Spengler for the eighteenth century[3] are a little higher than the corresponding English rates.[4]

(ii) The rapid increase in population in colonial America was said to be due primarily to a high birth-rate. But data provided by Lotka[5] do not justify this conclusion. He had no information about eighteenth-century mortality rates, and merely estimated the average number of live births per married woman, according to certain assumptions about mortality. From a medical viewpoint it seems more probable that the rapid increase in

---

[1] Habakkuk, op. cit., p. 123.

[2] The decline of the French birth-rate during the nineteenth century was attributed to control of conception, probably mainly by withdrawal. No opinion was expressed about the reason for the decline in the late eighteenth century. United Nations, op. cit., 1953, p. 72.

[3] J. J. Spengler, *France Faces Depopulation* (Durham, North Carolina, 1938), p. 41.

[4] Brownlee, 1916, loc. cit.

[5] A. J. Lotka, 'The Size of American Families in the 18th Century', *Journal of the American Statistical Association*, XXII (1927), 154.

population resulted from a relatively low incidence of infectious disease in a thinly populated country. The much publicized risk of death from violence in the new world was almost certainly less serious than the risk of death from infection in the old.

(iii) Attention was also directed to recent work on the acceleration of population growth in Ireland after 1780, which Connell attributes to economic improvements affecting age at and fertility of marriage.[1] But his only demographic data prior to the census of 1821 were estimates of population derived from hearth-money returns, and his argument is largely based on literary sources which do not consistently support it. It seems at least as likely that the agrarian improvements which he suggests occurred in the late eighteenth century, particularly the improvement in quality and quantity of the potato crop, were effective in reducing mortality in childhood.[2] Connell supports his views by reference to early nineteenth-century statistics, from which he infers higher fertility: (*a*) of earlier marriages in Ireland than in England, and (*b*) in rural than in urban Ireland. It is true that age at marriage was a little lower in Ireland in 1830–40 than in England and Wales in 1847;[3] but the difference was considerable only at ages under 20 (when proportions married were 28·1 and 11·3 per cent respectively) and was small at ages under 25 (66·5 and 62·2 per cent respectively). At a period when mortality was high, in the absence of birth control, differences in age at marriage of this order could be expected to have little influence on fertility. Connell's conclusion that fertility was substantially affected is based on a comparison which can scarcely be accepted, between fertility of Irish marriages in 1831 with that of English marriages in 1901[4] when measures of birth control were widespread. There is in fact little difference between crude birth-rates for Ireland in 1832–41[5] and for England and Wales in the same period.[6] Connell's data[7] suggest that in the early nineteenth century birth-rates were highest in rural areas, where there had been

---

[1] K. H. Connell, *The Population of Ireland 1750–1845* (Oxford, 1950).

[2] The infant mortality rate in Ireland in 1840 (129, estimated from data given by Connell: pp. 193, 267) compares favourably with that for England and Wales in 1841–5 (148: General Register Office, *Statistical Review, Tables, Part 1, Medical,* Table 3).

[3] Connell, op. cit., p. 39.   [4] Ibid., p. 31.   [5] Ibid., p. 261
[6] Brownlee, 1916, loc. cit.   [7] Connell, op. cit., pp. 247, 261

the greatest increase in population. But urban–rural differences were more marked in mortality than in fertility. The number of births in 1840 (per 1,000 women aged 16–45) was 14 per cent higher in rural than in civic districts,[1] and the infant mortality rate in 1840 (derived from Connell's data)[2] was 36 per cent lower.

(iv) As another example of the influence of the birth-rate on growth of population Habakkuk cites modern Brittany. It is true that Aries attributes the relatively dense population of Brittany to a high birth-rate,[3] but this is probably due to the absence of birth control in a modern community which has retained to a considerable extent a primitive way of life, and the observation has little bearing on growth of population in the eighteenth century.

In short, none of the pre-industrial societies to which we have referred seems to us to provide clear evidence of the influence of the birth-rate on population. Moreover, Swedish data, which are generally acknowledged to be the most reliable for any European country during the eighteenth century, suggest that the death-rate was more important than the birth-rate at the beginning of its industrial development. The population of Sweden increased by 28 per cent between 1761–5, and 1806–10, and by 54 per cent between 1811–15 and 1856–60.[4] For the two fifty-year periods respectively mean birth-rates (per 1,000 population) were 32·60 and 32·58, and mean death-rates 27·56 and 22·69.[5] Infant mortality (deaths in the first year of life per 1,000 live births) fell continuously from 216·1 in 1761–70 to 198·7 (1801–10), and from 183·4 (1811–20) to 146·0 (1851–60).[6]

We may now summarize our reasons for preferring a decrease in the death-rate to an increase in the birth-rate as an explanation of the rise in population in the eighteenth century. We have regarded the view that both rates changed as being established, our task being to decide whether the one was more

[1] Connell, op. cit., p. 36.
[2] Ibid., pp. 193, 267.
[3] P. Aries, *Histoire des Populations Françaises* (Paris, 1948), p. 32.
[4] From data provided by R. R. Kuczynski, *The Balance of Births and Deaths* (New York, 1928), p. 99.
[5] From data provided by A. Myrdal, *Nation and Family* (London, 1945), p. 20.
[6] Myrdal, loc. cit.

important than the other. Three observations are of first-rate importance: according to modern standards mortality was excessively high; the high death-rates were mainly due to infectious disease; and the highest risks were experienced by infants and young children. The level of the birth-rate seems to us to be less significant, although in general it was undoubtedly high.

Of the possible causes of an increase in the birth-rate, it is suggested that only a change in age at marriage requires serious consideration. The effect of postponement of marriage on fertility is probably less marked than has been thought, because when men delay marriage they usually marry women younger than themselves (in this context age of husband has no independent significance), and the decline in fertility with increasing age of wife is smaller than is commonly supposed. It is suggested that a change in mean age of marriage during the eighteenth century is unlikely to have been great enough to have had a substantial effect on the birth-rate. But perhaps more important, so long as mortality from infection remained high, a rise in the birth-rate would have relatively little effect on population, because a high proportion of children die shortly after birth. The proportion dying would be greater than the prevailing mortality rates suggest, because the additional children would chiefly be added to existing families, and mortality increases sharply with increasing family size.

Under the conditions which we have described, the fall in the death-rate could have been due to a reduction in the incidence of infectious disease, even in the absence of a specific medical contribution, as it was in the nineteenth century. It is hard to believe that it could have been secondary to a rising birth-rate, since an increase in the birth-rate would have been followed by an increase in mortality. Moreover, a primary reduction in mortality from infection would have a pronounced effect on population, both because the reduction is greatest in young age groups, where expectation of life is longest, and because a rise in the birth-rate is a probable secondary result.

These conclusions seem to us to be supported by the most reliable statistics available for a country in the same phase of its development, those for Sweden, and to be not contradicted by statistics of various pre-industrial societies which have been thought to show the influence of the birth-rate on population. We turn now to an examination of possible causes of a reduction in the incidence of infectious disease.

(5) POSSIBLE CAUSES OF A REDUCTION OF MORTALITY

We must now consider what is perhaps from a public viewpoint the most important question in medical history: To what do we owe the reduction of mortality from infectious disease? Having regard to its importance, it is surprising that this question has had so little attention; Greenwood[1] is one of the few epidemiologists who have seriously considered it.

The possible causes of a reduction of mortality can be grouped under three headings: (*a*) specific preventive or curative therapy; (*b*) improvements in the environment; and (*c*) a change in the balance between the virulence of the infective organism and the resistance of the host.

The relative importance of these three groups of causes is not the same in different infectious diseases. For example, it is probable that the disappearance of cholera resulted from purification of water supplies; that the virtual elimination of smallpox owes much to vaccination; that the prolonged decline in mortality from tuberculosis is mainly attributable to a general improvement in living conditions; and that the change in scarlet fever from a serious killing disease to a relatively trivial complaint owes little or nothing to therapy or environmental change, and is almost certainly the result of a modification of the virulence of the streptococcus, or of man's resistance to it. In short, to provide a satisfactory answer to the question about the cause of a reduction of mortality, we should require separate and detailed consideration of each infectious disease. Tuberculosis[2] is one of the few diseases in which such an examination has been made.

In these circumstances it may be asked whether any generalizations about the cause of the decline in mortality from infection are permissible. The conclusion which we regard as most important in the present context is a negative one: it is that the fall in the death-rate during the eighteenth and nineteenth

---

[1] M. Greenwood, *Epidemics and Crowd-Diseases* (London, 1935).

[2] V. H. Springett, 'An Interpretation of Statistical Trends in Tuberculosis', *The Lancet*, 1952, i, pp. 521, 575.

centuries was not the result of medical treatment, as Griffith and others have supposed. Only in the case of vaccination against smallpox is there any clear evidence that specific therapy had a substantial effect on the prevention or cure of disease earlier than the twentieth century. The decline in mortality from diseases other than smallpox was due to improvement in living conditions, and to changes in virulence and resistance upon which human effort had no influence.

About the relative importance of environment and of changes in virulence and resistance no firm opinion can be expressed. The relationship between an infective organism and its host is a constantly changing one, which reflects the inter-action of nature and nurture in both, and in centuries earlier than the eighteenth there were undoubtedly periods of increase and decrease in the incidence of infection which were largely independent of changes in the environment. The question arises: Is it possible that the reduction of the incidence of infec-tion during the eighteenth and nineteenth centuries was wholly the result of a natural change in infectivity and resistance?

Such a conclusion is plainly unacceptable. In earlier centuries, although the birth-rate was unrestricted, the excess of births over deaths was sufficient to permit only a slow increase in population. It seems most unlikely that the decline of mortality which resulted in a marked and consistent rise in population can be attributed to a modification in the character of the infectious diseases, and we conclude that it was mainly due to changes in the environment.

So far as the second half of the nineteenth century is con-cerned this conclusion presents no difficulty. By that time the influence of the environment on health was well recognized, and improvement in living conditions had been accepted as a major objective of public policy. Moreover, later knowledge and experience has shown that measures introduced even before the discovery of bacteria were such as would have had a profound influence on the incidence of infection. But it is not equally certain that living conditions improved during the late eighteenth and early nineteenth centuries, and it may be asked whether the same interpretation can be accepted for this period.

Before considering this question we should attempt to clarify what is meant in this context by an improvement in living conditions. We refer to any change which would have reduced the risk of infection, or increased the survival rate among those infected: under the first are such measures as improvement in housing, water-supply, or refuse disposal; under the second influences affecting the general standard of health, of which by far the most important was probably nutrition.[1] Indeed, at a time when infectious disease was widespread almost any change in economic or social conditions which could be regarded as an improvement would have some effect on the risk or fatality of infections.

Whether economic and social conditions did improve in the late eighteenth and early nineteenth centuries is a question for the economic historian, and not one to which there is as yet a clear answer. Let us note, however, that if we accept the view that the rise of population was not due to medical therapy, or to a change in the balance between immunity and infection, we must conclude that it resulted from an improvement in economic and social conditions. This is true whether we attribute more importance to the death-rate or the birth-rate; for in the latter case the only conceivable explanation is a substantial decrease in mean age at marriage of women in consequence of the economic developments of the period.

These conclusions have some bearing on the direction of future inquiry. So long as medical measures were believed to have been effective, it was considered unnecessary to look further for a cause of a decline in mortality. The decision that medicine had no influence reopens the question of the relative significance of birth- and death-rates. If the birth-rate is thought to be more important attention will be focused on such matters as changes in marriage rates and age at marriage. But if we accept the view that the rise in population was probably due to a fall in mortality it will be more rewarding to consider in what respects the social and economic environment changed in the late eighteenth century. Did economic conditions improve?

[1] In this context Lack's conclusion about the reason for limitation of growth of wild animal populations is of interest. He noted that control of numbers probably comes through variations in the death rate, the critical mortality factors being food shortage, predation, and disease. Any of these influences may be paramount; often they act together. In many species food supply appears to be the chief natural factor-limiting numbers. D. Lack, *The Natural Regulation of Animal Numbers* (Oxford, 1954).

Were the improvements in diet which resulted from the good harvests of the first half of the eighteenth century maintained in the second half? Did the teaching of Mead, Clarke, and others have a substantial influence on hygienic practice of the period? Were contemporary observers[1] correct in thinking that housing and clothing improved? If a positive answer can be given to any of these questions it would strengthen what we regard as already a strong case for believing that the rise in population in the last quarter of the eighteenth century was mainly due to a decline of mortality.

To sum up. Three possible causes of a reduction of mortality from infectious disease are considered: specific medical therapy; changes in the balance between the virulence of the infective organism and its host; and improvements in the environment. Reasons have been given previously for rejecting the first cause, and it is suggested that although there have undoubtedly been changes in the character of individual infections, it is unreasonable to attribute to this alone the progressive decline in mortality from infections as a whole, after many centuries in which mortality remained high. Improvements in the environment are therefore regarded as intrinsically the most acceptable explanation of the decline of mortality in the late eighteenth and nineteenth centuries.

It is well recognized that in the late nineteenth century living conditions improved in ways which quite certainly influenced the course of the infectious diseases. Although there is no equally good evidence that living conditions improved in the last quarter of the eighteenth century – in some respects they probably deteriorated – it is quite conceivable that there was a general advance in the standard of living in consequence of the economic developments of the period. It is noted that whether we accept the birth-rate or the death-rate as the more important influence on the rise of the population, the conclusion that conditions improved in the late eighteenth century must follow rejection of the effectiveness of medical effort.

[1] Blane, (1813), op. cit., *passim*; Hawkins, op. cit., p. 231; W. C. Heberden, 'Some Observations on the Scurvy', *Medical Transactions of the College of Physicians*, Vol. IV (1813), p. 70; T. Percival, 'Observations on the State of Population in Manchester', *Transactions of the Royal Society*, LXIV (1774), p. 58; LXV (1775), p. 327; W. White, 'Observations on the Bills of Mortality at York', *Transactions of the Royal Society*, LXXII (1782), p. 42.

4 A Demographic Study of the British Ducal Families

T. H. HOLLINGSWORTH

[This article was first published in *Population Studies*, Vol. XI (London, 1957).]

INTRODUCTION

A total of 1,908 individuals were traced who were the legitimate offspring of British kings, queens, dukes, or duchesses, and who were born between 1330 and the end of 1954. The former date was chosen because it was the birth-year of the first Duke created (the Duke of Cornwall). These 1,908 individuals form the population under study. Demographic data about each individual were collected, coded, and transferred to punched cards. The present paper presents the analysis of this information.

The amount of information available about such exalted people is very great, and since about 1700 seems to be almost as complete demographically as it is reasonable to desire. In 1676 Sir William Dugdale produced his *Baronage*, and in 1710 Arthur Collins his *Peerage*, and these works account for the great improvement in the completeness of peerage records at that time. Since 1780 the only information missing at all often relates to the birth dates of dukes' wives, and the families of dukes' daughters who married commoners. On the other hand, before 1500 it seems clear that quite large numbers of dukes' children are not mentioned at all.

Many studies using peerage records have been undertaken, particularly in the second half of the nineteenth century. The methods used were often fallacious and the results were sometimes very odd. A careful study of the complete peerage would be interesting from many points of view, historical, demographic, sociological, and biological. The dukes and kings have been chosen because they form a group just large enough for some significant results to emerge, and because data relating to that group are more complete than for any other. The work of Peller[1] on European ruling families is the only really comparable study, and our results have been compared with his.

It is extremely important that the data on which a study of this kind is based should be reliable. No conclusions can be drawn if suspicion rests upon the accuracy of the raw material on births, marriages, and deaths.

The major problem is posed by an entry stating that someone was, for example, 'born about 1500'. If we include such persons we need to be very careful how we mix them with those whose dates are exact. I have taken this course, although other workers, almost without exception,[2] have simply omitted all persons for whom the information was imperfect. It is possible that these omitted persons may form a special class, different from the rest. Yet the assumption that omitting 20 or 30 per cent of the population will make no difference is usually tacitly made – and is therefore never properly discussed: at the outset it is not easy to guess in what way they will be different, but that is no reason for assuming that no difference exists. In general, we might expect that the group with imperfect records, which I have included and most of my predecessors have not, and whose size we do not know, will tend to contain people with uneventful lives, the obscure, the unmarried, the short-lived, the childless, and that it will be mainly drawn from the early part of the period investigated. Everything depends on the care with which we attempt to reconstruct these partially recorded lives.

SYSTEM OF CLASSIFICATION OF INFORMATION

All dates, except those explicitly stated, were classified into four grades. There are thus really five grades in all, viz.

(i) 'Blank', or 'Z' – assumed correct.

[1] S. Peller, *Studies on Mortality since the Renaissance*: (A) 'General Mortality of Women', *Bulletin of the History of Medicine*, XIII (1943), 422–41; (B) 'Maternal Mortality', ibid., pp. 441–7; (C) 'Infancy and Childhood', ibid., pp. 447–61; (D) 'Twins and Singletons', *Bull. Hist. Med.*, XVI (1944), 362–81; (E) 'Man's Reproductive Activity', *Bull. Hist. Med.*, XXI (1947), 51–65; (F) 'Men's Mortality', ibid., pp.66–101; 'Mortality, Past and Present', *Population Studies*, I (1948), 405–56.

[2] One exception was T. R. Edmonds, 'On the Duration of Life in the English Peerage', *The Lancet*, 10 February 1838, pp. 705–9.

(ii) 'A' – known to within an interval of one year, e.g. 'Died 1731' will often be rendered 'Died A 1 July 1731'. This is the *worst* kind of 'A', because the possible margin of error is a *whole* year. In fact, owing to the old (pre-1752) calendar system, '1731' *might* mean the first three months of 1732 (sometimes written 1731/2). We should then have 15 months, with an ambiguous year number for the first three and last three of them. I have always regarded a year, however, as being the present kind of year.

There are better 'A' dates than this. 'Born August 1771', for example, would be rendered 'born A 16 August 1771', but the month is now recorded. Baptismal and burial dates were adjusted by 19 and 6 days respectively to give 'A' dates of birth and death, the month for which I assumed was then correct.[1]

(iii) 'B' – known to within 5 years. For example, 'About 1620' would be 'B 1 July 1620', and '1670 or 1671' would be 'B 1 January 1671'. The possible range of dates is only two years in the latter instance: in the former, it is an indeterminate, but presumably small, number. Many other considerations may lead to 'B' dates, but the accuracy is never as good as one year, or it would be 'A'.

(iv) 'C' dates are little more than guesses of a less wild kind than

(v) 'D' dates – a class which was introduced half-way through when it was found that many 'C' dates were correct to within 10 or 15 years, but a few were based on practically no evidence at all. Women, in particular, sometimes married outside the circle of the aristocracy, and were not traced after their marriage. Thus 'married 1736' may be the last information we know of a daughter. If she was stated to have had issue we know she must have lived a little longer at least, and perhaps her death would be 'D 1 July 1776' – a pure guess, liable to a 50-year range of possible error.

The division between C and D dates is thus arbitrary. For some purposes, where information in 5-year age groups was required, C and D dates or ages were not punched, but the

---

[1] Sometimes the month so found might be one out (A baptism on 19 June becomes a birth on A 31 May) because the 19- and 6-day intervals were chosen without any real investigation of the problem, but they are presumably sensible,

Z, A, and B grades were always punched. Sometimes a B age (say 29 years 11 months) would be put into a group (25–29 years in this case) which may easily have been in error, but no attempt was made to relate the certainty of the age to the actual 5-year groupings used.

I have been led to produce a more complete genealogical account of the immediate families of the British dukes than was in existence. This was not my main task, but I tried to perform it with great care. An extension to earls might take about three times as long, although the numbers would be about six times as large, since many of the books of reference need never be consulted, and the forms with slight modifications could be used as they stand.

MORTALITY

I. INTRODUCTION

We may divide the population into seven groups, by date of birth, viz. 1330–1479, 1480–1679, 1680–1729, 1730–79, 1780–1829, 1830–79, 1880–1954. The main considerations in deciding how to choose the groups were: (*a*) to have roughly the same number in each group; (*b*) to have equal intervals of time as far as possible; (*c*) to have sufficient numbers for sampling errors to be small; and (*d*) to have enough groups to show secular trends. This leaves some room for choice, particularly in the number of groups, but Peller's work[1] is similar to mine in some respects, and I have chosen groups which would correspond most closely with his, so that comparisons could be made. His groups were: 1480–1579, 1580–1679, 1680–1779, 1780–1829, 1830–79, 1880–1936. In my last cohort (born 1880–1954) some dukes' children do not contribute to a table (e.g. of mortality over the age of 20), and so the headings have been altered where this applies (to, for example, 1880–1934).

The simplest way of expressing mortality as a whole is the crude death-rate. However, the base population is difficult to compute from genealogical data, and no attempt has been made to calculate crude death-rates. The cohort expectation of life, on the other hand, can be found quite easily. It is, in fact, the average age at death of all the people in the cohort. Its

[1] S. Peller, loc. cit.

reciprocal, the death-rate in the corresponding stationary population, may be used as an alternative index of mortality trends.

Before proceeding further it may be well to emphasize the difference between the cohort expectation of life and the expectation of life in a hypothetical stationary population whose mortality is defined to be the same at every age as that prevailing at some prescribed epoch. This latter expectation is used by insurance companies, and it cannot be determined without careful manipulation of the death figures. Its great advantage is that it gives information about present mortality, whereas cohort expectations cannot be properly completed until the whole cohort has died. My 1830–79 birth group, nearly all of whom are dead, yields a reasonable life expectation, for example, but the post-1880 group can be dealt with only by making various assumptions – we can only guess their mortality after the age of 75.

Cohort life tables do, however, have the merit that they deal with actual people who really lived and died. Actuaries' life tables are artificial, in that they do not relate to actual persons.[1]

The expectation of life was not obtained by adding the ages at death of members of the cohort and dividing by their number. This would not yield sufficiently detailed information. Moreover, in the earlier cohorts most ages at death were not accurately known, and had to be dealt with carefully. Abridged life tables, giving the actual numbers surviving for successive quinquennia, were constructed. To estimate the years lived in the quinquennium, x to $x + 5$, the formula $2\frac{1}{2}(l_x + l_{x+5})$ was used. This procedure is not quite ideal, but it is good enough, and reduced the anomalies which would arise if single years had been taken. The only exception to the rule had to be made for the first quinquennium of life. A study of various life tables, in particular those of Russell,[2] suggested $l_0 + 4l_5$ as a suitable formula. This assumes that children dying under 5 die at a mean age of 1 year.[3]

---

[1] See L. I. Dublin and M. Spiegelmann, 'Current versus Generation Life Tables', *Human Biology*, XIII (1941), 439–56.

[2] J. C. Russell, *British Medieval Population* (Albuquerque, 1948), pp. 175–91.

[3] In modern times the mean age at death of this group will be less than 1 year, but since only a few die, the difference in the years lived by the population during the ages 0–4 becomes negligible whether an age of 1, $\frac{1}{2}$, or $\frac{1}{4}$ year is assumed.

In the two last cohorts some people are still alive; the rule for finding the years lived by the population in each quinquennium was not altered, but the numbers surviving were found from the successive quinquennial mortality rates.

2. CORRECTIONS TO THE DATA

It is highly likely that many children dying in infancy in the early groups will not have been enumerated. There will not, however, be many omissions at older ages, although the ages at death are not very accurately known for the first cohort of males and the first three cohorts of females.

It seems reasonable to assume, therefore, that the only errors of omission are of children who died before reaching the age of five and who tend to be ignored by published peerage records. After considerable thought, the following numbers were added to correct for this tendency:

Cohort born 1330–1479	25 boys	30 girls
Cohort born 1480–1679	0 boys	8 girls

Every figure in the paper which includes these additional children has been marked with an asterisk. The main considerations used in finding the numbers were: the sex-ratio at birth, the ratio of child mortality rates between the sexes, and the child mortality rates in the third cohort. We have implicitly assumed that the proportions of children who died under the age of 5, and who were in fact noticed in the peerages were:

Cohort born 1330–1479	Boys 44%	Girls 14%
Cohort born 1480–1679	Boys 100%	Girls 81%

The accuracy of the age at death is crucial to a study of mortality. The proportion of ages at death in each of the five classifications, Z, A, B, C, and D are therefore given (per cent):

Cohort born	Males					Females				
	Z	A	B	C	D	Z	A	B	C	D
1330–1479	22*	15*	26*	15*	22*	7*	18*	10*	16*	49*
1480–1679	36	27	20	14	3	24*	22*	17*	22*	15*
1680–1729	56	22	12	10	—	36	22	17	19	7
1730–1779	83	10	6	2	—	76	12	7	3	1
1780–1829	94	3	2	1	—	96	2	1	1	—
1830–1879	100	—	—	—	—	99	1	—	—	—
1880–1954	100	—	—	—	—	99	—	1	—	—

Group D includes the additional children added as a correction for incompleteness.

This table may be used as a guide to the relative value of the estimates of expectation of life quoted.

3. RESULTS

(i) *Expectation of Life at Birth*

Cohort born	Expectation of life at birth (in years)		Corresponding death-rate per 1,000 living		
	Males	Females	Males	Females	Both Sexes
1330–1479	24·0*	32·9*	41·7*	30·4*	35·2*
1480–1679	27·0	33·1*	37·1	30·2*	33·4*
1680–1729	33·0	33·6	30·3	29·7	30·0
1730–1779	44·8	48·2	22·3	20·8	21·5
1780–1829	47·8	55·4	20·9	18·0	19·5
1830–1879	49·8	61·5	20·1	16·3	18·2
1880–1954	54·6	70·1	18·3	14·3	16·2

Except in the third and fourth cohorts, the excess expectation for females is surprisingly large. An obvious explanation is the high incidence of deaths from violence, both in the early years, when civil wars and executions for treason were fairly frequent, and in the later years, when a large number of young men were killed in world wars. It is therefore instructive to remove all violent deaths from the calculations, and assume that the later mortality of such people would have been the same as for the rest of the population.

One hundred and four men and nine women suffered deaths from violence: among the men who died over the age of 15 the proportion of violent deaths to all deaths was:

	Cohort born						
	1330–1479	1480–1679	1680–1729	1730–79	1780–1829	1830–79	1880–1939
Percentage of violent deaths	46	19	10	4	5	8	48

The figure for the last cohort is particularly high, because most of the members are still alive and will presumably die peaceful deaths.

The revised expectations of life, omitting all violent deaths, are:

	Cohort born						
	1330–1479	1480–1679	1680–1729	1730–79	1780–1829	1830–79	1880–1954
Males	31·0*	30·1	34·7	45·8	49·5	51·5	62·4
Females	33·0*	33·9*	33·7	48·2	55·4	61·7	70·2

The table shows that violent deaths would account for the difference between males and females in the early groups, but since 1780 the discrepancy is still rather large.

The other features of the table are the relative stability of the figures in the first three cohorts, the great increase taking place about 1730, and the steady increase since that time. In the last cohort the numbers become small when violent deaths are omitted, and the increase over the previous cohort's expectation should be treated with caution.

The most remarkable variation is the increase in the expectation of life at birth shown between 1680–1729 and 1730–79. Deaths from violence were very few at that time, and it makes little difference whether or not they are included when considering the change that had occurred. For male babies the increase in expectation of life at birth was 11·8 years or 36 per cent, for female babies, 14·6 years or 43 per cent.

(ii) *Child Mortality*

Deaths under the age of 5 have already been mentioned in connection with adjustments for under-enumeration. The proportions of all children born who died before their fifth birthdays are (per cent):

	Cohort born						
	1330–1479	1480–1679	1680–1729	1730–79	1780–1829	1830–79	1880–1954
Males	36*	34	27	20	18	14	6
Females	29*	29*	28	15	9	6	5

It will be seen that the reduction in child mortality began early in the eighteenth century and has continued ever since. In contrast, there was very little decrease in child mortality in

the general population of England and Wales from the time
registration of births and deaths began in 1838 until 1901.[1]

The great difference between the sexes in the cohorts born
1780–1879 is peculiar. In the general population the ratio of
female to male child mortality fell with falling mortality rates,
but not by nearly as much as it did in the cohorts born from
1680 to 1879. The numbers are so small, however, that it is just
possible that the very low ratios are caused by chance.

(iii) *Mortality over the Age of 5 years*

The expectations of life at the age of 5 years are important, as
distinguishing between the effect of child mortality and other
mortality. They are (in years):

	Cohort born						
	1330– 1479	*1480– 1679*	*1680– 1729*	*1730– 79*	*1780– 1829*	*1830– 79*	*1880– 1949*
Males	31·9	35·8	40·0	50·7	53·1	52·9	52·9
Females	40·9	41·0	41·5	51·5	56·1	60·1	68·6

Deaths from violence account for a great deal of the difference between the expectations of life of the two sexes. If they
are omitted, the figures are:

	Cohort born						
	1330– 1479	*1480– 1679*	*1680– 1729*	*1730– 79*	*1780– 1829*	*1830– 79*	*1880– 1949*
Males	42·8	40·3	42·4	51·9	55·1	54·9	61·2
Females	41·0	42·1	41·6	51·4	56·1	60·3	69·2

The difference between the two sexes is now small until the
cohort born between 1830 and 1879 is reached, most of whom
died in the present century. The difference of 5·4 years compares with 4·9 years at the same age in the 1952 life table[2] for
England and Wales. The last cohort shows a widening of the
gap between the sexes to 8·0 years, a very large amount, but
liable to considerable error, since the number of non-violent
deaths is relatively small.

[1] The 1838–54 life table shows 26 per cent dying under 5, the 1891–1900 life
table 23 per cent.
[2] *United Nations Demographic Yearbook*, 1954.

The change in expectation of life at age 5 between the third and fourth cohorts is as marked as the change in expectation of life at birth. A great decline in adult mortality must have been taking place during the second half of the eighteenth century. The further increase in expectation of life after the fourth cohort is relatively small until the last cohort is reached. Although the number of deaths on which the last expectations of life are based is small, the increase is probably real, reflecting improvement in public health, particularly since 1919.

The variations in expectation of life and probability of survival at higher ages are what we should expect. Exclusion of violent deaths considerably reduces the difference between male and female mortality. The actual expectations of life are:

Cohort born

Age	1330–1479	1480–1679	1680–1729	1730–79	1780–1829	1830–79	1880–1934 (etc.)
				Males			
20	21·7	26·3	30·0	39·9	42·7	39·8	39·8
40	13·1	18·3	22·4	25·7	27·0	27·2	29·4
60	10·0	9·2	13·2	12·7	13·3	13·4	14·7
				Females			
20	31·1	29·1	35·4	44·2	44·8	46·2	54·3
40	19·2	18·3	24·9	29·9	32·8	31·5	37·4
60	8·2	10·3	12·3	16·1	17·6	16·6	21·2

If we exclude violent deaths, the corresponding expectations of life are:

Cohort born

Age	1330–1479	1480–1679	1680–1729	1730–79	1780–1829	1830–79	1880–1934 (etc.)
				Males			
20	31·5	30·5	32·8	41·3	44·1	41·9	49·4
40	18·7	19·9	23·0	26·0	27·4	28·0	31·8
60	12·3	9·2	13·3	12·7	13·3	13·4	18·1
				Females			
20	31·1	29·6	35·5	44·2	44·8	46·4	54·9
40	19·3	18·5	25·1	29·9	32·8	31·8	37·4
60	8·4	10·3	12·6	16·1	17·6	16·6	21·2

After the age of 40 the difference in expectation of life between the cohorts born 1680–1729 and 1730–79 is slightly less

than between those born 1480–1679 and 1680–1729. The centre
of the period of rapidly falling mortality was thus about 1755.

(iv) *Survivors per* 100 *born*
(*a*) *Including violent deaths*

				Cobort born			
Age	1330– 1479	1480– 1679	1680– 1729	1730– 79	1780– 1829	1830– 79	1880– 1954 (*etc.*)
				Males			
0	100	100	100	100	100	100	100
5	64*	65	73	80	82	86	94
20	54*	54	63	73	74	82	90
40	28*	33	41	61	66	66	68
60	8*	15	23	42	47	49	50
Median age	23*	22	29	53	58	58	60
				Females			
0	100	100	100	100	100	100	100
5	71*	71*	72	85	91	94	95
20	61*	65*	59	72	84	92	94
40	43*	44*	43	62	69	80	87
60	19*	17*	29	48	56	63	77
Median age	36*	36*	32	55	64	68	78

(*b*) *Excluding violent deaths*

				Cobort born			
Age	1330– 1479	1480– 1679	1680– 1729	1730– 79	1780– 1829	1830– 79	1880– 1954 (*etc.*)
				Males			
0	100	100	100	100	100	100	100
5	64*	66	73	80	82	86	94
20	58*	56	63	73	76	82	90
40	44*	40	45	63	69	69	84
60	19*	21	26	44	50	53	62
Median age	30*	26	32	56	60	61	72
				Females			
0	100	100	100	100	100	100	100
5	71*	71*	72	85	91	94	95
20	61*	67*	59	72	84	92	94
40	43*	45*	43	62	69	80	88
60	19*	18*	29	48	56	64	78
Median age	36*	37*	32	55	64	69	79

COMPARISON WITH PELLER'S RESULTS[1]

Peller's rates for 1480–1579 and 1580–1679 have been averaged to give a comparable figure. The data related to the ruling families of Europe.

(i) EXPECTATION OF LIFE
(a) *At age 15*

| Cohort born | British ducal families | | European ruling families | |
	Males	Females	Males	Females
1480–1679	27·7	33·2	31·2	35·9
1680–1779	37·8	41·6	36·8	39·7
1780–1879	45·0	49·6	43·7	45·6

(b) *At age 50*

| Cohort born | British ducal families | | European ruling families | |
	Males	Females	Males	Females
1480–1679	15·0[2]	13·7	13·4	14·8
1680–1779	19·3	21·5	16·5	17·8
1780–1879	20·5	24·2	18·7	21·0

The British ducal families have had an advantage over the European ruling families for the last two centuries. Previously the position seems to be reversed.

(ii) SURVIVAL RATES
(a) *The first 15 years*
Peller does not distinguish between boys and girls, and the data are tabulated by date of the parents' marriage. The best comparison we can make is therefore with the mortality under 16 of the children of dukes' sons.

Father born	British ducal families % children dying under 16	European ruling families Parents married	% children dying under 15
1480–1679	31·1	1500–1699	34·1
1680–1779	21·1	1700–1799	32·3
1780–1829	15·9	1800–1849	21·3
1830–1879	7·7	1850–1899	9·0
1880–1934	5·3	1900–1930	3·6

[1] Loc. cit., Papers C and F.
[2] Based on only thirty-four men.

The mortality is decidedly lower in Britain than on the Continent, except in the last group, where the number of deaths involved is very small (8 out of 151), so that the rate is liable to considerable random error. If only about 90 per cent of dukes' children born between 1480–1679 and dying under the age of 5 were noticed in the peerages, however, as we have assumed, then the figure of 31·1 per cent of dukes' sons' children in that group is likely to be too low by at least one-tenth. The British and European mortalities would then be almost the same.

(b) The years 15 to 50

We consider the proportions dying in the period, as percentages:

Cohort born	British ducal families		European ruling families	
	Males	Females	Males	Females
1480–1679	62·9	54·5	57·0	45·9
1680–1779	44·7	37·5	43·4	37·3
1780–1879	29·2	23·4	27·3	26·5

Male mortality has always been rather higher among British dukes' sons, but dukes' daughters' mortality has fallen more rapidly than that of the women of the ruling families of Europe, and is now the lower of the two.

(c) The years 50 to 70

The treatment is the same as in (b) above, but the numbers, especially in the first period, are rather small.

Cohort born	British ducal families		European ruling families	
	Males	Females	Males	Females
1480–1679	67·6	80·0	77·4	69·9
1680–1779	52·1	43·1	65·9	56·3
1780–1879	48·3	33·7	56·1	45·7

Mortality among the British aristocracy may have been higher in the first 200 years, but it has since been lower than among the European princes.

NUPTIALITY AND FERTILITY

I. AGE AT MARRIAGE

The age at marriage of the dukes' children has varied considerably over the years, but is presumably typical of the age at marriage of the aristocracy in general. The method of analysing nuptiality most suitable to study such changes is to consider the depletion of the number of bachelors and spinsters through marriage. Thus in the 1330–1479 female cohort there were 51 spinsters at the age of 15, and during the next five years 17 of them married and 2 died, leaving 32 spinsters at the age of 20. The number 'at risk' was 51 — (half the number dying) = 50, and so the probability of marriage was 0·34. The probability of continued spinsterhood was accordingly 0·66.

The product of these last probabilities for each age-group up to 15 was 0·64, and so 0·64 × 0·66 = 0·42 is the probability that a girl, living up to the age of 20, would remain single.

The proportions (per cent) of those still single at five-year intervals are:

Age	Cohort born 1330–1479	1480–1679	1680–1729	1730–79	1780–1829	1830–79	1880–1939
			Males				
15	91	95	99	100	100	100	100
20	70	79	93	97	100	100	100
25	50	49	73	63	80	77	73
30	35	32	57	40	52	44	42
35	14	23	38	34	37	28	30
40	9	19	30	30	26	24	21
45	9	17	24	21	24	22	7
50	9	14	23	21	22	20	5
Eventually	9	7	17	14	16	12	5
			Females				
15	64	89	97	100	100	100	100
20	42	45	75	76	89	80	93
25	15	19	37	44	46	53	47
30	12	16	22	26	24	35	22
35	7	11	18	20	20	25	12
40	7	6	17	17	15	25	10
Eventually	7	6	17	14	12	22	7

There is an obvious decline in frequency of marriage of men under 20 and women under 15, but beyond that, marriage by the age of 25 (or 35) has become steadily less common for dukes' daughters until the last cohort, which reflects twentieth-century conditions. The men show a correspondingly high proportion of bachelors at the age of 35 in the three cohorts born between 1680 and 1829.

The mean ages at marriage were, in years:

	Cohort born						
	1330–1479	1480–1679	1680–1729	1730–79	1780–1829	1830–79	1880–1939
Males	22·4	24·3	28·6	28·6	30·5	30·0	30·0
Females	17·1	19·5	22·2	24·0	24·7	24·2	24·9

The general increase is to be expected, but the women show no decrease in the last cohort.

2. RELIABILITY OF THE DATA

Only legitimate live births were considered, the data for illegitimate births being too incomplete, and not so important, demographically. It should be remembered, however, that all rates of reproduction and fertility will appear smaller than they really were, because illegitimate births would contribute a small amount (perhaps 10 per cent) to the total fertility of the population. Although reproduction and fertility rates are usually calculated in terms of births per woman, they have also been expressed as births per man, both because there will be greater completeness in the basic information and because sociologically the population consists of great families governed by male descent, giving the sons a special importance.

In 11 instances, a daughter married and simply 'left issue'. These can be used to estimate the incompleteness of the birth numbers. I have kept such cases separate from those where she 'left with other issue, a son John', for example. This is not a very useful distinction, but it may be used when estimating the proportion of childless marriages. Study of the apparent proportions dying young and of the families known to be incompletely enumerated suggests that in the first cohort, perhaps 25 per cent more births should have been found; in the second about 7 per cent more; in the third 4 per cent more; and in the fourth 2 per cent more. No rates have been corrected to allow for such additional births.

D

3. GENERATION REPRODUCTION RATES

A simple measure of the fertility of each cohort would be the total number of children born to it, divided by the original number of individuals.

For example, the 100 males in the first cohort had 154 children, and the 91 females (their sisters) had 216 children. Thus 370 children were produced by 191 parents. The ratio, 1·94, is a possible measure of fertility. However, only one parent of each of the 370 children is included in the total of 191, so that a clearer idea of fertility is found by halving the ratio. This halved ratio can be called the generation reproduction rate, and it has the property of being unity when the population is exactly reproducing itself. For the cohort born 1330–1479 the generation reproduction rate is 0·97. The figures are affected by under-enumeration, but this reproduction rate is probably fairly accurate. In the section on mortality, as a correction for under-enumeration, the number of persons in the cohort was increased to 246, and the 370 births recorded should presumably be increased by 25 per cent to 462. In the second cohort the effect of under-enumeration of the base population is negligible.

The corresponding results for the other cohorts are:

1480–1679	1·04
1680–1729	0·80
1730–1779	1·51
1780–1829	1·52
1830–1879	1·16
1880–1939[1]	0·98[1]

These figures give a general view of the rates of increase or decrease among the aristocracy. The population was apparently stable until 1700 or so, when it began to decrease. It is thought by historians that in the second half of the sixteenth century there was a rapid increase in the general population: as there were very few dukes at that time, only a small proportion of the 1480–1679 cohort were born in 1530–79, the relevant period.

---

[1] The figure is approximate, those born 1880–1929 being taken as the base, and all the births to members of the cohort being included. Thus the eventual figure is somewhat reduced by those people over 25 who may have further children, but somewhat exaggerated by those under 25 who have already had any. The probable effect is to underestimate fertility.

Thus any possible high fertility among the aristocracy at that time cannot appear in our figures.

After a time of failing to reproduce, a great change took place during the middle of the eighteenth century, and the average rate of generation increase was over 1·5 [1] for a century. The consequence of this high rate of increase between about 1760 and 1860 would be to multiply the numbers of the aristocrats by about 4·3 during the hundred years. The general population also increased, but not perhaps quite so rapidly. In the later nineteenth century the rate of increase declined, and at present the aristocracy is probably decreasing slightly.

This superficial treatment gives us the general picture. The period when the great increase was beginning, around 1760, will be especially interesting, since the rise appears to have been much more rapid than the subsequent fall a hundred years later.

In a more thorough analysis a host of factors affecting fertility suggest themselves, not all of which can be considered with such a small body of data. The difference between the reproductivity of the two sexes, mortality, age at marriage, and social position (in this group, well defined), should certainly be considered.

If the sex ratio among children born to a cohort is assumed to be 105, which is roughly in accordance with general observation, we can produce male and female generation reproduction rates separately. The actual numbers of children by sex are known, but assuming a sex ratio of 105 will tend to give a fairer picture, as it removes some of the chance tendencies towards one sex or the other. The generation reproduction rates are:

Cohort born	Male	Female	Combined (as above)
1330–1479	0·79	1·16	0·97
1480–1679	0·95	1·14	1·04
1680–1729	0·76	0·83	0·80
1730–1779	1·53	1·48	1·51
1780–1829	1·31	1·75	1·52
1830–1879	0·96	1·35	1·16
1880–1939	0·84	1·12	0·98

[1] N. H. Carrier has shown that a female rate of 1·416 was found among the general population, born 1838–43 ('An Examination of Generation Fertility in England and Wales', *Population Studies*, IX (1955), pp. 3–23).

The difference is remarkable. Dukes' sons must have had fewer children than dukes' daughters, since incompleteness in the data will tend to occur in the daughters' families rather than in the sons', the daughters sometimes marrying obscure men, while the sons' families, being in the line of succession, would be kept under observation. Sons also remained unmarried more frequently than daughters.

The peak was reached earlier for males than females: we may guess that the cohort born around 1770 for males, and that around 1800 for females, had the highest reproductivity. It is clear, moreover, that we cannot safely take the two sexes together, especially for the period 1730–1829.

Mortality may be the key to understanding the changes in the generation reproduction rate before the nineteenth century, when birth control began to be important. Griffith[1] had this opinion with respect to the general population. Habakkuk[2] suggested that during the eighteenth century a considerable increase in fertility may also have occurred. For the aristocracy as defined by our population of dukes' children we may hope to decide what was the cause of the great rise in the reproduction rate, so that in theory the population would be doubled in about 45 years, after a long period of comparative stability.

We have already seen that mortality fell sharply between the 1680–1729 and 1730–79 cohorts. Did it, however, fall enough almost to double the generation reproduction rate?

I have calculated the proportions surviving the age-periods 20–54 for males and 15–49 for females for each cohort. Because these ages correspond roughly to the reproductive age-group we should be able to judge how much mortality affected fertility. The percentages who reached the end of each age-period of those who were alive at the beginning of it were:

Cohort born	Males (20–54)	Females (15–49)
1330–1479	18	50
1480–1679	34	45
1680–1729	45	57
1730–1779	66	69
1780–1829	72	75
1830–1879	64	78
1880–1939, etc.	66	87

[1] G. T. Griffith, *Population Problems of the Age of Malthus* (Cambridge, 1926).
[2] H. J. Habakkuk, 'English Population in the Eighteenth Century', *The Economic History Review*, 2nd series, VI (1953), 117–33.

The low reproductivity of males in the early periods was clearly affected by heavy mortality.

The rise between the third and fourth cohorts is less than 50 per cent for males and less than 25 per cent for females. This is hardly sufficient to account for rises of 100 and 80 per cent in the reproduction rate, although the reproductive performance of each sex is affected by the chance that the spouse will die, thus terminating the marriage, as well as by the chance of the individual's own death. Frequent remarriage would tend to eliminate this effect.

Mortality before the reproductive period must also be taken into consideration. A sharp fall in childhood mortality would help to raise the generation reproduction rate, since a higher proportion would reach marriageable age.

The percentages of males surviving the first 20 years of life, and of females surviving the first 15 years, were:

Cohort born	Males	Females
1330–1479	67†	88†
1480–1679	54	71†
1680–1729	63	63
1730–1779	73	79
1780–1829	74	86
1830–1879	82	94
1880–1954	90	94

The figures marked with a dagger seem affected by incompleteness, and again the big improvement in mortality took place between the third and fourth cohorts.

4. MARRIAGES OF COMPLETED FERTILITY

We define a marriage as being of completed fertility if at its conclusion the wife had reached the age of 45. A very few marriages in which the wife was over 45 at the time of the marriage are thus included in the completed group. There are about 3 per cent of marriages for which our information is so poor that we cannot even guess whether fertility was complete or not: they are allotted in proportion to the two definite groups in order to produce comprehensive results.

In the last cohort many marriages are still in existence, although their fertility is as yet incomplete. The difference

between the cohorts born 1680–1729 and 1730–79 is remarkable, particularly since men married rather younger in the
fourth cohort than in the third.

*Proportion of Marriages in which Fertility was Complete
(Per Cent)*

	Cohort born						
	1330–1479	1480–1679	1680–1729	1730–1779	1780–1829	1830–1879	1880–1939
Dukes' sons' marriages	15	27	35	60	74	71	44
Dukes' daughters' marriages	24	34	39	58	71	70	44

There is some tendency for the marriages of completed
fertility to be those which were contracted when the wife was
older than the mean for the cohort. The mean ages in years
were:

	Dukes' sons		Dukes' daughters	
Cohort born	Fertility completed	Fertility not completed	Fertility completed	Fertility not completed
1330–1479	23·2	22·3	20·6	16·0
1480–1679	24·2	24·3	21·7	18·4
1680–1729	31·2	27·3	23·0	21·7
1730–1779	28·8	28·2	25·2	22·2
1780–1829	30·1	31·4	25·5	22·9
1830–1879	30·7	28·2	24·8	22·9
1880–1939	28·6	28·4	26·1	24·0

The ages of 20 per cent of the wives of dukes' sons are not
known: the two worst cohorts being born 1680–1729 (30 per
cent) and 1880–1934 (36 per cent). However, using only those
whose ages were known, their mean ages at marriage were (in
years):

Husband's cohort born	Fertility completed	Fertility not completed	All marriages
1330–1479	26·0	16·2	17·9
1480–1679	22·9	17·7	19·3
1680–1729	26·4	20·1	22·4
1730–1779	24·2	21·8	23·4
1780–1829	25·1	22·5	24·5
1830–1879	25·3	22·0	24·3
1880–1934	25·8	22·9	24·4

The figures for all marriages agree very closely with those for dukes' daughters, which is satisfactory. The constancy, to within $3\frac{1}{2}$ years, of the mean age at marriage when the fertility of that marriage proved to be complete is largely accidental: the figure for the first cohort might well have been 20·0 or thereabouts.

5. FERTILITY

The fertility of each cohort may be divided into that which arose from marriages of completed fertility and that which arose from marriages of incomplete fertility. The mean family sizes are:

| | Dukes' sons | | Dukes' daughters | |
Cohort born	Fertility completed	Fertility not completed	Fertility completed	Fertility not completed
1330–1479	3·7	1·8	4·6	1·5
1480–1679	5·9	2·7	4·6	2·8
1680–1729	4·3	2·7	4·5	3·1
1730–1779	5·6	2·7	5·4	3·7
1780–1829	4·3	3·9	5·6	3·7
1830–1879	3·0	2·2	4·0	3·4
1880–1939	2·4	2·2	2·9	2·2

The marriages for which completeness was not known are omitted, since the sizes of such families are almost certainly understated.

When the first marriage was not of completed fertility it was sometimes followed by a second marriage from which there were children. The total fertility (of all marriages) of the dukes' daughters whose first marriages were not of completed fertility is considerably higher than that first-marriage fertility.

The mean ultimate family sizes, when fertility was not completed with the first marriage, are:

| | Cohort born | | | | | | |
	1330–1479	1480–1679	1680–1729	1730–79	1780–1829	1830–79	1880–1939
Family size	2·8	3·5	3·3	4·5	3·8	3·7	2·6

Those born 1330–1679 and 1730–79 are affected most.

6. CHILDLESSNESS

Where the first marriage was of completed fertility, the proportions childless are:

	1330–1729	Cohort born *1730–1829*	*1830–1934*
Males	16%	20%	20%
Females	17%	18%	13%

These rates seem rather high. The social system may be partly
responsible for these large proportions of childless marriages
among the aristocracy.

Now, if we take *all* marriages, first and subsequent, fertility
completed or not, the proportions of people who never had
offspring are:

	1330–1729	Cohort born *1730–1829*	*1830–1939*
Males	27%	19%	17%
Females	23%	19%	12%

For persons born since 1730, these rates, which allow for remarriage, are remarkably similar to those for the first marriages
which were of completed fertility. Apparently after about 1760
the absence of children in a first marriage was quite often made
good if the spouse died before the fertile period was completed.

7. CONCLUSIONS

The mean family size for females whose first marriage lasted to
the end of the fertile period suggests strongly that there was a
real rise in fertility in the fourth and fifth cohorts. The rise was
from about 4·6 to about 5·5 children, and occurred quite
suddenly amongst the group born round about 1730, the dividing date between the third and fourth cohorts. The later fall
was even more abrupt, and began amongst the group born
about 1830. Thus 1760 and 1860 are the rough limits of the
period of high fertility.

Those whose first marriage was not of completed fertility
show a high average family size at the same period.

The dukes' sons do not show quite such a clear pattern, but
apparently the cohort born 1730–79 had a considerably higher

level of fertility than the cohort born 1680–1729. The first marriages of completed fertility do not show a similarly high fertility in the cohort born 1780–1829, but those marriages for which fertility was not completed nevertheless show a remarkable fertility. The only feature which does not conform to the pattern of fertility established for their sisters is the high fertility of dukes' sons in the cohort born 1480–1679. The period is so long that it may well contain fluctuations in fertility, and historical evidence would suggest a high level of fertility for people born about 1530–79.

Age-specific Fertility

We may also study the age-specific fertility of first marriages. The punched cards contain the data required where they were known to within five years. The remainder, which is a relatively small number except in the two earliest cohorts, has been distributed among the groups, for trying to estimate the actual dates (C and D) from the original forms would be tedious. There is a danger of placing all the births at the most likely age, and it would lend more respectability to the figures than they deserve.

Using Tait's law,[1] we may fit a regression line to the age-specific fertility rates of each female cohort. We thus obtain some idea of the range within which the actual fertility of the cohort should be. The total fertility between the ages of 20 and 49 is shown in the following table, which takes no account of possible under-enumeration of births:

Female Fertility, 20–49, Births per Married Woman

Cohort born	Regression estimate	95% confidence range	Direct calculation
1680–1729	5·12	4·80 to 5·44	4·98
1730–1779	7·00	5·84 to 8·16	7·29
1780–1829	7·84	7·49 to 8·19	7·91
1830–1879	5·87	5·12 to 6·62	5·67
1880–1939	4·82	3·81 to 5·83	4·81

[1] J. Matthews Duncan, *Fecundity, Fertility, Sterility and Allied Topics* (Edinburgh, 1866), p. 213. Also P. G. Tait, 'Note on Formulae representing the Fecundity and Fertility of Women', *Transactions of the Royal Society of Edinburgh*, XXIV (1866), 481–90.

The effect of the regression technique is to reduce the two highest estimates and raise the three lowest ones.

Tait's law, using single years of age, sterility at age 50, and $k = 1 \cdot 5$ per cent per year, gives a value of 6·975 for Edinburgh and Glasgow women in 1855 aged 20–49. At that date the fertility of dukes' daughters was falling rapidly from 7·84 to 5·87; it may well have been close to that of ordinary women of 1855.

We notice that the only two pairs of consecutive cohorts where pooling of the data would be statistically tenable are the second and third and the fourth and fifth. 1680–1729, 1730–1829, and 1830–1939 are thus possibly natural periods in the demographic history of the highest social class.

It would be agreeable if we could show that the fertility of women born before 1830 had always been at the same high level, averaging about 7½ children per woman who married at 20 and neither died nor lost her husband until she was past 50. When we remember that other evidence[1] suggests that about one-eighth of marriages in this social class are naturally sterile this represents a very high level of fertility among the remainder.

Lorimer et al.[2] found that about 8 births per woman was the highest average fertility ever observed in practice among a large number of people. Under-enumeration of births, and marriage before 20 place the 1730–1829 dukes' daughters in just this class. Is there any evidence that the 1680–1729 cohort should also be placed so high? Now 5 out of the 87 women in the cohort who married, or about 6 per cent, left 'issue', number not stated. Of the remaining 82, 17 were sterile. The 65 fertile women had, at least, 307 children by all marriages, or 4·72 per woman. Thus the remaining five may be allowed 23·6 children between them: say 22 by their first marriages (I have not checked whether any of them married twice). This would only raise the number of children by first marriages from 293 to 315, or by about 7½ per cent. The consequent rise in the estimate of total fertility (20–49) is from 5·12 to 5·51. Moreover, the same argument would raise the fertility of the

---

[1] E.g. T. B. Sprague, 'On the Probability that a Marriage entered into by a Man of any Age will be fruitful', *Proceedings of the Royal Society of Edinburgh*, XIV (1887), 327–46.

[2] F. Lorimer (ed.) *Culture and Human Fertility* (Unesco, 1954).

1730–79 cohort by about 3 per cent (7·00–7·24 children per woman). The 1730–1829 cohorts now appear more uniform than ever, and almost as markedly different from the 1680–1729 cohort as before.

The second possible explanation of the difference is the kind of husband married. Peers have large families, and there are complete records of their number; commoners seem to have smaller families, and records are poor. However, the average number of children born to dukes' daughters marrying peers rose from 4·1 (1680–1729) to 6·3 (1730–79). This will be partly explicable by falling mortality and earlier marriage, but the smaller increase from 3·4 to 4·5 observed for the total number of marriages was, as we have seen, too large to be explained in such ways. The proportion of daughters who married peers remained constant at 52 per cent over the two cohorts.

Age-specific Fertility Rates

	Males Ages							Total
Cohort born	20–4	25–9	30–4	35–9	40–4	45–9	50–4	20–54
1680–1729	1·94	1·68	1·56	1·31	0·88	0·47	0·30	8·14
1730–1779	1·84	2·03	1·91	1·32	0·98	0·40	0·08	8·52
1780–1829	1·81	1·99	1·65	1·32	0·70	0·34	0·08	7·89
1830–1879	1·94	1·71	1·02	0·73	0·45	0·14	0·09	6·08
1880–1934	1·83	1·18	1·07	0·54	0·37	0·16	0·04	5·19

	Females Ages							Total
Cohort born	15–9	20–4	25–9	30–4	35–9	40–4	45–9	15–49
1680–1729*	1·99	1·70	1·44	1·01	0·65	0·18	0·00	6·97
1730–1779*	1·84	2·13	2·09	1·64	1·04	0·36	0·03	9·13
1780–1829	2·63	2·58	2·15	1·52	1·10	0·54	0·02	10·54
1830–1879	2·31	2·09	1·66	1·16	0·51	0·23	0·02	7·98
1880–1939	0·00	1·97	1·32	0·76	0·58	0·18	0·00	4·81

* The rates for the female cohorts born 1680–1729 and 1730–1779 should probably be about 7·5 per cent and 3·3 per cent higher respectively, to allow for families described as 'issue', number not stated.

A third possible explanation of the rise would be the omission of large numbers of children who 'died young' born to the first cohort. Interpreting 'died young' as died under 16, the apparent proportions dying young were successively 28·7 and

16·3 per cent. The fall in apparent mortality was thus very great; the fall in real mortality can hardly have been any greater.

We conclude that the higher fertility of dukes' daughters born after 1730 compared with those born before 1730 was real, and it remained at a high level for a century before it began to fall.

FURTHER TOPICS

Four minor demographic aspects of the population are discussed briefly:

(1) *The Marriages of Eldest Sons and their Brothers*. We know whether a duke's son was the eldest or not. Since the whole life of the eldest son was a preparation for the time when he would inherit, eldest sons should be treated as a distinct class. The problem immediately arises of what to do when the actual first-born son died in infancy, and his next brother became the heir. In the eighteenth century a large proportion – about 30 per cent – of eldest sons never grew to maturity, and so some younger sons were virtually eldest sons. I therefore made the following rule: when the eldest son died under 16 the next living brother at the time of his death is counted as a 'virtual' eldest son. It is possible for several brothers to be successively 'eldest' in this way. This procedure is not ideal, but it removes most of the anomalies.

Eldest sons married younger than the other sons. The marriage of a duke's eldest son was the occasion on which the estate was settled on him, and the fathers may have encouraged their eldest son to marry early. The younger sons, on the other hand, had no great fortune, and would tend to delay marriage, or not marry at all.[1] This is borne out by the present study.

We may construct tables of the proportion surviving who were still bachelors at five-year intervals of age, in the same manner as we earlier did for dukes' sons and daughters.

It is obvious that eldest sons marry younger than do their brothers and are much less likely to remain bachelors. Over the

---

[1] A. Goodwin (ed.), *The European Nobility in the Eighteenth Century* (London, 1953), Chap. I, by H. J. Habakkuk.

six centuries, eldest sons have married progressively later, but their younger brothers, since about 1855, show a tendency to be married rather sooner than formerly.

Age	Born 1330–1679 Eldest	Born 1330–1679 Younger	Born 1680–1829 Eldest	Born 1680–1829 Younger	Born 1830–1954 Eldest	Born 1830–1954 Younger
0	100	100	100	100	100	100
5	99	98	100	100	100	100
10	96	98	100	100	100	100
15	88	97	100	100	100	100
20	64	81	96	97	100	100
25	39	56	55	83	63	83
30	19	42	29	63	33	49
35	4	28	18	47	14	37
40	4	21	14	37	14	29
45	4	19	10	31	8	22
50	4	17	10	29	6	20
Eventually	4	9	8	20	3	14

The ratio of younger sons to eldest sons at the age of 15 has been almost constant:

Born 1330–1679	177 per 100 eldest sons
„ 1680–1829	170 „ 100 „ „
„ 1830–1939	154 „ 100 „ „

The reproductivity of the younger sons is considerably reduced by their tendency to marry late or remain single.

(2) *Heiress Marriages*. It has been suggested[1] that marriages with bourgeois heiresses are detrimental to fertility in peerage families. We may classify wives into three categories: peerage families, commoners, and foreigners. (The last group is very mixed – German princesses and American heiresses, for example.)

First wife's origin	Born 1330–1679 No.	Born 1330–1679 Children	Born 1330–1679 Av.	Born 1680–1829 No.	Born 1680–1829 Children	Born 1680–1829 Av.	Born 1830–1934 No.	Born 1830–1934 Children	Born 1830–1934 Av.
Peerage	72	202	2·8	121	562	4·6	62	203	3·3
Commoner	29	77	2·7	97	314	3·2	67	135	2·0
Foreign	19	57	3·0	20	66	3·3	26	59	2·3
Total	120	336	2·8	238	942	4·0	155	397	2·6

In the two latter periods the advantage of the wives from peerage families is unmistakable. The proportion of marriages with daughters and grand-daughters of peers has fallen from

[1] F. Galton, *Hereditary Genius* (London, 1869), pp. 130–40. Also, for example, W. Wagner-Manslau, 'Human Fertility', *Eugenics Rev.*, XXIV (1932), 195–210 and 297–304.

60 to 40 per cent, however. This has contributed to the decline in fertility, but each class shows reduced fertility in the third period compared with the second. The first period is liable to various errors of omission of births, but all three classes seem equally fertile. There is no difference between the wives of eldest and younger sons in this respect, except that eldest sons, marrying earlier, always had rather larger families.

The same kind of analysis for the daughter cohorts, in which we must remember that a few births from non-peerage marriages are missing, yields a similar pattern.

First husband's origin	Born 1330–1679 No.	Children	Av.	Born 1680–1829 No.	Children	Av.	Born 1830–39 No.	Children	Av.
Peerage	109	351	3·2	159	850	5·3	81	318	3·9
Commoner	35	70	2·0	81	215	2·7	69	173	2·5
Foreign	17	33	1·9	19	64	3·4	22	73	3·3
Total	161	454	2·8	259	1129	4·4	172	564	3·3

The omissions cannot account for the great difference in average family size between peerage marriages and commoner marriages. The age at marriage, being perhaps lower for marriages with peers, may explain some of the difference.

(3) *Actual Family Size*. Here we consider all the marriages of an individual. Childlessness has declined, but there have also been fewer large families in the modern period. No attempt was made to allow for differing durations of married life. Falling mortality since 1680 will therefore exaggerate any real decline in the incidence of large families. However, the changing proportions of small and of large families have an intrinsic interest.

Eldest sons had more children than did their brothers, but not because they were less frequently childless. A remarkable fact is that the sons, and even the eldest sons, appear to have been more inclined to have no children than the daughters. The percentages of dukes' sons ever married having families of stated size are:

Family size	Born 1330–1679 Eldest	Younger	Born 1680–1829 Eldest	Younger	Born 1830–1934 Eldest	Younger
None	26	31	23	20	17	18
1–4	30	40	25	44	51	69
5–9	26	22	38	26	30	13
10 and over	18	7	14	10	2	0
Total	100	100	100	100	100	100

Similarly, for all dukes' sons and for dukes' daughters:

Family size	Born 1330–1679 Sons	Daughters	Born 1680–1829 Sons	Daughters	Born 1830–1939 Sons	Daughters
None	29	22	21	19	17	12
1–4	36	49	36	37	62	60
5–9	23	21	31	30	20	25
10 and over	12	8	12	14	1	3
Total	100	100	100	100	100	100

Proportions of over 20 per cent of married people dying child-less seem high. Under-enumeration of births is not an impor-tant cause of this high rate, since although Peller[1] found only 15 per cent of married men childless among the ruling families of Europe, who had a fairly similar marriage system, and a similar desire for children, it is hard to believe that after 1700 the family of many eldest sons of dukes would not be fully chronicled: yet 23 per cent of the eldest sons born 1680–1829 married without apparent issue.

The lateness of some marriages and early termination of marriages would be quite a common reason for childlessness. (See section on marriages of completed fertility.)

(4) *Sex ratio.* It has often been remarked that the first child has a tendency to be male.[2] We can see how far it is true of the present cohorts (first marriage children only), since simple χ^2 tests of association can be made:

	Male cohorts Male	Female	Total	Female cohorts Male	Female	Total
First child	209	172	381	247	202	449
Other children	659	637	1,296	869	829	1,698
Total	868	809	1,677	1,116	1,031	2,147
	$\chi^2 = 1\cdot89$			$\chi^2 = 2\cdot09$		

Grouping the two cohorts together would not be valid, since there were a number of marriages between the sons and daugh-ters of dukes, so that the two tables are not independent. All we can say is that the observed first child sex-ratio is about 122 males per 100 females, and the observed other children sex-ratio is about 104, but even with such large numbers, the dif-ference is not statistically significant.

[1] S. Peller, 'Man's Reproductive Activity', *Bull. Hist. Med.*, XXI, 1947, pp. 51–65.
[2] For example, R. C. Punnett, 'On Nutrition and Sex Determination in Man', *Proceedings of the Cambridge Philosophical Society*, XII (1903), 262–76.

SUMMARY

The available records of the ducal families of the British Isles have been studied in order to determine fertility and mortality among the highest social class.

The expectation of life was considerably higher for females than males, but a large part of the difference could be explained by deaths from violence. Mortality fell rather abruptly about the middle of the eighteenth century, and perhaps again in the twentieth century. At other times mortality has fallen gradually.

The mortality of the aristocracy was similar in Britain and the Continent. The differences are rather in favour of Britain, especially for children and old people.

The mean age at marriage rose from 22 to 29 for men, and from 17 to 24 for women, between the fourteenth and the eighteenth centuries. Thereafter it has scarcely varied. Eldest sons have always married at younger ages than did their brothers.

Between about 1760 and 1860 the rate of fertility was remarkably high. To a large extent falling mortality accounts for the sudden rise in fertility in the mid-eighteenth century, but it does not explain all the increase. After 1860 or so fertility fell, as in the general population, and at present ducal families are probably just failing to reproduce themselves.

In every period roughly one in six of all marriages of completed fertility were childless. The decline in fertility was thus brought about by a reduction in the proportion of large families.

Especially since 1700, marriages into another peerage family produced more children than did other marriages. There is no evidence that the first child was significantly more often male than were subsequent children.

ACKNOWLEDGEMENTS

My thanks are due to Professor D. V. Glass for suggesting the subject of this work and subsequent advice; to Professor A. L. Banks for his kind help and encouragement throughout; to the East Anglian Regional Hospital Board for punching my cards; and to the staff of the Department of Human Ecology of the University of Cambridge for their constant assistance.

5 Some Neglected Factors in the English Industrial Revolution

J. T. KRAUSE

[This article was first published in the *Journal of Economic History*, Vol. XIX (New York, 1959).]

The economic differences between the Europeans on the eve of industrialization and the currently less developed peoples has assumed a certain degree of importance in the recent literature. It has been argued that West Europeans had significantly higher *per capita* incomes than do most of the peoples of the world today and that the levels of living of many people fell off during the process of early industrialization. Obviously, the argument is important in that the levels of living found in most of today's less developed peoples could not decline significantly without the risk of disaster.

Partially contradicting this argument is the generally held theory of the demographic transition. The view that all populations prior to about 1750 were characterized by a mortality which was sufficiently high to make demographic growth exceedingly slight minimizes the differences between past and present less developed societies. And given the relatively well-established generalization that high mortality, in the absence of modern methods of public health, results largely from low levels of living, it appears that there was little difference between the Europeans and the presently less developed peoples on the eve of industrialization.

Although the current theory of the demographic transition has been challenged recently, I shall develop the argument somewhat differently in this paper.[1] I shall try to make the

[1] K. H. Connell, *The Population of Ireland, 1750–1845* (Oxford: Clarendon Press, 1950); K. H. Connell, 'Some Unsettled Problems in English and Irish Population History, 1750–1845', *Irish Historical Studies*, VII (1951), 225–34; H. J. Habakkuk, 'English Population in the Eighteenth Century', *The Economic History Review*, 2nd series, VI (1953), 117–33; J. T. Krause, 'Changes in English Fertility and

following points: pre-industrial Western fertility was generally limited by economic considerations, especially among the lower classes; most of the populations of the currently less developed areas have not controlled their fertility in the interests of relatively high levels of living; the contrast between the attitudes towards fertility led to differences in levels of living and mortality before the Industrial Revolution occurred; and indeed, Western demographic traits favoured industrialization and those of the currently less developed countries hindered it.

I should stress, however, that I am not putting forward another single-cause explanation of all human history. I am presenting a much simplified model in the interest of brevity, and obviously many variables have been omitted. I should also stress the tentative nature of much of the argument. It will be a long time before we have enough satisfactory data to deal with the various problems which will be raised in the discussion.

I

Current demographic theory has stressed the constantly high fertility of the pre-industrial West; however, recent work has emphasized the great variability of that fertility. Crude birth-rates ranged from a high of between 55 and 60 per 1,000 in the United States and French Canada of the eighteenth century to a low of about 15 per 1,000 in Iceland in the ten or fifteen years surrounding 1703, a range much greater than that found in the currently less developed world. For most Western countries the birth-rate seems to have hovered about

Mortality, 1781–1850', *The Economic History Review*, 2nd series, XI (1958)), 52–70; J. T. Krause, 'Some Implications of Recent Work in Historical Demography', *Comparative Studies in Society and History*, I (1959), 164–88; J. T. Krause, 'Western Demographic History and the Current Situation in the Less Developed Countries', which will appear in *Population Studies*.

In the effort to avoid a needless multiplication of footnotes, I might mention that my 'Some Implications of Recent Work' and 'Western Demographic History and the Current Situation' provide the statistical basis for my discussion of the demographic differences between past and present less developed peoples. The latter article also contains a brief analysis of some eighteenth-century English local materials. Then those parts of the following discussion which relate to England and Wales between 1781 and 1850 are based on my 'Changes in English Fertility and Mortality'.

the mark of the low thirties, as was the case in the Northern European countries between 1735 and 1800; in other words, well below the rates of over 40 per 1,000 which are found in so many underdeveloped countries today.

Also, long-term changes have been noted within some Western countries. K. H. Connell has argued quite persuasively that the rapid growth of the Irish population between 1780 and 1840 resulted from an increased birth-rate; unfortunately, however, there are few statistics on which to support his hypothesis.[1] English statistics are far superior to the Irish, and have been used recently to suggest that English birth-rates were about 30 per 1,000 between 1700 and 1750, that they rose to about 42 per 1,000 in the decade 1811–20, and eventually fell to the level of 35 per 1,000 in the 1840s. These crude rates understate the actual changes in fertility, because the age structure in the 1810s was probably least favourable to a high crude birth-rate. Also it has been suggested that Swedish birth-rates rose from about 32 per 1,000 in the period 1721–36 to nearly 36 in the decade 1751–60 and then fell off. And it would be most surprising if the high Canadian and American birth-rates had been matched by their ancestors in their respective homelands.

Demographically speaking, variations in fertility were caused by either changes in the numbers of married women or of births per married woman. It has long been known that short-term movements in the marriage rates were greatly affected by grain prices. According to the first report of the Swedish Tabellkommission:[2]

It is obvious that crop failures and hard years prevent many persons from marrying. But it is also easy to understand why, at the same time, existing bridal beds will be less fruitful if it is remembered that an increase of a couple of *daler* in the price of corn will immediately result in an addition to all the burdens imposed on farmers, compelling

[1] Connell, *The Population of Ireland*. While the Irish statistics leave much to be desired, Connell's approach to the effect of institutions on fertility and his argument which rules out mortality as a variable in Irish demographic growth are excellent.

[2] The material is cited in H. Gille, 'The Demographic History of the Northern European Countries in the Eighteenth Century', *Population Studies*, III (1949), 49.

them to cut down their other expenses in order to fill their own stomachs. They grow sad and worried and both husbands and wives have to earn their own living. In 1747 and 1748 the price of corn was 30–28 *daler* per Tunna in most parts of Sweden . . . but in 1750 the price was only 17 *daler*. At once girls and boys were ready for the bridal bed, and for married couples love began to burn more vigorously.

There is reason to believe that these comments are also applicable to long-run changes. Certainly, the people of French Canada had easy access to large amounts of vacant cultivatable land, and their marriage rates were the highest known in the pre-industrial West. The Finns had higher marital rates than the other Northern Europeans and also had, as a result of the murderous devastation of the Great Northern War, relatively large tracts of cultivatable land available. But availability of land was certainly not the only factor. Changing use of the land, new crops, and rack-renting have been cited by Connell as factors which reduced the Irish age of female marriage after 1780. And in England it is relatively certain that the marriage rate rose sharply in the late eighteenth and early nineteenth centuries and then fell in the 1830s. The suggested causes of this development are many: early industrialization, with its child labour; the poor laws; enclosure; and mining. Little has been done as yet to study changes in the age of marriage, but in each of three southern agricultural areas the age of first marriage for women was about 27 years between 1700 and 1750. In each area the age fell so that by 1801–12 it was only 20 in one parish (a famous poor-law parish), 22 in another, and 25 years in three Suffolk parishes. I hasten to add, however, that by 1841–50 the age of first marriage for women in these Suffolk parishes had fallen to 21 years.

There is another way of demonstrating the effect of economic conditions on marriage. Since Marcus Rubin's study of the Danish census of 1787, it has been known that, broadly speaking, the higher the class, the greater the percentage of males who were married, a finding which is confirmed by some Italian data.[1] Also, a recent study of Polish peasant women

[1] M. Rubin, 'Population and Birth Rate, Illustrated from Historical Statistics', *Journal of the Royal Statistical Society*, LXIII (1900), 596–625, especially 596–606; R. Mols, *Introduction à la démographie historique des villes d'Europe du XIV e au XVIII e*

shows that the larger the holding, the earlier the age of female marriage.[1] And some English data are important in this connection. Evidence taken from the allegations for marriage licences of seventeenth-century Gloucestershire and eighteenth-century Nottinghamshire shows that the median age of marriage of the wives of gentlemen was about 22 years.[2] On the other hand, the median age of marriage for husbandmen's wives, the lowest landed category available for Gloucester, was about 26–27 years. In the Nottingham sample the median age of marriage for the wives of labourers was about 25 years, the highest age for any group in that sample. A further consideration makes this evidence more impressive. Often editors of the allegations for marriage licences warn the reader of the numerous errors to be found in such documents. In comparing ages given in the allegations with those derived from the parish registers, I have found that the allegations very often understate the ages of those persons who were 25 years of age or older. Thus, the ages of marriage for the lower classes in these samples are probably too low.[3]

Existing evidence makes clear that differences in marriage do not explain all the variations in pre-industrial Western birthrates.[4] For example, the total fertility ratio, the average number

---

siècle, 3 vols. (Louvain: Editions J. Duculot, 1954–6), II, 303–5. While both bodies of data suggest that marriage among the lower classes was later and less frequent than that of the upper classes, several writers on historical demography have none the less used small samples from the upper class to argue that marriage was early and almost universal among all classes.

[1] W. Stys, 'Influence of Economic Conditions on the Fertility of Peasant Women', *Population Studies*, XI (1957), 136–48.

[2] The Gloucester data is summarized in the review by J. D. Chambers in *The Economic History Review*, 2nd series, IX (1956), 145–6. For the Nottingham data see J. D. Chambers, *The Vale of Trent 1670–1800*, Supplement No. 3 of *The Economic History Review*.

[3] It is unfortunate that the tabulations of the Nottingham and Gloucester materials do not discriminate between first marriages and other marriages. One might expect that widows and widowers would constitute an abnormally high percentage of those marrying by licence. One should also remember that Nottingham probably had a higher rate of economic growth during the eighteenth century than did England as a whole; thus, the age of marriage in that county might be expected to have been lower than the English average. There is another possibility which is involved in the use of marriage-licence allegations: the labourers and husbandmen who married by licence may have been somewhat better off than their fellows who married by bans.

[4] In addition to the materials which are mentioned in my first footnote, see L. Henry, 'Charactéristiques démographiques des pays sous-développés; natalité,

of children born to a woman who was married at age 15 and who lived to be 50 years old, was about 30 per cent higher in French Canada than it was in eighteenth-century Sweden. Gille has also shown that Finnish marital fertility was somewhat higher than the Swedish, but it is clear that the Swedish rates were similar to those found in Norway, England, Iceland, Denmark, and Brandenburg-Prussia.

It has been argued that conscious family limitation was an important factor in bringing about the observed differences in pre-industrial Western marital fertility rates. Interestingly enough, most of the evidence suggests that poverty was a major cause of family limitation and that it was the poor who often restricted the size of their families.[1] While this evidence it scarcely overwhelming in its bulk, it is consistent with the findings of G. Utterström, H. Gille, D. Thomas, and P. Goubert, who have suggested that the sharp falls in the birth-rates during times of high grain prices were the results of the practice of family limitation.[2]

The evidence on family limitation, taken in combination with the data on class-differentials in marriage, thus suggests that pre-industrial Western class fertility patterns were quite different from those found in the West today. Instead of the

---

nuptialité, fecondité', in *Le 'Tiers Monde'. Sous-développement et développement*, ed. by G. Balandier (Paris: Presses Universitaires de France, 1958), pp. 149–73.

[1] In addition to the materials which are cited in Krause, 'Some Implications of Recent Work', pp. 184–5, see A. Venard, 'Saint de Sales et Thomas Sanchez', *Population*, IX (1954), 683–92. The material from Sanchez is especially interesting.

Admittedly I am venturing on to very treacherous ground in suggesting that the poorer classes practised family limitation to a greater extent than did the upper classes. But such data as I have examined on family limitation stresses poverty as a major factor, and obviously family limitation could have been carried out by a variety of means: abstinence, extended nursing, coitus inter-ruptus, primitive chemical and mechanical methods of contraception, abortion, exposure, infanticide, and other means. Given the very slow rates of economic growth which were characteristic of the pre-industrial West, there were certainly incentives for the poor to limit the size of their families. Had they not done so, it is difficult to see how the West could have avoided the poverty which is found in India today, because even late marriage can lead to exceedingly high birth-rates.

[2] G. Utterström, 'Some Population Problems in Pre-Industrial Sweden', *Scandinavian Economic History Review*, II (1954), 103–65, especially 159; Gille, 'The Demographic History of the Northern European Countries', p. 49; P. Goubert, 'Une richesse historique en cours d'exploitation. Les registres paroissiaux', *Annales: économies, sociétés, civilisations*, IX (1954), 83–93, especially 86.

poorer groups having the highest reproduction rates, as today, they possibly had the lowest. If this observation about the low reproduction rates of the lower classes is verified there will be many ramifications, not only for income distribution but for social structure as well. However, it will be some time before it will be possible to test the idea adequately.

Although we are still quite far from understanding the various aspects of the complex problem of pre-industrial Western demography, it seems apparent that economic factors exercised a strong influence on fertility. However, to avoid too over-simplified a view, I might mention that the English birth-rate apparently reached 42 per 1,000 in the decade 1811–20, a far from prosperous decade which featured harvest failures and widespread unemployment. Real expenditures on the poor increased by 277 per cent between 1776 and 1817–21, and by the latter period at least 20 per cent of the entire population was probably receiving parish aid. While early industrialization, with its child labour, the poor law, and other economic factors have been advanced as causes of high fertility in this decade, it is possible that cultural disorganization also played a role. After all, illegitimacy was increasing sharply at a time when marriage rates were rising significantly. And while I doubt that the fall in fertility between the 1810s and the 1840s was the result of any change in the standard of living, as was apparently the case in the late nineteenth century, workers in historical demography must always be on the watch for such changes.

In sharp contrast to the consciously limited fertility of the pre-industrial West is the relatively uncontrolled fertility of most currently less developed countries. Although there are some exceptions, marriage is far earlier and far more frequent than it was in the West. To take the areas of high nuptiality, the percentages of married women in the age-group 15–49 of India (1931) and Taiwan (1930) were 79 and 74 per cent respectively. On the other hand, the extreme instance of postponed Western marriage was Iceland in 1703, in which only 28 per cent of the women between the ages of 15 and 49 were married. In the probably typical instance, Sweden in 1800, 49 per cent of the women in the same age-group were married. And it is even doubtful that French Canada of the eighteenth century, with the highest marriage rates of the pre-industrial West, matched the precocity and frequency of marriage which is found in most of the world today. With rare exception, contemporary investigators find no evidence of conscious limitation of demographic growth in the currently less developed countries, although there is evidence of many customs which do limit fertility to some extent.[1] While there is some evidence of differentials in fertility, they appear to be much less than those which characterized the pre-industrial West.

II

Assuming that the pre-industrial West and the currently less developed peoples did differ sharply in regard to controls over fertility and that there was a long period of relatively slight technological improvement, it is easy to see that the economic differences between the two demographic types would become very great. In those lands in which fertility was unchecked the relatively fixed quantity of good agricultural land would soon prove insufficient to feed the rapidly growing population. Hence more and more marginal lands would be brought into production, and less and less land would be available for dwelling purposes and for livestock and forest products. Animals thus played a small economic role as sources of food, fertilizer, and labour power. Also, the increasing population led to a decreased size of holding, whether of individuals or of families. In the absence of communal cultivation the decrease in the size of the holding would in the long-run result in under-employment and, considering the large amounts of poor land under cultivation, a very low productivity per worker. While one could mention other consequences of fertility unchecked by economic considerations, the above are sufficient for the present purpose. On the other hand, one can easily see that the societies which limited fertility in the interests of a relatively

---

[1] The action of at least some social customs have quite different effects from the economically controlled fertility of the pre-industrial West. For example, it has been argued the Hindu taboo on remarriage of widows acts as a damper on the Indian birth-rate, yet it is primarily an upper-caste taboo. Also, if extended nursing acts to restrict fertility in many currently less developed societies one might expect that the measure would be mainly effective in the relatively well-nourished classes.

high level of living would not fall to the levels found in most of the world today.

Such evidence as we possess confirms these inferences about the economic differences between the pre-industrial West and the presently less developed peoples. Bert Hoselitz recently pointed out that agricultural densities in the latter are roughly three or more times higher than those which prevailed in European countries on the eve of industrialization.[1] Examination of the very sketchy evidence on income per worker also suggests that the pre-industrial West enjoyed considerably higher levels than do most currently less developed countries.[2] Perhaps better than the quantitative evidence is the virtually unanimous judgement by eighteenth-century European observers that the mass of Indians and Chinese had a level of living which was well below that of Europeans of the day. Many of these observers also pointed to uncontrolled fertility as a cause of Indian and Chinese misery.[3]

Perhaps our most precise evidence on differentials between pre-industrial populations refers to diets. Materials for Sweden, Ireland, and England show that these pre-industrial Western peoples had relatively adequate diets, diets which were far superior to those of the presently less developed countries.[4] These materials, having been available in print for some time now, require no comment on my part; however, I might stress a small body of data which has not previously been used, the budgets of the English poor which were collected by Frederick Eden.[5]

[1] B. Hoselitz, 'Population Pressure, Industrialization and Social Mobility', *Population Studies*, XI (1957), 123–35, especially 125.

[2] For example, see S. Kuznets, 'Population, Income and Capital', in *Economic Progress*, ed. by L. H. Dupriez (Louvain: Institut de Recherches Economiques et Sociales, 1955), pp. 27–46, especially pp. 33–4.

[3] T. R. Malthus, *The Principle of Population*, 7th edn. (London, 1872). R. Cantillon, *Essai sur la nature du commerce en général* (Paris: Presses Universitaires de France, 1954). Other examples are cited in K. Davis, *The Population of India and Pakistan* (Princeton: Princeton University Press, 1951), pp. 203–5.

[4] E. F. Heckscher, *Sveriger Ekonomiska Historia från Gustav Vasa*, 2 vols. (Stockholm: Albert Bonniers förlag, 1936–49), II, appendix, 16–19; Connell, *The Population of Ireland*, pp. 151–6; R. N. Salaman, *The History and Social Influence of the Potato* (Cambridge University Press, 1949); J. C. Drummond and A. Wilbraham, *The Englishman's Food* (London, 1939).

[5] The most convenient source of this material is F. M. Eden, *The State of the Poor*, abridged and edited by A. G. L. Rogers (London: G. Routledge and Sons Ltd., 1928).

The value of the data is increased by the fact that they refer to the year 1795, a year which, as H. J. Habakkuk has pointed out, seems to have been as severe as those of the late seventeenth and early eighteenth centuries.[1] Further, the budgets do not include items of food for which no money was spent. Yet the incomplete data for the English poor in a harsh year reveal a *per capita* consumption of dairy goods which was about twice as great as the estimated Indian *per capita* production in 1940.[2] Then, of the 31 families for which Eden had detailed information, 27 families had meat or fish included in their diets, sometimes in sizeable quantities. Of the four families without any meat listed in their budgets, three of the men were given some victuals by their employers, and thus may have had meat. One curious feature of the budgets is that nowhere is there any mention of fowl or eggs. It is not impossible that many of the families supplied these foods by home production.

The consequences of these differences in food consumption, together with other results of poverty, are many. Some are relatively easy to pin down and prove, others are not capable of proof in the present state of our knowledge, but their possible importance merits a brief discussion. A definite consequence of the differences in levels of living is a difference in levels of mortality. *Chronic* shortages of calories and protective foods have led to the multiple deficiency diseases so common in the world today and to lowered resistance to infection. The high densities of settlement make for rapid spread of disease, and of course poverty aggravates the situation. In contrast to the estimated Indian death-rate of about 41 per 1,000 between 1871 and 1941, the Northern European rate between 1735 and 1800 was about 28 per 1,000. And there is some reason to believe that the English death-rates of the first half of the eighteenth century were in the low twenties. The difference between the English and the Northern European rates may well be explained in part by the higher English levels of living.

Another fairly obvious consequence of low levels of living is

[1] H. J. Habakkuk, 'The Economic History of Modern Britain', *Journal of Economic History*, XVIII (1958), 486–501, especially 499.

[2] V. N. Patwardhan, *Nutrition in India* (Bombay: The Indian Journal of Medical Sciences, 1952), pp. 11–12.

a decline in fecundity. Food shortages and disease result in late sexual maturation and in a relatively short and sub-fecund maturity.[1] Thus, even though eighteenth-century Swedes practised some forms of family limitation, an average Swedish woman who married at age 15 and lived through the reproductive period had nearly twice as many children as a comparable woman of Mysore in the twentieth century. No doubt social custom plays some role in reducing Indian fertility, but clinical and experimental evidence shows that physiological factors are quite important.

Thus, there are two major types of demographic regime among pre-industrial populations. The Western type, which also included Japan and many tribal groups, controlled fertility by means of postponement of marriage and family limitation for the purpose of maintaining a level of living.[2] It is possible that England was the country in which the tightest controls were exercised over fertility during periods of slight economic growth. On the other hand, uncontrolled fertility in the currently less developed countries has led to a situation in which an equilibrium was reached by means of high mortality and low fecundity. On the basis of available statistics India would appear to be the ideal type of this category, in that India has the fewest controls over fertility.

Both types of demographic regime, however, have the possibility of rapid increase of population, although by different means. In the West there is reason to believe that favourable economic conditions brought about an increase of nuptiality and a decrease of family limitation. A different mechanism may explain J. Durand's recent finding that the Chinese population had grown more rapidly than the European during the century 1751–1851.[3] Presumably there was no hygienic

[1] Krause, 'Some Implications of Recent Work', pp. 181–4. In addition to the comments which I made in that article on the work of J. de Castro, *The Geography of Hunger* (Boston: Little, Brown and Company, 1952), one should note that the demographic part of his argument is based on official crude birth-rates, many of which are quite inaccurate.

[2] A. Okasaki, *Histoire du Japon: l'économie et la population* (Paris: Presses Universitaires de France, 1958), pp. 36–8; A. M. Carr-Saunders, *The Population Problem* (Oxford: Clarendon Press, 1922).

[3] J. D. Durand, 'Some Remarks on the Population Statistics of Ancient China and the Outlines of Chinese Population History', which will appear in *Population Studies*.

revolution or any revolutionary medical advances in China at that time, but it is quite possible that an important improvement took place in the food supply. Such an improvement, by reducing mortality and increasing fecundity, would have made possible an explosive rate of demographic growth.

The pre-industrial Western demographic pattern has many advantages over that found in most of the world today. Relatively few Western children were brought into the world, but most of them survived to be educated, to use that education as mature workers, and to enjoy a relatively long period of maturity. To use H. Singer's language, there was not the over-investment in children characteristic of today's underdeveloped areas.[1] A recent writer has estimated that the direct losses caused by the high Indian infant and child mortality amount to about 3 per cent of the annual national income, as compared with a loss of less than 1 per cent in the United Kingdom today. Considering India's great poverty, a direct loss of even 3 per cent and the indirect losses (loss of the mother's services, maternal mortality, effects of repeated pregnancies, and the like) are of great importance.[2]

And from another point of view, high fertility leads to a type of age structure which does not promote high *per capita* production. Not only does India have a much larger percentage of its population under the age of 15 than did pre-industrial England, given comparable rates of demographic growth, but we should expect that the productive period of Indian labourers would be shorter and less efficient than that of the corresponding group in England. High mortality implies high morbidity, which in combination with the nutritional diseases reduces the efficiency of Indian labour.

The consequences of uncontrolled fertility possibly also extend to the problem of rationality so much discussed by Max Weber and others in the controversy about the relationships between Calvinism and capitalism. Generalizing on the

[1] H. Singer, 'Problems of Industrialization of Underdeveloped Countries', in *Economic Progress*, ed. by L. H. Dupriez (Louvain: Institut de Recherches Economiques et Sociales, 1955), pp. 171–92.
[2] W. L. Hansen, 'A Note on the Cost of Children's Mortality', *Journal of Political Economy*, LXV (1957), 257–62. I am indebted to Prof. R. E. Gallman for this reference.

Swedish population in the eighteenth century, Eli Heckscher wrote:[1]

> It is usual to look upon the new regime which was the outcome of the Industrial Revolution as stamped by unrest and insecurity. It would be more to the point to say this of pre-revolutionary society, for the lives of pre-revolutionary people were insecure and irregular; they fell helpless victims to the inexplicable and unpredictable freaks of Nature. . . .
> What cannot be stressed too strongly, however, is that this old 'static' order was accompanied by a frequency and a depth of *fluctuations* with which the following century had nothing to compare.

The inadequately fed people of the East who were so closely packed together must have known more intense, if not also more numerous, fluctuations than the eighteenth-century Swedes. Given such a social environment, one would not expect much evidence of long-term economic planning, at least of the type that Weber singled out as a result of the Reformation. Life was simply too unpredictable.

There is also another aspect of the problem of rationality: the intellectual capacity of the individual. I grant that we know very little about the effects of malnutrition and low health levels on intelligence. The problem is clouded by the many definitions of the term 'intelligence', by the difficulties of constructing cross-cultural tests, and by other factors. None the less, some competent observers argue that malnutrition and poor health leads to a stunting of the intellect.[2] While such a position is not capable of proof now, it is quite plausible because of the well-known effects of these factors on the

---

[1] E. F. Heckscher, 'Swedish Population Trends before the Industrial Revolution', *The Economic History Review*, 2nd ser., II (1950), 266–77, especially 272.

[2] J. Gillman and T. Gillman, *Perspectives in Human Nutrition* (New York: Grune and Stratton, 1951), pp. 484–5; S. Peller, 'Nature and Nurture in Mental Development', *Sociological Review*, XXIX (1937), 103–8; S. Peller, 'Growth, Heredity and Environment', *Growth*, IV (1940), 277–89. I might mention at this point that I am *much* indebted to Dr Peller for his advice on medical and demographic matters. Not only has he shown great willingness to discuss these questions with me but he has read and criticized most of my articles. Naturally he is not responsible for any errors that may remain in my treatment of these questions.

nervous system.[1] There is thus the possibility that the pre-industrial Westerners could learn and think more accurately than can the mass of today's less developed peoples. While the upper classes in these countries may have had relatively adequate diets, it is hard to see how their behaviour would not have been affected in one way or another by the behaviour of the lower classes.

Finally, in connection with the question of rationality is the direction of planning. Cheap labour supplies provided little incentive for the development of labour-saving machinery, and low *per capita* income meant little effective demand for mass-produced goods. If investments were made in industry they would be in the production of luxury goods which were labour-intensive. And with the great pressure on the land landed investment would perhaps have yielded a higher and a securer return in the East than in the West.

III

A number of consequences flow from the contrasts which I have argued exist between the pre-industrial West and the currently less developed countries. Whereas the West had a labour force which adjusted its numbers in a rough way to economic conditions, the presently underdeveloped countries do not. It is thus possible that the eradication of many diseases and improved nutrition will lead to rates of demographic growth which are higher than the world has ever seen. For example, the birth-rate in the malarial regions of Ceylon prior to the DDT campaign was 39 per 1,000, and the rate is now 50 per 1,000.[2] What will happen when nutritional levels improve

[1] Many medical texts on nutrition deal with this question, but note Gillman and Gillman, *Perspectives in Human Nutrition*, pp. 444–66. I think that the work of these researchers is especially important to those working on the less developed countries, because the two men are not only able clinicians but also have considerable experience with an underdeveloped people, the Bantus. Another interesting work which touches on the psychological consequences of malnutrition is M. G. Wohl and R. S. Goodhart (eds.), *Modern Nutrition in Health and Disease* (Philadelphia: Lea and Febeger, 1955), especially pp. 135–9.

[2] Department of Census and Statistics, Ceylon, *Fertility Trends in Ceylon*, Monograph No. 3 (Government Press, 1954). I would hazard a criticism of the explanation of the rise of the birth-rate in the malarial region. While it is true that quinine impairs fecundity, there is also evidence that malaria reduces the ability to have children, see Krause, 'Some Implications of Recent Work', p. 183. I am indebted to Dr Sarkar for this reference on Ceylon.

markedly? Without a rapid spread of the practice of family limitation, demographic growth might even cancel out gains in *per capita* production.

However, if the rates of natural growth are successfully brought down the prospects for an improved labour force are much greater than they were in the West. It is arguable that health levels declined in England during early industrialization and stayed low for a long time.[1] Yet, with modern methods of public health and improvements in nutrition, the modern labour forces will probably show an unprecedented increase in efficiency.

While much of my argument is tenuous and indicates the need for additional research, it is interesting to note that England, perhaps the Western country with the strongest controls over fertility, was the first nation to industrialize and that Japan, one of the few pre-industrial Asian nations to control fertility, was the first industrial power in the East. By drawing sharply the differences between past and present less developed countries, and by providing a possible explanation of at least part of those differences, I believe the paper partially confirms the conclusion of Simon Kuznets and others that the process of industrializing the currently less developed world cannot simply follow the Western experience.

[1] Krause, 'Changes in English Fertility and Mortality'. On the deterioration of the quality of urban food and on the increase of rickets in nineteenth-century England, see many references in Drummond and Wilbraham, *The Englishman's Food*.

6 English Population Movements Between 1700 and 1850[1]

J. T. KRAUSE

[This article was first published in the *International Population Conference, New York, 1961*, Vol. I (London, 1963).]

Since the 1920s it has generally been thought that high infant mortality prevented rapid English population growth in the first half of the eighteenth century. About 1750 infant mortality supposedly began to fall and fell very sharply about 1800, with the result that high rates of population growth were reached in the first two decades of the nineteenth century. Then, according to this hypothesis, infant mortality began to climb enough so that general mortality rose to the level of the 1840s.

However, the idea that mortality fell significantly during the eighteenth century has been challenged in recent years. Some have argued that a rising birth-rate was mainly responsible for the rapid growth of the first two decades of the nineteenth century, and that the birth-rate fell somewhat after 1821. The tentative explanations of this phenomenon have centred mainly on early industrialization and the poor law. I should note that proponents of this view also allow for some fall in the death-rate, but not importantly until after 1821.

Writers who argue that the death-rate was the major factor in population growth between 1700 and 1850, although they may differ on various matters, nevertheless agree on one crucial assumption: the rates of omission of births and deaths in the available ecclesiastical statistics were virtually constant for the whole period from 1700 to 1837. On the other hand, the proponents of the birth-rate as the major factor in the demographic changes of the period argue that Anglican statistics after 1780

[1] I wish to thank the Rockefeller Foundation, whose grants for the years 1959–61 made this paper possible.

became increasingly inadequate guides to the totals of births and deaths and that improved registration of burials was responsible for the rise in the burial rate after 1821.

Considering the volume of research on English population history, it is astonishing that so little has been done on the basic problem of registration. Unfortunately, it is a difficult problem, and much of this paper will be taken up with it. In particular, I should stress the fact that I shall not present any precise, long-term series of decadal statistics because the data are insufficient both at the national and the local level. Nor can the present paper be said to prove my conclusions. Limitation of space and the peculiarities of all the statistics which I have gathered preclude such an attempt. The paper, then, is merely an attempt to give a broad outline of my findings, which suggest that death-rates changed but little during the period 1700–1820 and that the birth-rate was the major variable.

With these preliminary observations out of the way, let us consider the main statistics. Firstly, there are decadal national censuses which began in 1801, some of which contain age distributions, as in 1821, 1841, and 1851. While all agree that the first two censuses were rather defective, they are quite invaluable and there is nothing to equal them for the whole of the eighteenth century. Fortunately there are a fair number of local censuses for the period between 1695 and 1801, but nothing that would permit the calculation of a long series of rates.

Secondly, the national totals of baptisms, burials, and marriages are available for much of the period 1700-1840. The numbers of the first two are given only for each tenth year between 1700 and 1780 and for each year thereafter. Marriage totals, however, are given for each year after 1754. Numerous parish registers can be used to supplement national data or to do local studies. The grave difficulty with these records is that they provide mainly totals of Anglican ceremonies, totals which bear uncertain relationships to the numbers of births and deaths. Many observers have been struck by the fact that the number of burials was virtually unchanged between the 1780s and the first decade of the nineteenth century, at a time when the population was growing rapidly, and have concluded that the death-rate had fallen sharply.

However, the problem of changing adequacy of registration

E

cannot be simply dismissed, even though it is difficult. For example, percentages of omissions in 1838-9, the earliest possible direct test, varied from less than 1 per cent in Rutland to about 50 per cent in Lancashire. Not only were regional variations important but so were temporal, of which the best example is London, whose Bills of Mortality have so often been cited to show a major fall in infant and child mortality during the eighteenth century. But such arguments depend on the relative constancy of omissions in London, a false assumption. In the 1690s registration of burials was virtually complete. By 1729 registration had deteriorated somewhat, about 9 per cent of the total burials went unregistered in the Bills. By 1780 omissions increased quite considerably, reaching a figure of at least 30 per cent of the total deaths. Omissions undoubtedly continued to increase especially about 1800, but it is impossible to estimate even vaguely the degree of omission by that time.

However, London was certainly atypical in regard to the early deterioration of registration. Only about 5 per cent of the total burials in Manchester in the 1770s were omitted by the Anglican registers. However, by 1830 at least 73 per cent of the burials were omitted from these registers. On the other hand, only a few per cent of the burials in Carlisle were omitted in Carlisle's Anglican registers during the 1780s and the situation had not apparently changed much by the 1820s. Clearly, there were important regional and temporal variations in the adequacy of registration.

The best starting-point for the study of registration is the period 1811-20. Given the backwardness of methods of public health, the usually accepted birth- and death-rates clearly pose the issue. To take the somewhat extreme [instance, T. R. Griffith's estimates imply that the infant and child death-rate for the period 1816-20 was about the same as that which prevailed in the early 1930s, a situation which should occasion some little astonishment.

However, I think that we can reject the view that mortality was so low, that we can make a *relatively* precise estimate of the levels of the birth- and death-rates in that decade, and thus arrive at an estimate of the omissions. We have an age distribution for 1821 and a reasonable idea of age-specific death-rates in the period 1838-54. Thus the survival ratios of the later period can be applied to the respective age-groups in 1821 to estimate the size of the population in 1811. The calculation results in an estimated population which is quite close to 1811's census total. However, when one considers that immigration exceeded emigration, that the census of 1811 probably omitted 250,000 people, and that the age groups over age 60 were probably exaggerated in the census of 1821 it is obvious that mortality in the 1810s was higher than that of the 1840s.

Another approach is the comparison of the ratios between the total populations of 1811 and 1841 with the populations aged ten and above in the suceeding censuses. 83 per cent of the census total of 1811 were aged 10 and above in 1821, whereas the corresponding percentage for the population of 1841 was 85. Again, the biases of the data understate the differences between the two periods. Mortality was thus undoubtedly higher in the 1810s than in the 1840s. To guess that the death-rate in the 1810s was only 27 per 1,000 by contrast with the 23 per 1,000 of the 1840s is probably to understate. If we accept this guess, then the birth-rate must have been about 40 per 1,000, given the probable rate of increase between 1811 and 1821. These estimates imply that 33 per cent of the deaths and 28 per cent of the births escaped registration. That the proportion of deaths escaping registration exceeded that of births during this decade, a most unusual situation, may become clear in the following discussion.

This high percentage of unregistered deaths is plausible if one examines some basic sources, which have hitherto been neglected. While there were non-Anglican burial grounds during the eighteenth century, outside of London, about 1800 the number began to increase rapidly, and neither these nor the older non-Anglican burial grounds gave totals to Anglican clergymen or to John Rickman, the official who collected these statistics. Not until 1831 did he make a serious effort to obtain totals from Non-Anglican grounds, and even then it was sloppy. As a result, the national burial totals for the 1810s omit what I would guess to be about 250,000 burials from some 3,000 non-Anglican burial grounds. Here too, one must note that the war deaths abroad must have been numerous, not so much from enemy action as from disease.

However, burials in non-Anglican grounds do not by any

means make up the only major cause of leakage of deaths from the Anglican totals in the 1810s. To be precise, an Anglican burial register then was not a register of burials, but of Anglican funeral services, which could not be given for those who had died without the sacrament of baptism.

While eighteenth-century registers had often recorded the burials of those who had not had the funeral service, very few did so in the early nineteenth century. However, one register is indeed precious because it did so. However, these totals were not included in the national statistics because the entry did not specify the sex of the unbaptized child. And in Kempston fully 25 per cent of the total burials which took place in the *churchyard* were not included in the national statistics because they were burials of unbaptized children. How many Kempstoners were buried in non-Anglican grounds is unknown. In official terms, Kempston's infant burial rate for the period 1801-10 was 45 per 1,000, whereas if one assumes that all the unbaptized were infants, an unlikely assumption, the rate rises to 225 per 1,000 baptisms. By 1801-10 Kempston's median time between birth and baptism was 87 days, as compared with only 13 days in the 1740s. There is abundant evidence to show that Kempston was by no means atypical. Many parishes and even whole counties had absurdly low infant burial rates between 1800 and 1820. So far, the lowest such rate I have found is 14 per 1,000 baptisms, but even lower ones will probably turn up. In Cornwall at least 70 per cent of infant deaths must have been omitted between 1813 and 1830. Not only did infant burial rates fall from relatively plausible levels to absurd ones but the unprinted comments which the clergy made on registration in 1811 and 1831 show that the burials of unbaptized children constituted an important source of omission in all regions.

Unfortunately, neither the numbers of those buried in non-Anglican grounds nor those who were buried in Anglican churchyards without record can be counted. However, it is quite clear that Griffith's allowance of 10 per cent to arrive at the total of deaths for the 1810s is definitely far too low. Even Brownlee's allowance of 18 per cent seems far too low. While it is impossible to arrive at a definite figure, a third of the deaths may well have been omitted.

It is certain that omissions had not been nearly as great in the eighteenth century. There had been few non-Anglican burial grounds until about 1800, and where they did exist, their burials were often entered in Anglican registers or else totals were obtained from them for the national statistics. An examination of many parish registers and of the comments which the clergy made on registration in 1811 show that the burials of unbaptized children had only become a major problem a few years before. That registration should have collapsed in such a short time need not surprise us unduly because Dissent and Dissenting opinions spread very rapidly after 1795. Further Anglican church building lagged very badly behind the growth of the rapidly growing new industrial centres, with the result that most churches and Anglican burial grounds were located in areas where they were least needed. While educated guesswork is needed to estimate the omissions in the 1780s and earlier, it seems unlikely that more than ten per cent had been omitted in the 1780s, and the figure must have been lower before 1780. If this guess is correct, then the number of deaths increased by about 50 per cent between the 1780s and the 1810s, which was quite possibly more than the population grew. Here, it must be remembered that Brownlee's estimated totals for 1781 and 1791 must be raised considerably because he did not make allowances for the deficiencies of the first two censuses. Likewise, baptismal registration must have been much better in the 1780s than it became in the 1810s. Even if the birth-baptism ratio was as high as 1·2 in 1781-90 (Farr placed it at 1·1), the number of births increased by over 70 per cent between the 1780s and the 1810s, which is certainly far more than the population increased.

If changing adequacy of registration can account for the apparent fall in the death-rate after 1780, can it also account for rising burial rates after 1821 when mortality was in fact falling? I think that the answer is 'yes'. Two major factors resulted in rising burial rates after 1821. Firstly, even John Rickman began to realize that burials in non-Anglican grounds were important. The result was that some 126,000 such burials were included in the totals of the 1820s, fully enough to explain the increased burial rate. An even larger number was included in the totals of the 1830s, and in neither case was the public given adequate warning of the changing basis of the statistics. Secondly, by the 1820s, and more so by the 1830s the Anglican Church had done something to readjust itself to the changed distribution of population, to improve the quality of its personnel, and to restore the laymen's belief in the desirability of early baptism. Thus the apparent rise in infant mortality after 1820 was probably nothing more nor less than the fact that more infants who died received funeral services, and hence were recorded in the parish registers.

TABLE I *English Local and National[1] Crude Birth- and Death-rates (per 1,000)*

Area	Total population	Birth-rate	Death-rate	Death-rate, 1838–44
21 rural parishes, East Kent, 1700–9	4,614	33	24	21
54 rural parishes and 7 market towns, 1720s and 1730s	43,629	33	29	25[2]
14 rural parishes, 1760s and 1770s	23,799	33	20	25[2]
Manchester, 1770–79	29,151	40	36	33
Carlisle, 1779–87	8,177	31	25	23
England and Wales 1811–20 (est.)		40	27	
England and Wales, 1841–50		35	23	

Sources: Kent County Record Office, Q/CTz2 T; Short, *New Observations, Natural, Moral, Civil, Political and Medical, on City, Town and Country Bills of Mortality* (London, 1750); R. Price, *Observations on Reversionary Payments*, 6th edn., 2 vols. (London, 1803); T. Percival, *The Works, Literary, Moral, and Medical*, 4 vols (London, 1807); J. Milne, *A Treatise on the Valuation of Annuities and Assurances*, 2 vols. (London, 1815); J. T. Krause, 'Changes in English Fertility and Mortality', *The Economic History Review*, XI (1958), 52–70; D. V. Glass, 'A Note on the Under-Registration in Britain in the Nineteenth Century', *Population Studies*, V (1951), 70–88.

The foregoing analysis thus implies that a falling death-rate did not play a significant part in the emergence of the demographic gap in England, although after 1820 the death-rate did fall somewhat. This conclusion can be reinforced by a variety of local materials, which suggest that no important secular fall occurred in mortality between 1700 and 1820 (see Table I). No one has suggested that the first decade of the eighteenth century had high mortality, so that the figure for the East Kentish parishes is not surprising. I should note that the data contain a crisis year in which mortality rose to more than twice the

[1] Of course, the rates for the period before 1811 are baptismal and burial rates.
[2] Rates are for the counties of Lancashire and West Riding, in which most of the parishes are located.

normal, and yet the decadal death rate was only 24 per 1,000. Data for the 1720s and 1730s show effects of the century's greatest epidemic. But we should remember that pre-industrial populations were not stable, and hence crude rates are often misleading. In this case evidence suggests that an abnormally high percentage of the population was over the age of 50. For those parishes whose data refer only to the post-epidemic period the death-rate was 23 per 1,000. Likewise the crude rates of the period 1760-87 are similar to those of the 1840s.

A few refined rates can also be cited. Using data from fifteen parishes which recorded the burials of still-births and unbaptized persons, I find an infant burial rate of 170 per 1,000 baptisms in the early eighteenth century. Allowing for still-births and for the fact that the term 'infant' often included those under age two, we can see that rural infant mortality was similar to that of the 1840s. In 1757-67 female life expectation at age 5 in rural Ackworth was 52 years, or higher than that shown by English Life Table No. 3. And as is well known, Carlisle's life table, based on the years 1779-87, was used by English insurance companies until the 1870s.

While there is much additional evidence, I should note the plausibility of my findings. If Swedes had a life expectation at birth of 36 years in 1751-1800, a figure of about 40 seems plausible for eighteenth-century England. English living levels were higher than the Swedish, and the English climate presumably had fewer deleterious direct and indirect effects on health than did the Swedish. Also, England was less disturbed by the direct and indirect results of war than were most continental countries.

As noted earlier, birth-rates rose significantly between the 1780s and the 1810s. The dating of this change is difficult because of the breakdown of registration. However, the marriage totals yield a clue. Between 1755 and 1800 marriages increased slowly, but between 1801 and 1803 the increase was more than 40 per cent, an unparalleled increase. Further, the subsequent trough was higher than any peak of the period before 1801. If we examine the regional totals the areas north of the coal line, the areas of most rapid modernization, were those in which the number of marriages had increased most rapidly after 1754, and in which the greatest jump occurred between 1801 and 1803. Further, the rapidly growing cotton and woollen centres of the North showed the fastest growth.

That every large region participated in the 'great leap forward' of 1801-3 is evidence that differential migration is an unsatisfactory explanation. Fortunately there are statistics on all civilian males aged 17-55 for 1803, which show that areas of rapid growth in the number of marriages were those in which high percentages of men between the ages of 17 and 29 were married. For example, 40 per cent of these men in the cotton areas of Lancashire were married, whereas the corresponding figure for the backward areas of North Wales was 23. Nor were the rapidly expanding woollen and worsted centres of the West Riding far behind the early marriage of the cotton areas. Further, early marriage was accompanied by high probability of ultimate marriage. However, I should stress that the textile areas at this time were *not* factory areas, domestic production dominated.

While English agricultural counties did not match the early marriage of the new textile areas, they also had much earlier marriage than did backward northern Wales. Many agricultural counties were being transformed by enclosure, which often resulted in a more labour-intensive agriculture than had been the case and by the breakdown of the custom of living-in, i.e. agricultural labourers no longer lived with their employers, but set up their own households.

The age distribution of 1821 shows the high fertility of the 1810s. There were 605 children aged 0-4 per 1,000 women aged 15-49 as compared with 506 in 1851. Again, the local figures are of some interest. The cotton and woollen areas, as might be expected, had the highest ratios in the country, but the woollen areas had the higher of the two. I suspect that Lancashire's fertility started to fall in the 1810s as the factory began to be important. It is interesting to note that the fertility ratios of the cotton areas fell far more sharply than did the national average between 1821 and 1851. And, as woollen production entered the factory during the 1830s, so, too, did fertility fall sharply. Another aspect of the 1821 fertility ratios was the height of these ratios in the poor-law counties. As with the textile counties, these ratios did not result from peculiar sex ratios, but must have resulted from high fertility. And after the poor law was changed fertility in these counties also fell more than did the national average.

To account for the national fall in fertility ratios between 1821 and 1851 is not very difficult. As T. H. Marshall pointed out long ago, marriage rates which had increased between 1781 and 1821 declined between 1821 and 1851.

To conclude this paper, there is little reason to believe that mortality changed significantly between 1700 and 1821 and much reason to suppose that birth-rates increased. In particular, it seems obvious that birth-rates went up for some forty years after the early 1780s, when the English economy took off into sustained economic growth. Of course, English modernization had many unique features which are not characteristic of under-developed countries today. There is clearly no necessary reason why the English experience should be repeated, but one has to consider the possibility.

SUMMARY

There are two schools of thought on the demographic history of England between 1700 and 1850. The first holds that movements in infant mortality were sufficient to explain the rapid demographic growth of the early nineteenth century and that after 1821 infant mortality rose sharply, although not to its eighteenth-century levels. The second school holds that the birth-rate rose sharply after the 1780s and fell after 1821.

The study of registration is one means of deciding on the claims of the two schools. The first has assumed that omissions of births and deaths were relatively constant between 1700 and 1837, and the second has argued that registration deteriorated sharply between 1780 and 1821 and improved thereafter.

Using new sources, I have found that the argument of the second school is substantially correct. The fall of the death-rate after 1780 is a statistical mirage. The apparent rise in the death-rate after 1821 is merely the result of better registration. Eighteenth-century local data also confirm the unlikeliness of a fall in the death-rate before 1821. Then movements in the numbers of marriages, regional variations in nuptiality in 1803, and fertility ratios of 1821 suggest that rising fertility was the cause of rapid population growth in the early nineteenth century and that both birth- and death-rates fell somewhat between 1821 and 1851.

7 Population Change in Eighteenth-Century England : a Re-Appraisal

P. E. RAZZELL

[This article was first published in *The Economic History Review*, Vol. XVIII (Utrecht, 1965).]

There have been two traditional explanations of the acceleration in population growth which occurred during the middle of the eighteenth century: (1) the Malthusian view that it was a consequence of the Industrial and Agricultural Revolutions through an improved standard of life; (2) that it was the result of various medical innovations independent of these Revolutions. The problem posed by these competing interpretations is central to English economic and social history: did the Industrial and Agricultural Revolutions create their own future labour force and expanding numbers of consumers, or were they themselves children of a Population Revolution which preceded them?

Economic historians have attempted to answer this question by estimating population, birth- and death-rates at decennial intervals throughout the eighteenth century. Professor Krause, however, has questioned the validity of the traditional method for the period before 1781 when aggregate statistics of Anglican baptisms and burials are available only for every tenth year from 1700 to 1780. He has pointed out that the use of one conventional assumption about English demographic data with reference to Sweden would exaggerate the amount of actual increase of population in that country between 1750 and 1780 by over 61 per cent.[1] Krause has attempted to use the statistics of annual baptisms and burials from 1780 onwards by making certain questionable assumptions about changes in the baptism/birth and burial/death ratios during the period 1781-1850. He concluded that a rise in the birth-rate rather than a fall in the death-rate was 'the major variable in English demography'.[2]

---

[1] J. T. Krause, 'Changes in English Fertility and Mortality, 1781–1850', *The Economic History Review*, 2nd series, XI (1958–9), 53.   [2] Ibid., p. 69.

This has led the medical historians McKeown and Record to state that 'the data (on mortality and natality) are so treacherous that they can be interpreted to fit any hypothesis, and it seems preferable to rely on assessment of the sensitivity of the birth-rate and death-rate, and their relative effectiveness, in a period when both rates were high'.[1] This they had done in their own work and after reviewing the history of all the major diseases and preventive measures taken against them, concluded that the 'fall in the death-rate during the eighteenth and nineteenth centuries was not the result of medical treatment as Griffiths and others had supposed. Only in the case of vaccination against smallpox is there any clear evidence that specific therapy had a substantial effect on the prevention or cure of disease earlier than the twentieth century. The decline in mortality from diseases other than smallpox was due to improvement in living conditions, and to changes in virulence and resistance upon which human effort had no influence.'[2]

Krause, however, has pointed out that vaccination did not become really widespread until the 1840s and has argued that the average standard of living probably deteriorated slightly between 1780 and 1821 when population was increasing very rapidly.[3] Chambers, in his study of the Vale of Trent region, examined the relationship of food-supply to mortality-rates and concluded that population 'was vulnerable to disease, but not as a result of famine. Epidemics could do their own work without its aid, nor, it would seem, did they require the assistance of gin.'[4] A similar conclusion was reached by Pickard after analysing the relationship between food prices and changes in mortality and natality in eighteenth-century Exeter.[5] It should also be remembered that from 1838 to 1875, when the standard of living was undoubtedly rising rapidly, the overall death-rate was virtually constant.[6] It is in the light of all these contradictory

[1] T. McKeown and R. G. Record, 'Reasons for the Decline of Mortality in England and Wales during the 19th Century', *Population Studies*, XVI (1962), 94–5.

[2] T. McKeown and R. G. Brown, 'Medical Evidence Related to English Population Changes in the 18th Century', *Population Studies*, IX (1955), 139.

[3] Krause, op. cit., pp. 63–5.

[4] J. D. Chambers, 'The Vale of Trent, 1670–1800', *The Economic History Review*, Supplement 3, p. 29.

[5] R. Pickard, *Population and Epidemics of Exeter* (Exeter, 1947), p. 67.

[6] See B. R. Mitchell and P. Deane, *Abstract of British Historical Statistics* (Cambridge, 1962), pp. 36, 343–58.

facts that McKeown and Record have been reduced to making
the following desperate statement: 'When we have eliminated
the impossible (medical explanations of population growth),
whatever remains (economic explanations), however improbable, must be the truth.'[1]

I

This paper is intended as a summary of research to date on the
cause of the increase in population in eighteenth-century England.[2] Before discussing these causes it is necessary to estimate
the size of population during the eighteenth and early nineteenth centuries, in order to appreciate the magnitude of change
during this period. The estimates of population used in this
paper are those derived from the returns of marriages made
from several thousand parishes which were published by Rickman in 1841.[3] These estimates have several advantages: (1) unlike baptisms and burials, the overwhelming majority of dissen-
ters' marriages took place in the Anglican church;[4] (2) the
registration of marriage is generally considered to have been the
most reliable;[5] (3) the estimates are based on three-year
clusters of returns rather than single years, a procedure which is
much more likely to reduce fluctuations of the marriage-rate
from one time to another.[6] The basis of Rickman's own estimate
was the assumption that the ratio of the number of marriages to

---

[1] McKeown and Record, op. cit., pp. 94, 95.

[2] The paper is really a series of hypotheses illustrated occasionally by statistical
and other evidence. It is hoped to incorporate detailed evidence into a monograph at a later date.

[3] Rickman's figures for marriages were generally derived from over 4,000
parish registers. See G. Talbot Griffiths, 'Rickman's Second Series of Eighteenth
Century Population Figures', *Journal of the Royal Statistical Society*, 92 (1929), 263.

[4] The best confirmation of this is to be found in the *Report on Non-Parochial
Registers*, Parliamentary Papers 1837–8 (28), where it is seen that there were
virtually no non-Anglican marriage registers kept for the eighteenth century.

[5] See J. C. Cox, *The Parish Register of England* (1910), p. 76; W. E. Tate, *The
Parish Chest* (Cambridge, 1946), p. 65; G. Talbot Griffiths, *Population Problems of
the Age of Malthus* (Cambridge, 1926), p. 33.

[6] An examination of the Swedish statistics for the eighteenth century, for
example, shows that three-yearly clusters fluctuated far less than single years in
terms of the marriage-rate. See *Historical Statistics of Sweden, 1720–1950* (Stockholm, 1955), pp. 39–41. The long-term marriage-rate in Sweden was remarkably
stable between 1751 and 1825. See G. Sundbärg, *Sweden, Its People and Its Industry*
(Stockholm, 1904), p. 96.

total population in 1800, was the same for the periods 1699–1701 and 1749–51, i.e. that the marriage-rate was constant between 1700 and 1800. It is impossible to test this assumption in any detail, although there are a few scattered statistics available to suggest that it is not too unreasonable.

The Marriage-rate throughout the Eighteenth Century

Place	Total population	Approximate period	Marriage-rate/ 1,000 population
7 Market towns [1]	27,043	1724–36	8·7
54 Villages [1]	19,607	1724–36	8·4
11 Towns [2]	37,541	1770s	8·5
England and Wales [3]	8,892,436	1795–1805	8·8

These figures must not be taken too literally, as they refer to places of different sizes and locations; the figure for 1795–1805 is somewhat arbitrary because of the flaws in the registration of both marriages and population.

Be that as it may, the figures for marriage-rates indicate that there were no marked long-term changes in the marriage-rate throughout the eighteenth century. This conclusion is confirmed by at least one local study of population change during the same period.[4] The estimates of population size from the returns of the number of marriages are as follows:[5]

Period	England and Wales Estimated population (nearest 1,000)	Average annual rate of change, %
1700	5,307,000	
1750	5,895,000	+0·2
1801	9,337,000	+1·1
1851	17,719,000	+1·8

[1] Thomas Short, *New Observations On Bills of Mortality* (1751), p. 133.

[2] J. Howlett, *Observations On the Increased Population . . . of Maidstone* (Maidstone, 1782), p. 82.

[3] I have excluded from this population figure the numbers in the army and navy; also I have not corrected for under-enumeration, as a few marriages were also not registered because of the non-Anglican marriage of Quakers, Jews, and Roman Catholics, as well as various illicit marriages in sea-ports and elsewhere. For the source of the population figure see *Census of Great Britain, 1851*, pp. xxiii, xxvi.

[4] Chambers, op. cit., pp. 54, 55.

[5] These estimates are recomputations of Rickman's figures. The following adjustments were made: (1) 5 per cent was added to the 1801 enumerated population because of estimated under-enumeration. See Krause, op. cit., p. 60. (2) Rickman took the number of marriages in the single year 1800 as the basis of his

Although we have indicated that the marriage-rate was only stable during the eighteenth century, it is possible to check the earlier population estimates with estimates derived from an independent source. Gregory King estimated the population of England and Wales to be 5·5 millions in 1695, an estimate which Professor Glass thinks may be slightly too high.[1] King's estimate was based on hearth-tax returns and local censuses conducted in connection with the tax on marriages, etc.; it is similar to the one we have made for 1700 on the basis of the marriage returns.

The Age at Marriage of Spinsters, 1615–1841

Period	Region	Mean age at marriage	Number in sample
1615–21	Wilts, Berks, Hants, and Dorset[2]	24·6	280
1662–1714	Yorkshire[3]	23·76	7,242
1701–36	Nottinghamshire[4]	24·5	865
1741–45	Surrey[5]	24·9	333
1749–70	Nottinghamshire[4]	23·9	700
1796–99	Sussex[6]	24·1	275
1839–41	England and Wales[7]	24·3	14,311

marriages/population ratio. This has been recomputed on the basis of the years 1800–2 so that the basic ratio is derived from a three-year cluster of marriages like all the previous periods. The original estimates are those Rickman arrived at by treating England and Wales as one unit, and may be found in Griffiths's article in *Journal of the Royal Statistical Society*, 92 (1929), 263. See also J. Rickman, *Parishes Possessing Registers Extant 1570 and 1600 with their Population in 1801*, Document M. 74·10 in the General Register Office Library. (3) No allowance was made for the numbers in the armed service. The population figures are not intended as exact estimates, but rather as indications of the magnitude of change in the size of the population during the eighteenth and early nineteenth centuries. For the source of the 1801 and 1851 figures, see *Census of Great Britain, 1851*, pp. xxii, xxiii, xxvi.

[1] D. V. Glass, 'Gregory King's Estimate of the Population of England and Wales, 1695', *Population Studies*, III (1950), 358.

[2] Rev. E. Nevill (ed.), *Marriage Licences of Salisbury, 1615–1682*.

[3] M. Drake, 'An Elementary Exercise in Parish Register Demography', *The Economic History Review*, 2nd series, XIV (1962), 444.

[4] T. M. Blagg and F. A. Wadsworth (eds.), 'Nottinghamshire Marriage Licences', *The Index Library, British Record Society*.

[5] A. R. Bax (ed.), *Allegation for Marriage Licences Issued by the Commissary Court of Surrey, 1673–1770* (Norwich, 1907).

[6] D. Macleod (ed.), 'Sussex Marriage Licences, 1775–1800', *Sussex Record Society*, XXXV (1929).

[7] *Fourth Annual Report of the Registrar General* (1842), p. 10.

The population increased relatively slowly up to 1750, after which it increased rapidly and steadily right through to the end of the nineteenth century. It is the causes of this rapid and consistent increase which are the subject of this paper.

Ideally, we should want to analyse the aggregate birth- and death-rates, age-specific fertility and mortality-rates, etc. Unfortunately, the paucity of accurate information means that we can only collect data of a piecemeal kind, which at least points in the direction of certain conclusions. It has already been indicated that the aggregate marriage-rate changed but little during the eighteenth century. This conclusion is consistent with the fact that the age at marriage of spinsters was virtually constant during the same period. Our findings indicate that the population explosion in the eighteenth century was not caused by a lowering of the age at marriage or by an increase in the marriage-rate due to any possible increase in the standard of living, or the level of employment associated with the Industrial and Agricultural Revolutions.

Another source of demographic information is to be found in life-expectancy tables. These were constructed for a group of Northamptonshire and Hertfordshire 'county families'.

Changes in the Average Age Lived (County Families)[1]

Cohort born	Expectation of life at birth (males)	Number of sample
1681–1730	37 years	138
1731–1780	48 years	130
1781–1830	50 years	162

The results of this study were compared with those published by Hollingsworth in his paper on the demographic history of ducal families,[2] as well as the results of his unpublished research into the whole of the aristocracy. All these studies point to the same conclusion: that expectation of life for cohorts born from *circa* 1740 onwards rose significantly, the saving of life occurring mainly among infants, children, and young adults. A more

[1] Samples were taken from the Northants and Herts. genealogical volumes of the *Victoria County History* series published in 1906 and 1907. Figures were computed to the nearest year.

[2] T. H. Hollingsworth, 'A Demographic Study of the British Ducal Families', *Population Studies*, XI (1957).

detailed analysis of the 'county family' material illustrates the sharpness of this rise.[1]

Changes in the Average Age Lived (County Families)

Cohort born	Expectation of life at birth (males)	Number in sample
1680–99	36 years	92
1700–19	38 years	89
1720–39	35 years	86
1740–59	48 years	76

Unfortunately it is impossible to construct similar tables for the general population during the same period.[2] It is probable that there was a similar rise among the general population, for the mean expectation of life at birth derived from Gregory King's life-table for Lichfield in about 1695 was 32·0 years,[3] whereas according to the English life-table constructed by Farr in 1841 it was 41·2 years.[4] If these figures are representative the aristocracy and gentry always had a higher life expectancy than the general population, but managed to increase their relative advantage slightly throughout the eighteenth and early nineteenth centuries.

What are the possible causes of the increase in expectation of life throughout the eighteenth century? For obvious reasons, an explanation in terms of increased food supplies is inappropriate for social groups such as the gentry and aristocracy. The rise in expectation of life was too rapid among the 'county families' to be explained in terms of changes in environment. There is, however, one major plausible explanation: the introduction and use of *inoculation* against smallpox during the eighteenth century. Inoculation must formally be contrasted with the nineteenth-century practice of vaccination. Inoculation is the injec-

---

[1] Hollingsworth's figures for the whole aristocracy, which are based on much larger cohorts, indicate that the rise in life expectancy was somewhat more gradual than this.

[2] Although Finlainson analysed mortality-rates from annuities and tontines, his findings apply essentially to the aristocracy and gentry. His results confirm those of Hollingsworth's two studies and my own, i.e. there was a very sharp rise in the expectation of life beginning sometime during the middle of the eighteenth century. See 'Report of John Finlainson on the evidence and elementary facts on which the Tables of Life Annuities are founded', Parl. Pap. 1829 (3).

[3] See Glass, op. cit., p. 368, for the reliability of this figure.

[4] *Fifth Annual Report of the Registrar General* (1843), p. 29.

tion of smallpox virus taken from the vesicle of a person suffering from smallpox, whereas vaccination is the injection of cowpox virus. The two injections are conventionally distinguished by the different symptoms they produce. Inoculation is thought of as giving rise to pustular eruptions in different parts of the body as well as at the site of injection, and is viewed as a mild form of natural smallpox, inasmuch as it is believed to spread the natural disease from the inoculated person to other unprotected people. Vaccination only gives rise to a vesicle at the site of the injection and is not infectious to other unprotected people.

II

Inoculation was originally practised sporadically and on a very limited scale as a part of folk medicine, mainly in Oriental and African countries. It was introduced into England in 1721, when Lady Mary Wortley Montagu had her daughter inoculated in London, although it had been known by report for some years previously. It was practised on only a very limited scale during the 1720s and 1730s, owing mainly to the fact that the very severe technique of inoculation caused several deaths. Between 1721 and 1728 there were 897 people known to have been inoculated, 17 of whom were suspected to have died from inoculated smallpox. In the early 1740s the practice was revived again mainly as a result of the use of a safer technique involving milder injections of virus. However, because the medical profession had elaborated inoculation from its original simplicity into a very complex operation involving both a fortnight's preparation and convalescence, often in a special isolation hospital, the practice became very expensive, and was consequently restricted to the rich. Although the London Smallpox Hospital was founded in 1746 to offer charitable inoculations to the poor, most of its clients in the early period tended to be servants of the subscribers to the foundation of the hospital.

During the 1750s the overseers of the poor began to pay the cost of inoculation for all the poor within their parish; this usually took place as a response to the threat of a smallpox epidemic which provoked mass inoculation among all members of the parish. In addition to these mass inoculations there were many individuals who were inoculated at their own expense. Thus Kirkpatrick wrote in 1754: 'But since we have certain accounts that the populace, who were at first strongly predisposed against this practice, and who so rarely stop at the Golden Mean, are rushing into the contrary extreme; and go promiscuously from different distances to little Market Towns, where without any medical advice, and very little consideration, they procure inoculation from some operator, too often as crude and thoughtless as themselves ... '[1] This popularization of inoculation was made possible by its cheapness through the activities of local surgeons and apothecaries.[2]

However, inoculation did not become really widespread until after the 1760s, for, according to one source, only 200,000 people had been inoculated in England by 1766.[3] The main reason why inoculation was not more widespread was the occasional mortality still associated with the operation. This situation was changed in the 1760s when the Sutton family began to inoculate by injecting the minimal amount of virus into the arm with the very lightest of scratches. The result was that 'if any patient has twenty or thirty pustules he is said to have the smallpox very heavy',[4] thus ensuring a negligible risk of death. The Suttons claimed in 1768 'that about fifty-five thousand had been inoculated by them since the year 1760; of which number only six had died'.[5] The 'Suttonian Practice' consisted of Robert Sutton, an apothecary and surgeon at Framlington Earl, Norfolk, and several of his sons, as well as a very large number of non-family partners; the practice extended to most counties and several foreign countries.[6] The most famous son was Daniel Sutton, who, because of his very

[1] J. Kirkpatrick, *The Analysis of Inoculation* (1754), pp. 267, 268.
[2] This was achieved through the simplification of inoculation, culminating in the abandonment of preparation and convalescence by Lewis Paul Williams (a Leicestershire surgeon) in 1763. See *Northampton Mercury*, 15 December 1768; *The British Medical Journal*, 11 (1910), 633–34.
[3] See A. C. Klebs, 'The Historic Evolution of Variolation', *Bulletin of the Johns Hopkins Hospital*, XXIV (March 1913), 82. The basis of this estimate is unknown.
[4] Creighton, op. cit., p. 476.
[5] R. Houlton, *Indisputable Facts, Relative To The Suttonian Art Of Inoculation* (Dublin, 1768), p. 10. The negligible risk of death from inoculation after the 1760s is confirmed by a great deal of evidence.
[6] Ibid., pp. 21–3.

spectacular feats of inoculation,[1] was chiefly responsible for popularizing the Suttonian method. By the end of 1776 they claimed to have inoculated 300,000 people,[2] a claim which is very plausible in the light of the very large number of partners they had. They offered to inoculate the rural poor *gratis* on the condition presumably that the rest of the parish were also inoculated by them; certainly the Suttons appear in the account books of innumerable overseers who paid them for mass inoculations in their parishes.

The Suttonian method was soon taken up by the rest of the medical profession, as well as by amateur inoculators who began to proliferate very rapidly. Thus Houlton wrote in 1768 'that in every county of England you meet advertisements of these pretenders and itinerants . . . . Some of them as before observed, advertise that they inoculate according to the *Sutton method*; while others have the modesty to deck their imposition with the style of "*The Suttonian art improved*" . . . '[3] Some of these 'pretenders and itinerants' were undoubtedly professional surgeons and apothecaries, such as Dimsdale, who was converted to the Suttonian method by its superiority over the older technique; another professional medical practitioner who later inoculated with the Suttonian method before discovering vaccination was Edward Jenner, who had been inoculated in the old method as a boy during the mass inoculation at Wootton-under-Edge in 1756. Others of the imitators of the Suttonian method were 'a certain tribe of empirics and other unexperienced Practitioners',[4] such as the livery servant who left his employment in about 1768 to become a full-time inoculator[5] and the farrier and blacksmith who inoculated 170 people in the neighbourhood of Norwich in 1769.[6] The occupations of the amateur inoculators ranged from farmer to customs-officer, and some set up schools in their own method of inoculation.

Inoculation was practised much more extensively and earlier

[1] During a mass inoculation at Maldon, Essex, he inoculated 487 people in one day, none of whom died.

[2] W. R. Clayton, 'Notes on the history, incidence and treatment of smallpox in Norfolk', *Norfolk Archaeological Society*, XXX, 7.

[3] Houlton, op. cit., p. 24.

[4] M. G. Hobson, *Otmoor and its Seven Towns* (Oxford, 1961), p. 20.

[5] W. Watson, *An Account . . . of Inoculating the Small Pox* (Dublin, 1768), pp 71, 72.

[6] *Gentleman's Magazine*, XXXIX (1769), p. 167.

in rural areas and small towns than in large towns and cities. Haygarth, writing in 1780, stated that

> whole villages in this neighbourhood (Chester) and many other parts of Britain, have been inoculated with one consent. And it cannot be supposed that the inhabitants of towns are more ignorant or more obstinate. There is not a reasonable doubt that our poor fellow citizens would eagerly and universally embrace a proposal to preserve their children from death and deformity, if the intelligent and the opulent would humanely exert their influence and assistance to carry it into execution.[1]

Although the relative lack of provision of charitable inoculation was one of the major reasons why it spread only slowly in the large towns, another reason was because of the differing structure of smallpox epidemics in town and countryside. In the large towns where the disease was endemic all smallpox deaths were of infants and young children; this tended to engender a fatalistic attitude about the inevitability of catching the disease. This was recognized by Haygarth when he wrote that

> the lower class of people (in Chester) have no fear of the casual (natural) smallpox. Many more examples occurred of their wishes and endeavour to catch the infection, than to avoid it. This . . . prejudice . . . probably prevails in other large towns, especially in those which are so large as perpetually to nourish the distemper, by so quick a succession of infants as constantly to supply fresh subjects for infection . . .[2]

This he contrasted with 'small towns and villages, especially where placed in remote situations, the young generation grow up to have a consciousness of the danger before they are attacked by the dreadful disease'.[3] This consciousness was also based on the greater fatality of smallpox in isolated areas. One of its results was seen at Blandford, Dorset, in 1766 when a very malignant epidemic of smallpox broke out and 'a perfect rage

---

[1] J. Haygarth, *An Enquiry How To Prevent The Smallpox* (Chester, 1785), p. 164.
[2] J. Haygarth, *A Sketch of A Plan to Exterminate the Casual Smallpox* (1793), p. 186.
[3] Ibid., p. 186.

for inoculation seized the town'.[1] In the small town or village it was possible for everybody to compare the spectacular differences in mortality of the inoculated and uninoculated during a smallpox epidemic, whereas in a large town it was very difficult to familiarize the poorer classes with the benefits of inoculation owing to the dispersed and piecemeal nature of smallpox mortality.

The relatively slow spread of inoculation in the large towns must not be exaggerated in importance, for only a small minority of the total population lived in such areas. Also it appears that inoculation was making rapid headway in the large towns by the very end of the eighteenth century.[2] In the small towns and villages inoculation appears to have been universally practised well before the end of the century. There are innumerable references to mass inoculations in local histories and medical writings for every decade from about 1750 onwards.[3] One of the reasons why parish authorities were so willing to pay for inoculation of their poor was because of the great expenses involved in isolating and nursing the sick during an epidemic of the natural smallpox. The costs were sufficiently great to make many parishes *compel* everyone within their jurisdiction to be inoculated.[4]

One observer noted in 1771 'that inoculation, which was heretofore in a manner confined to people of superior ranks, is now practised even in the meanest cottages, and is almost universally received in every corner of this kingdom'.[5] According to Dimsdale, writing in 1776,

> in the county of Hertford, there have been two methods of public or general inoculation; one to inoculate, at a low price, as many of the inhabitants of any small town or village, as

[1] Creighton, op. cit., p. 513.

[2] Many of these large towns founded dispensaries during the late eighteenth century which provided charitable inoculation. Although the London Smallpox Hospital only inoculated 36,378 people between 1746 and 1805, practitioners such as Daniel Sutton specialized in the inoculation of 'the families of artificers, handicraftsmen, servants, labourers, etc.' in the Metropolis.

[3] See the Appendix.

[4] See S. and B. Webb, *English Local Government – English Poor Law History*, I (1927), 306; M. F. Davies, *Life in an English Village* (1909), p. 74; E. G. Thomas, *The Parish Overseer in Essex, 1597–1834* (London M.A. Thesis, 1956), p. 394.

[5] *Medical Transactions*, II (1772), p. 279.

could be persuaded to submit to it, and at the same time were able to pay, refusing all those who had it not in their power to procure the money demanded. The other method has been, where the inhabitants of a town, or a district, of all denominations, have agreed to be inoculated at the same time, the parish officers or some neighbouring charitably disposed persons, having first promised to defray the expense, and provide subsistance for such of the poor, as unable to pay for themselves.[1]

To some extent the emergence of the amateur inoculators served the needs of the poor, who were unable to afford the price of professional inoculation and whose parish was unwilling to pay for a mass inoculation. A supporter of inoculation summed up the extent of the practice by writing in 1805 that 'smallpox inoculation was a well-known, proved, and absolute prevention from receiving the *natural Smallpox* infection, as millions of people now living can testify'.[2] Inoculation did not disappear with the introduction of vaccination. On the contrary, it remained very popular, especially with the poorer classes, who were very prejudiced against vaccination. Ironically, inoculation and vaccination appeared to have supplemented one another, in that virtually all of the population during the first half of the nineteenth century were protected by one injection or the other, sometimes by both.[3] Inoculation was eventually banned by law in 1840 at the instigation of the supporters of vaccination, who accused inoculation of spreading natural smallpox to the unprotected.

Inoculation was very extensively practised in other countries, several of which encouraged it by legal enactments during the latter half of the eighteenth century, e.g. Sweden, Russia, and Austria. It appears to have been particularly popular in Ireland,

---

[1] T. Dimsdale, *Thoughts On General and Partial Inoculations* (1776), p. 29.

[2] W. Rowley, *Cowpox Inoculation no Security Against Smallpox* (1805), p. 4.

[3] See Dr J. Forbes, 'Some Account of the Small Pox lately Prevalent in Chichester and its Vicinity', *London Medical Repository* (September 1822), pp. 211–15, for an invaluable description of the history of inoculation and vaccination during the first two decades of the nineteenth century. Vaccination was not introduced into the area until 1812, although all the population appeared to have been protected by inoculation at least as early as the beginning of the nineteenth century.

where itinerant tinker inoculators proceeded 'from village to village several times during the year for the purpose of *inoculating* the infantile population'.[1]

III

In order to determine the significance of inoculation it is necessary to discuss the history of smallpox mortality before its effective introduction. By smallpox mortality we mean the proportion of every 100 children born who died from the disease during their lives. There are two methods of estimating such smallpox mortality: (1) multiplying the extent of the disease by its case-fatality rate (allowing for children who would have died before they had a chance to catch the disease); (2) counting the number of smallpox deaths and expressing it as a proportion of the number of births, such information being occasionally found in parish registers – in a period of static population growth the proportion of smallpox deaths to all deaths will approximate to the ratio of smallpox deaths per number of births. In order to estimate smallpox mortality we will use both methods outlined above. First, however, it is necessary to discuss the problem in interpreting smallpox statistics.

There are five major difficulties in using figures of smallpox mortality: (1) The existence of a type of smallpox, known as fulminating smallpox, which does not manifest the classical pock symptoms because of the rapidity with which it kills its victims. It has been discovered only relatively recently, for as a current medical authority on smallpox has observed, 'this is "sledge-hammer" smallpox, and the diagnosis both clinical and at autopsy is impossible unless smallpox is thought of and unless laboratory facilities are available and used to grow the virus'.[2] It is impossible to estimate what proportion of all smallpox deaths were of the fulminating kind; generally it would be highest in very isolated communities which lacked a pool of antibodies derived from frequent epidemics. (2) The variation in fatality of smallpox in different types of area. This was recognized by Lettsom when he wrote 'that in some

---

[1] W. Wilde, 'Report on Tables of Deaths', *Population Census of Ireland 1851*, Parl. Pap., 1843 (24), p. xii.

[2] C. W. Dixon, *Smallpox* (1962), p. 9.

countries, and even some counties of England, the infection does not appear for the space of some years; but when it does appear, it is more fatal; owing probably to this, that in great towns the infection being always prevalent, it is caught without the accumulated changes of air peculiarly favourable to epidemics; whereas when it comes at stated periods its malignity seems to be augmented by some unknown but deleterious state of the atmosphere.'[1] This, we now know, was due to the creation of a pool of antibodies in the large towns through constant recurrence of smallpox epidemics, which it has already been noticed occurred to a lesser extent in isolated areas. (3) A large number of smallpox deaths were unregistered for other reasons. Lettsom, who had a great deal of experience with the health of the poor in London, estimated that smallpox mortality was nearly twice that recorded in the Bills of Mortality, 'the genetic article "convulsions" having swallowed up, in his opinion, a large number of the smallpox deaths of infants'.[2] Very young infants are known to be vulnerable to fulminating smallpox[3] – and it appears that this could be partly the explanation of this mis-registration.[4] Lettsom also pointed out that from smallpox 'some have been deprived of sight; many have been afflicted with the evil and scrofulous complaints, to which they had previously been strangers; many have been disabled in their limbs . . . at length, emaciated and debilitated, they have sunk under their miseries, and filled up the amazing list of consumptions; many of which originated from the violence of Natural Smallpox'.[5] Smallpox mortality was also much higher when the disease converged with epidemics of other diseases; some of the increased mortality would be ascribed to the other disease. (4) Pregnant women are particularly vulnerable when attacked by smallpox,[6] the great majority of their children

---

[1] T. J. Pettigrew, *Memoirs of the Life and Writings of the late John Cockley Lettsom* (1817), II, 121, 122.

[2] Creighton, op. cit., p. 534.

[3] Dixon, op. cit., p. 324.

[4] See J. Haygarth, *A Sketch of a Plan to Exterminate the Casual Small-Pox* (1793), p. 141: 'The disease most fatal to infants is convulsions, arising from various causes; one of them is the small-pox. The two circumstances will explain the reason why, under one year old, the proportion of deaths by the smallpox is less than in subsequent periods. . . .'

[5] Pettigrew, op. cit., I, 6.

[6] Dixon, op. cit., p. 326.

dying because of such an attack. According to Dixon, 'in forty-six cases where the infant's condition is recorded (when the mother has been attacked by smallpox), twenty-six were still-born, and of the twenty born alive, eleven died later'.[1] Most of the stillborn children and many of those infants which died soon after birth were probably not recorded in the parish registers, as they would not have been baptized; those deaths which were recorded were probably attributed to some causes other than smallpox, e.g. convulsions. Also according to a doctor of the Bristol Royal Infirmary during the middle of the eighteenth century, 'the female sex whose cases from about 12 years of age to 50 become more dangerous on account of their menstrual discharges, which sometimes coming on in the beginning or State of the Disease proves fatal'.[2] Thus the group of potential mothers was particularly vulnerable to death from smallpox, a fact that we shall discuss later in connection with changes in the birth-rate. (5) Many people who died of smallpox appear to have been buried in non-consecrated burial pits near the pest-houses or infirmaries used for isolating those sick of the disease. In the Maidstone parish register the incumbent summarized the burials for the year 1760 with the following entry: 'Total Burials – 223. Of the Small Pox from Dec. 13–59. besides. These carried out of Town 102.' It is quite clear from examining the average number of burials in Maidstone that these 102 smallpox victims were not a part of the total 223 burials, a conclusion confirmed by examining the ages of those buried in the churchyard. It is thought that they were buried out at the pest-house because it was quite common practice in the eighteenth century for hospitals to bury their own dead. Both the Northampton and London bills of mortality had yearly returns of the number of people buried in local infirmaries. People responsible for isolating and nursing smallpox victims were also considered responsible for burying them,[3] and this was because people were so terrified of smallpox that they feared the corpses themselves; there are references in the literature of incumbents refusing to perform the burial rites,

[1] Dixon, op. cit., p. 113.
[2] *Bristol Infirmary Biographical Memoirs*, I, 59.
[3] See, for example, W. Le Hardy (ed.), *Calendar to The Herts Session Books, 1752–1799*, VIII (Hertford, 1935), 226.

and relatives refusing to attend funerals.[1] The existence of these non-consecrated burial grounds not only poses a problem for the construction of smallpox mortality statistics but also for those demographic studies which assume that burials entered in the parish register represent the total number of deaths.

We are now in a position to estimate total smallpox mortality. As earlier stated, there are two methods in arriving at such estimates, the first being to multiply the extent of smallpox by its case-fatality rate. As to the extent of the disease, most writers regarded it as a universal affliction to which all were subjected at some time or other, e.g. D'Escheray, in his writings on smallpox in England, observed in 1760 that 'this distemper spares neither Age nor Sex, Rich and Poor are equally exposed to its influence. What is the most unaccountable, and so wide from all other fevers, is, that the Difference of Constitution is no preservative against its Attack, insomuch, that very few escape it, at one time or other.'[2] This universality of smallpox is consistent with what we know about the nature of the disease; e.g. Dr J. F. D. Shrewsbury, the bacteriologist, has written that smallpox is 'the most highly infectious of the transmissible diseases of man'.[3] It appears from statistical evidence that smallpox was endemic in London as early as at least the sixteenth century; in fact, the disease was so endemic as to be found regularly every week in the bills of mortality during the seventeenth and eighteenth centuries. Smallpox deaths occurred in other large towns during the eighteenth century at least every year. Thus London, and other large towns to a lesser extent, were smallpox reservoirs from which the disease was constantly exported to the countryside.

The case-fatality rate of smallpox may be estimated from a series of smallpox censuses conducted during the 1720s. The figures compiled were for the number of total cases of smallpox sickness with the resulting numbers of deaths in thirty places. Of the 13,192 cases of people suffering from smallpox, 2,167 died i.e. an average case-fatality rate of 16·5 per cent.[4] This figure must be interpreted in the light of the difficulties in using smallpox statistics that we have already discussed. Three of the

[1] See, for example, Document I.C. 1185, 1679 in the Northampton Record Office.
[2] D. D'Escheray, *An Essay on the Smallpox* (1760), p. 2.
[3] Private communication, 1964.
[4] For details of the censuses see Creighton, op. cit., 518, 519.

difficulties are relevant: (1) the figures would exclude cases of fulminating smallpox, the mortality from which is nearly 100 per cent; (2) large numbers of unregistered deaths would have been excluded, in the ways described by Lettsom; (3) variations in the fatality of smallpox varied from one type of area to another. With reference to the last difficulty, most of the censuses were conducted in market towns, many of them in Yorkshire and centres of industrial activity. These were towns of very frequently recurring epidemics, which consequently had a lower case-fatality rate than places such as the isolated villages in Worcestershire studied by Eversley.[1] He has written that during the smallpox epidemic of 1725–30 in the area of Bromsgrove 'a conservative estimate of the net loss of population at Hanbury is 164 out of the 716 alive in 1715'.[2] This was similar to the epidemics in the Shetland Islands, where 'formerly the smallpox occasioned the most dreadful ravages in these islands frequently carrying off a fifth part of the inhabitants',[3] 'in 1720, the disease was so fatal as to be distinguished by the name of the mortal pox. On this occasion tradition tells us, in the remote Island of Foula, probably inhabited by about two hundred people, it left only four to six to bury the dead.'[4] This type of spectacular smallpox mortality was to be found in other extremely isolated places where the population had no pool of antibodies to protect them.[5] It was noted by one contemporary medical observer 'that when the smallpox is epidemic, entire villages are depopulated, markets ruined, and the face of distress spread over the whole country'.[6] Certainly epidemics of the fatality of the one in Hanbury occurred quite often.[7] As about

[1] D. E. C. Eversley, 'A Survey of Population in an Area of Worcestershire', *Population Studies*, X (1956–7).

[2] Ibid., p. 267.

[3] J. Sinclair, *The Statistical Account of Scotland*, II (1792), 569–70.

[4] Robert Cowie, *Shetland: Descriptive & Historical* (Aberdeen, 1871), pp. 73–5. See also Sinclair, op. cit., XX (1798), 101, for another description of this epidemic.

[5] See E. W. and A. E. Stearn, *The Effect of Smallpox on the Destiny of the American Indian* (Boston, U.S.A., 1945); also *Royal Commission on Vaccination*, 1st Report (1889), pp. 109, 110.

[6] James McKenzie, *The History of Health* (1760).

[7] See the *Parish Register of Burford* in 1758; also *Gentleman's Magazine*, XLII (1772), 542. Many of the mass inoculations suggest that a very large proportion of village populations were vulnerable to smallpox, e.g., at Irthlingborough, Northants, 'upwards of Five Hundred People' were inoculated in 1778, whereas the total population was only 811 by 1801.

23 per cent of the total population of Hanbury was wiped out, the case-fatality rate must have been considerably higher than this, for many of the older members of the village must have had smallpox when they were younger. Thus it appears that the case-fatality rate of 16½ per cent derived from the smallpox censuses in the market towns is much too low for the country as a whole. It is impossible to estimate total smallpox mortality for the whole countryside using the present method; suffice it to say that smallpox was a universal disease with a recorded case-fatality rate varying from 16½ per cent to 97 per cent.

The other method of estimating smallpox mortality is to use the parish registers and bills of mortality. Ideally, we would like to express the number of smallpox deaths as a proportion of the number of births. This is not always possible because of the lack of information about births, the deficiencies in registration, etc. When it is not possible the proportion of smallpox deaths to all deaths will be used, as it will generally approximate to the smallpox deaths/births ratio because of the relatively equal number of births and deaths during a period of static population. The smallpox mortality-rate in the eighteenth century varies from 11·6 smallpox deaths per 100 births in London during 1730–39,[1] 20 per 100 deaths in Dublin during the two approximate 30-year periods 1661–90 and 1715–46,[2] to an extreme proportion of 50 per 100 deaths in Great Chart, Kent, during 1688–1707.[3] The majority of records (mainly for towns) yield an average figure of about 15 per cent of all births and deaths due to smallpox during the first half of the eighteenth century. All of the difficulties outlined earlier in the paper apply to these statistics, and all of them would tend to increase actual smallpox mortality over recorded mortality, e.g. Lettsom's estimate of the true smallpox mortality in London would raise the figure for 1730–39 from 11·6 smallpox deaths per 100 births to over 20 per 100, this being in an area where smallpox mortality was at its lowest due to the endemic nature of the disease. Once again it is impossible to estimate exactly the

[1] J. Marshall, *Mortality of the Metropolis* (1832).

[2] J. Fleetwood, *History of Medicine in Ireland* (Dublin, 1951), p. 65; Dr J. Rutty, *A Chronological History of the Weather and Seasons, and of the Prevailing Diseases in Dublin* (Dublin, 1770).

[3] M. C. Buer, *Health, Wealth, and Population in the Early Days of the Industrial Revolution* (1926), p. 190.

magnitude of smallpox mortality, but for the time being it will be sufficient to note that recorded smallpox deaths accounted for between 11·6 and 50 per cent of all those born and dying, and that actual smallpox mortality was possibly twice as large as that actually recorded.

IV

Why has the possibility of inoculation reducing smallpox mortality been rejected by previous historians? The two basic reasons for rejecting the effectiveness of inoculation have been: (1) the argument that inoculation spread natural smallpox to the unprotected; (2) the continuance of smallpox deaths in the bills of mortality of some of the large towns.

There are several reasons why the objection that inoculation spread natural smallpox is spurious: (*a*) smallpox was already a universal disease before the introduction of inoculation; (*b*) inoculation had become so widespread by the end of the eighteenth century that only a relatively small proportion of the population was left unprotected; (*c*) experimental and other evidence is available to show that inoculation did not spread natural smallpox to the unprotected. This conclusion is supported by the fact that *vaccination is in reality a more attenuated form of inoculation*.[1]

Smallpox did continue to kill substantial numbers of children in some of the large towns during the late eighteenth century, but this has misled medical historians for two reasons: (*a*) the total population increased very rapidly in these places, and if the number of smallpox deaths is expressed as a proportion of the number of children at risk a marked reduction in smallpox mortality is seen to have taken place; (*b*) as we have already seen, these large towns were atypical, in that inoculation spread much later in them than elsewhere. This was stated quite explicitly by Howlett in 1781:

> It may be thought, at first sight, that the healthiness of London is more increased than that of country towns . . .

[1] It is impossible in this paper to document this very controversial statement. The subject is of sufficient importance to warrant a separate paper. Suffice it to say that the inoculators were able to produce a single vesicle at the site of injection identical to that of vaccination, through a process of attenuation. Inoculation was superior to vaccination in that it conferred life-long immunity against further attacks of smallpox, owing to the larger amount of virus injected.

But it must be remembered that the diminished mortality in the latter appears to be chiefly owing to the salutary practice of inoculation; whereas in the former, for want of universality, it has hitherto been of little advantage . . . In provincial towns and villages, as soon as this disorder makes its appearance, inoculation takes place amongst all ranks of people; the rich and poor, from either choice or necessity, almost instantly have recourse to it; and where two or three hundred used to be carried to their graves in the course of a few months, there are now perhaps not above 20 or 30.[1]

Smallpox Mortality at Maidstone, 1754–1801[2]

Period	Smallpox burials	All burials
1752–63	252	1,703
1762–71	76	1,426
1772–81	60	1,549
1782–91	91	1,676
1792–1801	2	2,068

An illustration of this reduction of smallpox mortality is to be found at Maidstone in Kent.

A mass inoculation was conducted by Daniel Sutton in 1776, and its effects were described by Howlett in a pamphlet by him in 1782.

Upon casting an eye over the annual lists of burials, we see that, before the modern improved method of inoculation was introduced, every 5 or 6 years the average number was almost doubled; and it was found upon enquiry, that at such intervals nearly the smallpox used to repeat its periodical visits . . . in the short space of 30 years it deprived the town of between five and six hundred of its inhabitants; whereas in the 15 or 16 years that have elapsed since that general

[1] Rev. J. Howlett, *An Examination of Dr Price's Essay on the Population of England and Wales* (Maidstone, 1781), p. 94.

[2] Taken from the *Parish Register of Maidstone*, lodged in All Saints Church, Maidstone. Smallpox deaths disappeared from the register after 1797. This gradual decline of smallpox cannot be attributed to a decrease in the virulence of the disease, as all the evidence points to the opposite conclusion, i.e. an increase in its virulence, e.g. the case-fatality rates at the London Smallpox Hospital were as follows in 1746–63, 25%; 1775–99, 32%; 1836–56, 35%. See the *Royal Commission on Vaccination*, 1st Report (1889), p. 74, and the *Royal Commission on Vaccination*, 3rd Report (1890), p. 100.

inoculation it has occasioned the deaths of only about 60. Ample and satisfactory evidence of the vast benefits the town has received from that salutary invention.[1]

There are many other statistical tables which can be produced to prove the effectiveness of inoculation,[2] the most detailed being for Boston, USA, during the eighteenth century, from which it is possible to attribute the reduced mortality directly to inoculation.[3]

The effects of inoculation were described in contemporary literature; e.g. in *She Stoops to Conquer* written in 1773, Mrs Hardcastle says to Hastings: 'I vow since Inoculation began, there is no such thing to be seen as a plain woman. So one must dress a little particular; or one may escape in the crowd.' Arthur Young, writing an essay on population in 1781, wrote:

In several of these parishes where population had for some periods been rather on the decrease, a great change has taken place lately, and the last ten years are found to be in a rapid state of progression; as considerable drains of men have been made from almost every parish in the kingdom for the public service in that period, I should not have expected this result, and know nothing to which it can be owing, unless the prevalence of inoculation, which certainly has been attended with a very great effect.[4]

There are also references to the effects of inoculation on mortality in the reports on agriculture made by local observers to the Board of Agriculture at the end of the eighteenth century,

[1] J. Howlett, *Observations on the Increased Population . . . of Maidstone* (Maidstone, 1782), p. 8.

[2] For the sources of these statistics see: the parish registers of Basingstoke (Hants), Calne (Wilts.), Milton Ernest (Beds.), Whittington (Salop), Selattyn (Salop), Boston (Lincs.). For other statistics see 'An Abridgement of the Observations on the Bills of Mortality in Carlisle, 1779–87; by Dr Heysham in W. Hutchinson, *The History of Cumberland* (Carlisle, 1794), pp. 668–75.

[3] The number of inoculations in this town increased from 287 in 1721 to 9,152 in 1792, which was the vast majority who had not had smallpox before. Smallpox mortality fell from 175 smallpox deaths per 1,000 living population in 1677–8 to 10 per 1,000 in 1792, and this was in spite of the fact that the virulence of the disease generally increased throughout the period. See J. Blake, *Public Health in the Town of Boston (Mass.), 1630–1822* (Cambridge, U.S.A. 1959), p. 244; H. R. Viets (ed.), *A Brief Rule to Guide the Common People of New England* (1937), p. xxxv; *Royal Commission on Vaccination*, 6th Report, Parl. Pap. 1896 (47), p. 762.

[4] A. Young, *Annals of Agriculture*, VII (1786), 455.

e.g. 'I may further add, that since the year 1782, when these observations were made, the population of this parish has been increasing: most certainly inoculation for the Smallpox . . . has been most essential to population throughout this kingdom.'[1] Similarly John Holt of Lancashire wrote in 1795: 'One reason, why persons in large manufactures in Lancashire, do not frequently die in great numbers . . . is that they have (in general) been inoculated in their infancy. Inoculation is the most effectual of all expedients for preserving the short lived race of men – many gentlemen pay for inoculation of the children of the poor in their own neighbourhood.'[2]

In 1796 it was observed that

the increase of people within the last 25 years is visible to every observer. Inoculation is the mystic spell which has produced this wonder . . . before that time it may be safely asserted, that the malady, added to the general laws of nature, did at least equipoise population. It is now 30 years since the Suttons and others under their instructions, had practised the art of inoculation upon half the kingdom and had reduced the chance of death to 1 in 2,000.[3]

Similarly, another gentleman observed later in 1803 that 'one very great cause of increasing population may be ascribed to the success of inoculation for the Smallpox. One in four or five, or about 200 to 250 in a thousand, usually died of this loathsome disorder in the natural way of infection . . . so that this saving of lives alone would account for our increasing number, without perplexing ourselves for any other cause.'[4]

It is necessary to attempt to evaluate the claims that some contemporaries made of the effect of inoculation on population growth. Unfortunately there is virtually no reliable demographic data available with which we can do this. An analysis of the 'county family' life tables suggests that a reduction of about 25 per cent in mortality among the younger age-groups could account for the whole increase in expectation of life between 1681–1730 and 1781–1830. The same conclusion probably applies to both the ducal families and the whole of the

[1] J. Plymley, *General View of the Agriculture of Shropshire* (1803), pp. 343, 344.
[2] J. Holt, *General View of the Agriculture of Lancaster* (1795), p. 208, n. 2.
[3] *Gentleman's Magazine*, LXVI, 1 (1796), n. 112.
[4] *Gentleman's Magazine*, LXXIII, 1 (1803), 213.

aristocracy. For the population as a whole there is no data sufficiently reliable to test the hypothesis directly. However, it is possible to construct a simple hypothetical model whose limits are defined by the small amount of reliable information that we do possess. In 1697 Gregory King constructed a 'life table' for Lichfield; Professor Glass has written that 'it would appear that by taking Lichfield as a basis, King began with a collection of statistics which were probably not markedly untypical, and then adjusted more acceptably as an indication of national structure'.[1] It is possible by using King's 'life table' to construct a hypothetical population reproduction model for our period.

Female Population Reproduction, 1750–1855

Numbers surviving to the following ages (*years*)	Numbers surviving in the following years							
	1750	*1765*	*1780*	*1795*	*1810*	*1825*	*1840*	*1855*
0	1,000	1,071	1,237	1,468	1,762	2,116	2,538	3,045
15	620	680	793	952	1,138	1,366	1,640	1,967
30	450	480	559	659	798	956	1,146	1,376
45	315	325	357	422	498	603	722	866
60	190	190	196	215	255	300	364	435
75	50	50	50	52	57	67	79	85
90	0	0	0	0	0	0	0	0
Population Index [2]	2,125	2,260	2,573	3,034	3,627	4,350	5,220	6,251

The above model was constructed on the following assumptions: (1) increase in the female population was proportionate to the increase in total population; this ignores the effects of the relationship between the number of males and females, e.g. the proportion of married women who were widowed; (2) of 1,000 female children born before 1750, the numbers surviving to various ages were the same as in King's 'life table'; (3) the population was static before 1750, based on an age-specific birth-rate of 1 female child born for every 13·7625 women living between 15 and 45; (4) the age-specific birth-rate remained

---

[1] D. V. Glass, 'Gregory King's Estimate of the Population of England and Wales, 1695', *Population Studies*, III (1949–50), 368.

[2] This population index is the sum of the average number of people living in each age-period, i.e. I have not bothered to multiply by 15 throughout.

F

constant throughout the whole period; (5) of every 1,000 born, lives were saved in the following manner:

Ages (years)	Period 1750–65	1765–80	1780–95	1795–1810
Under 15	60	60	20	15
15–30	30	30	5	5
30–45	10	10	5	0

In all, it is assumed that 250 lives were saved out of 1,000 born. According to our earlier estimates of population growth, it almost exactly trebled between 1750 and 1851. In our model it does not quite do this, but we assumed that population was static before 1750, whereas according to the earlier estimates it was increasing about 0·2 per cent per annum between 1700 and 1750. If an allowance is made for this pre-1750 growth population in our model increases by 3·2 times between 1750 and 1851; the greater the allowance made for pre-1750 growth, the more the model population increase will exceed that as estimated. The point of the model is not to describe exact changes in the population structure, but rather to estimate the magnitude of lives required to be saved in order to generate the rate of increase in estimated population. The assumptions are thought to be realistic because: (1) the crude birth-rate appears to have been very similar between the 1690s and the 1840s;[1] (2) the saving of life (250 out of 1,000 born) assumed is very similar to that which took place among the gentry and aristocracy.

In order for inoculation against smallpox to account for the whole of the population increase, smallpox mortality before inoculation must have been about 310 deaths per 1,000 born, for of the 250 lives saved of every 1,000 born in our model, about 45 would have died of other diseases during the same

[1] The birth-rate was estimated as 34·5 births per 1,000 living during the 1690s by Gregory King and 35·2 per 1,000 during 1841–5 by Professor Glass from civil registration returns. See G. King, 'Natural and Political Observation 1696', in George Chalmers, *An Estimate of the Comparative Strength of Great Britain* (1804), p. 44; and D. V. Glass, 'A Note on the Under-registration of Births in Britain in the Nineteenth Century', *Population Studies*, V (1951), 85. Professor Glass has written about the basis of King's estimate: 'the statistics collected were more comprehensive than any provided previously and, indeed, than any subsequent statistics prior to the establishment of the full mechanism of censuses and civil registration in the nineteenth century'. See D. V. Glass, 'Gregory King and the Population of England and Wales', *Eugenics Review*, XXXVII (1946), 175.

age-period, while smallpox accounted for about 1½ per cent of deaths of all born during 1838–40,[1] when civil registration was first introduced. It is impossible to state definitely that smallpox mortality before inoculation was as high as 310 deaths per 1,000 born, but we may conclude from our earlier discussion that this is certainly a plausible figure. It must be remembered that much of this saving of life would have been indirect, in so much as the elimination of smallpox attacks probably increased the expectation of life of those who did not die of the disease. Also the vulnerability of mothers and other young adult females to smallpox could have meant that the elimination of the disease led to an increase in the birth-rate; e.g. at Basingstoke (Hants) the average number of baptisms in the ten years before the smallpox epidemic in 1741 was 69·6, whereas in the following ten years it fell to 45·5 (a much greater fall than the average number of deaths and therefore presumably the population), which was possibly due to the fact that one-half of the smallpox deaths occurred among adults.[2] A rise in the age-specific birth-rate was not allowed for in the population reproduction model for two reasons: (1) simplicity and economy; (2) the very long-term stability of the estimated crude birth-rate. Thus any increase in the birth-rate has been absorbed for analytical reasons into a fall in the death-rate.

Although it is not possible to analyse in any detail the history of other diseases, it is possible to draw some conclusions from bills of mortality. For example, in Northampton there was no major epidemic of any disease, other than smallpox, during the hundred-year period after 1736 when records were kept.[3] Smallpox epidemics occurred every seven years on average in Northampton before the introduction of inoculation; the listing of diseases and epidemics was very similar in a place like Maidstone; i.e. recurrent severe smallpox epidemics were the only causes of sharp rises in mortality-rates. This would indicate that the sharp peaks in mortality found in many local studies were due to smallpox and that they disappeared only with the introduction of inoculation.

---

[1] See Creighton, *op. cit.* This figure includes chickenpox deaths, which are assumed to approximate to omissions due to fulminating smallpox, etc.

[2] See the *Basingstoke Parish Register.*

[3] See the *Northampton Bills of Mortality* in the British Museum Library.

Ideally one would like to trace the history of all diseases in order to evaluate their importance in contributing to total mortality, but unlike smallpox, most other diseases prevalent in the eighteenth century are not sufficiently distinctive to be analysed statistically. Many incumbents in their returns to Sir John Sinclair for the *Statistical Account of Scotland* discussed the history of diseases in their parish. No disease, other than smallpox (due to inoculation), was described as having declined or disappeared, except ague (malaria), which is very frequently mentioned as having disappeared during the latter half of the eighteenth century. Recently one medical authority has questioned whether malaria was ever endemic in Britain.[1]

However, the incumbents so consistently mention that the disappearance of ague was linked with the draining of marshes, the reclamation of swamp-land, etc., that one is led to suspect that the disease they described was malaria; this is confirmed by any descriptions of the disease that they give. Buer, in her discussion of malaria, maintained that although 'its direct effect on the death-rate was small, its indirect effect must have been great'.[2] Certainly it rarely appeared in the bills of mortality and parish registers as a cause of death even during the early eighteenth century. Malaria in England is a subject which warrants further investigation.

Although this paper has laid great stress on the importance of inoculation against smallpox as a cause of the population explosion during the eighteenth century, this does not rule out the role of other explanations.[3] However, while there is no convincing evidence for any of these other explanations, we must provisionally reject them, and such a rejection can only be nullified by detailed and plausible evidence to the contrary. Inoculation against smallpox could theoretically explain the whole of the increase in population, and until other explanations are convincingly documented, it is an explanation which must stand as the best one available.[4] Although the Industrial and Agricultural Revolutions did not cause the population

---

[1] McKeown and Brown, op. cit., p. 124, n. 4.

[2] M. C. Buer, op. cit., p. 212.

[3] For example, the effects of the changing distribution of population between rural and urban areas has not been discussed in this paper.

[4] This is particularly true with respect to the increase in expectation of life of the aristocracy and gentry.

explosion, they at least enabled population to grow unchecked. In Ireland, where such Revolutions did not take place, the Malthusian check of mass starvation was the result of a rapidly increasing population without concomitant changes in the structure of the economy. The main achievement of the Industrial and Agricultural Revolutions in their earlier phases was the *maintenance* of the standard of living in a period when population was growing for reasons unconnected with the Revolutions themselves.

APPENDIX

In order to indicate the extent of mass inoculation, a sample was taken of those described in local histories, medical commentaries, accounts of the Overseers of the Poor, local newspapers, etc. The following list is in no sense comprehensive or representative, but merely a series of isolated examples culled from the literature, mainly from the South of England. The name of the town is given first, followed by the date of the mass inoculation:

Guildford, Surrey, 1740s. Salisbury, Wilts., 1751–2. Bradford-on-Avon, Wilts., 1752–3. Blandford, Dorset, 1753, 1766. Wootton-Under-Edge, Gloucs., 1756. First Regiment of Foot Guards, 1756. Beaminster, Dorset, 1758, 1780, 1791. Maldon, Essex, 1764. Maidstone, Kent, 1766. Marnham, Notts., 1767. Rye, Sussex, 1767. Neighbourhood of Norwich, 1769. Burton, Lincs., 1770. Berkhamstead and surrounding villages in Herts., 1770. Corsley, Wilts., 1773; Meopham, Kent, 1776. Bedford, Beds., 1777. Ware, Herts., 1777. Great Clivall, Essex, 1778. Irthlingborough, Northants., 1778. Villages in the neighbourhood of Carlisle, Cumberland, 1779, 1781. Cricklade, Wilts., 1783. Painswick, Gloucs., 1786. Knowle, Kent, 1787. Weston(?), 1788. Northwold, Norfolk, 1788. Cowden, Kent, 1788. Luton, Beds., 1788. Bozeat, Northants., 1789. Chislehurst, Kent, 1790, 1799. Toddington, Beds., 1790, 1801, 1824. Weston, Norfolk, 1791. Eaton Socon, Beds., 1793, 1800, 1808. Hevingham, Norfolk, 1794. Berkeley, Gloucs., 1795. Hastings, Sussex, 1796–7. Dursley, Gloucs., 1797. Three villages near Gillingham, 1797. Tenterden, Kent, 1798. Rayne, Essex, 1806. Chichester, Sussex, 1806, 1812, 1821.

Under Dimsdale's influence, mass inoculations increasingly became 'general' rather than 'partial'.[1] General inoculations usually involved a degree of compulsion, as was described by Cowper, the poet, in 1788: 'the smallpox has done, I believe, all that it has to do at Weston. Old folks, and even women with child, have been inoculated. . . . No circumstances whatsoever were permitted to exempt the inhabitants of Weston. The old, as well as the young, and the pregnant, as well as they who had only themselves within them, have been inoculated . . . .'[2] An example of the effects of general inoculation is to be found at Calne, Wilts. A local surgeon, Mr Wayte, described in 1795 a general inoculation as follows: 'in September, 1793, when the poor of the parish were inoculated . . . We inoculated six hundred and upwards . . . Besides the poor, I inoculated about two hundred (private) patients. . . . Now in inoculating a whole parish, we have no choice of patients, all ages, and the sickly as well as others, were inoculated; but these were mostly children, as I assisted in inoculating the whole parish, about twelve or thirteen years ago.'[3] According to the Calne parish register, the number of smallpox deaths declined as follows: 1723–42, 205; 1743–62, 122; 1763–82, 54; 1783–1802, 8. The last mention of smallpox deaths is in 1793 when there were 6; previous to this there had been a very minor epidemic in 1782 involving 10 deaths (this was the epidemic which provoked the earlier general inoculation mentioned by Wayte). These late-eighteenth-century epidemics should be compared with the major ones in the early eighteenth century, e.g. in 1732 there were 173 people registered as dying from smallpox.

[1] See, for example, T. Dimsdale, *Remarks on 'A Letter to Sir R. Barner . . .'* (1779), p. 13; and Walker, op. cit., p. 467, n.

[2] S. and B. Webb, *op. cit.*, p. 306, n. 2.

[3] Thomas Beddoes, 'Queries Respecting a Safer Method of Performing Inoculation', in Don A. De Gimbernat (Beddoes translated), *A New Method of Operating for the General Hernia* (London, 1795), pp. 56–9.

8 Family Limitation in Pre-Industrial England

E. A. WRIGLEY

[This article was first published in *The Economic History Review*, Vol. XIX (Utrecht, 1966).]

M. Louis Henry of the *Institut National d'Etudes Démographiques* in Paris has, by his development of the technique of family reconstitution, placed a powerful new weapon in the hands of historical demographers in those countries fortunate enough to possess good parish registers. By this method any running series of births (baptisms), deaths (burials), and marriages can be exploited to provide a detailed picture of many aspects of the fertility, mortality, and nuptiality of a community.

Family reconstitution is in principle a simple operation.[1] Information abstracted from the registers is transferred initially to slips, each event in each register being recorded on a separate slip. This in turn is collated on Family Reconstitution Forms (F.R.F.s), on each of which there is space to record the dates of baptism and burial of the two principals to the marriage, the date of the marriage itself, the names of the parents of the married couple, and, in the lower half of the form, the names and dates of baptism, marriage, and burial of all issue of the marriage. There is also space to record other information about residence, occupation, place of baptism and burial, and so on. Only a small proportion of families can be completely reconstituted in most parishes, but for many purposes partially reconstituted families can also be used. From the F.R.F.s a

---

[1] For a full description of the method and a discussion of the type of register to which it can be applied see E. A. Wrigley (ed.), *Introduction to English Historical Demography* (1966), Chapter 4. This in turn is largely based upon the earlier French manual of M. Fleury and L. Henry, *Des registres paroissiaux à l'histoire de la population. Manuel de dépouillement et d'exploitation de l'état civil ancien*, I.N.E.D. (Paris, 1956). A new and expanded edition of this work has recently been published.

wide range of demographic measures can be calculated, including such things as age at first marriage, age-specific marital
fertility, infant and child mortality, expectation of life (subject
to some margin of error), birth intervals, and the percentage of
pre-nuptial first pregnancies.

Only those registers in which there are few or no breaks are
suitable for family reconstitution. Nor is it always the case that
a register without any missing year is of use, since for successful
reconstitution the information given at each entry must normally be sufficient to allow the individual in question to be
identified with confidence. Many English registers fall short in
this respect. Nevertheless, by modifying French practice somewhat to take account of the idiosyncrasies of English parish
registers it is possible to apply Henry's family reconstitution
methods to some English registers. As a result, it is reasonable
to hope that in time the demographic history of England during
the period from the mid-sixteenth to the mid-nineteenth century will be seen much more fully and in much sharper focus.

Although in general it may be true that French parish
registers lend themselves more easily to family reconstitution
than English because the French *curés* were in the habit of
recording much more detail in their registers than the English
vicars in theirs,[1] in one respect England is very fortunate. A few
hundred English registers go right back to 1538, and a much
larger number is still extant from the early seventeenth century,
though of course it often happens that there are gaps, especially
for the Civil War years.[2] In France, in contrast, the registers are
seldom of use for family reconstitution purposes before the last
quarter of the seventeenth century. The middle years of the
seventeenth century both in England and on the Continent were
often a turning-point in demographic history when a period
of rapid population growth came to an end and a different

[1] The second chapter of E. Gautier and L. Henry, *La Population de Crulai*,
I.N.E.D. Cahier No. 33 (Paris, 1958), gives an account of the type of information
to be found in a good French register. See also E. A. Wrigley, *Some Problems of
Family Reconstitution using English Parish Register Material*, Proceedings of the
Third International Economic History Conference, Munich, 1965.

[2] No good general inventory of parish registers exists, though the Society of
Genealogists hopes shortly to publish a revised edition of the *National Index of
Parish Registers* which will cover both originals and transcripts. The inventory
which Rickman published in the 1831 Census is still the best starting-point for
work in many counties.

pattern of slower growth, stagnation, or decline set in. This occurred before most French registers are suitable for reconstitution, but some English parishes maintained good registers from a much earlier date. In them a complete cycle of demographic experience can be examined, beginning with a period of rapid growth in the sixteenth and early seventeenth centuries, followed by a check and decline, which in turn gave way to renewed growth during the eighteenth century.

I

The parish of Colyton in the Axe valley in east Devon possesses an exceptionally complete register. The record of baptisms, burials, and marriages is uninterrupted from 1538 to 1837 (the date of the beginning of civil registration) and beyond. Moreover, the degree of detail given at each entry varies considerably in different periods of the register. These two characteristics in combination made the Colyton register particularly suitable for a pilot study of family reconstitution using English parish registers. The second is important because it makes it possible to determine the threshold level of information necessary for successful reconstitution below which the identification of the people named (especially in the burial register, the most sensitive of the three in this respect) becomes in many cases impossible.[1] In the event Colyton proved to be a parish of the greatest interest from a general, as well as a technical, point of view, for Colyton's population history was very varied during these three centuries. The changes in fertility which occurred are especially striking. The bulk of this article is devoted to this topic. Other aspects of the parish's demographic history are touched on only *en passant*.

Figure 1 shows the totals of baptisms, burials, and marriages in Colyton plotted as nine-year moving averages. From them it appears that the population history of the parish fell into three phases: a first in which there was usually a substantial surplus of baptisms over burials and the total population rose sharply; a second during which burials usually exceeded baptisms and the population as a whole appears to have fallen somewhat; and a third beginning only in the 1780s when large surpluses of

[1] This question is dealt with in Wrigley, *Some Problems of Family Reconstitution*.

baptisms over burials again appear and the population rose sharply once more. The second period may be sub-divided about 1730, since after that date there was near balance between baptisms and burials, whereas before it there was usually a surplus of burials. The abruptness of the division between the first and second periods is masked by the moving averages, but is clearly revealed by annual figures. Between the beginning of November 1645 and the end of October 1646, 392 names are recorded in the Colyton burial register, in all probability as a result of a last and virulent outbreak of bubonic plague. This was perhaps a fifth of the total population. After this drastic mortality the number of baptisms stayed upon a much lower level. The average annual figure 1635–44 was 72·8, higher than in any subsequent period in the Colyton register. In the decade 1647–56 the annual average fell to 40·0. Apart from the first decade after the catastrophe the moving averages show that there were normally more burials than baptisms for two generations. The boundary between the second and third major periods is also quite sharp. In the decade 1776–85 the average annual surplus of baptisms over burials was only 0·5, a figure typical of the preceding half century. In the next ten years the average surplus rose to 7·8 and increased considerably thereafter.

Another feature of the moving averages is worth remarking. There was a well-marked inverse correlation between baptisms and burials until the end of the seventeenth century which can still be detected at times in the eighteenth. Periods which encouraged the formation of a large number of marriages and thus produced a rise in the number of baptisms were periods of low mortality, and vice versa. This may seem a very natural correlation to appear, but it is interesting to note that there were parishes in which marriages, baptisms, and burials were positively correlated in an equally marked fashion. This was true, for example, of Hartland on the northern coast of Devon. The further investigation of this issue may well throw much light on the question of the links between populations and their livelihood.[1]

The changes in the balance between births and deaths

---

[1] Hartland also possesses an unusually fine register. Mrs J. V. Stewart is at present engaged upon a family reconstitution study of this parish.

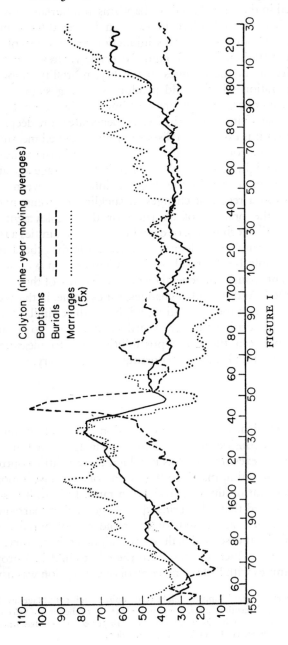

Colyton (nine-year moving averages)

Baptisms
Burials
Marriages (5x)

FIGURE I

revealed in the annual totals of baptisms and burials show that great changes took place in Colyton in the three centuries between Thomas Cromwell's injunction and the inception of civil registration. But although the crude figures may arouse curiosity about the changes in fertility, mortality, nuptiality, and migration which could produce such big swings in the relative numbers of baptisms and burials, they cannot go far towards satisfying that curiosity. To penetrate more deeply into the matter it is essential to dispose of more refined measures of demographic conditions. For example, a fall in the number of baptisms might be the result of a rise in the average age at first marriage, or a rise in the average interval between births (perhaps as a result of changes in suckling customs, perhaps through the practice of abortion or the employment of a contraceptive technique), or even in some communities a reduction in the number of illegitimate births.[1] On the other hand, it might simply be the result of heavy emigration without any significant changes in general or marital fertility of the type just mentioned. And still other changes, for example, in the age and sex structure of the population, might produce similar fluctuations in the relative number of births and deaths. To be able to decide between the many possibilities and to measure the changes accurately family reconstitution is necessary.

II

It is convenient to begin the discussion of fertility changes at Colyton by considering the fluctuations in age at first marriage of the two sexes. In societies in which there is little control of conception within marriage this is one of the most important variables bearing upon reproduction rates. Indeed, it is sometimes asserted that a lowering of the age of first marriage for women largely accounted for the rapid rise of population in England in the second half of the eighteenth century. The mean age at which women bore their last child in European communities with little or no control of conception was usually

---

[1] Registered bastard baptisms might reach quite a high percentage level even as early as the sixteenth century. For example, 135 out of the total of 876 children baptized at Prestbury in Cheshire 1581–1600 (16 per cent) were bastards. I am indebted to Dr Stella Davies for this information.

about 40,[1] and for some years before this their fecundity declined rapidly. It is clear therefore that a mean age at first marriage of 22 in these circumstances will give rise to twice as many births in completed families as a mean age of, say, 29 or 30. Table I shows that in Colyton there were remarkable

TABLE I *Age at First Marriage*

Men	No.	Mean	Median	Mode[2]
1560–1646	258	27·2	25·8	23·0
1647–1719	109	27·7	26·4	23·8
1720–1769	90	25·7	25·1	23·9
1770–1837	219	26·5	25·8	24·4
Women				
1560–1646	371	27·0	25·9	23·7
1647–1719	136	29·6	27·5	23·3
1720–1769	104	26·8	25·7	23·5
1770–1837	275	25·1	24·0	21·8

Note. The total numbers of marriages in the four periods were 854, 379, 424 and 888 respectively.

changes in the mean age at first marriage of women, though the mean age of men did not greatly vary. The strangest period to modern eyes was the period 1647–1719.[3] Immediately after the terrible mortality of 1646 the average age at first marriage of women shot up to almost 30 and was maintained at this very advanced age for some 70 years.[4] During this period, moreover, the mean age of women at first marriage was two years higher than that of men.[5] Table II shows the means for shorter periods.

[1] See, for example, L. Henry, *Anciennes familles genevoises*, I.N.E.D Cahier No. 26 (Paris, 1956), p. 88; J. Ganiage, *Trois villages de l'Ile de France*, I.N.E.D. Cahier No. 40 (Paris, 1963), pp. 71–2; Gautier and Henry, *La Population de Crulai*, p. 157.

[2] The mode was calculated here from the mean and median using Tippett's formula, Mean − Mode = 3(Mean − Median). See L. H. C. Tippett, *The Methods of Statistics*, 4th revised edn. (1952), p. 35.

[3] The time divisions used here and in subsequent tables were chosen to maximize the difference between the main periods of Colyton's demographic history.

[4] The difference between the two means 1560–1646 and 1647–1719 is 2·61 years. The standard error of the difference is 0·69 years. The difference of the means is therefore 3·8 times the standard error of the difference, and we may properly conclude that women in the second period were really marrying later in the first.

[5] See Wrigley, *Some Problems of Family Reconstitution*, for a full discussion of the accuracy of the figures of age at marriage. See K. M. Drake, *Marriage and Population Growth in Norway, 1735–1865*, unpublished Ph.D. thesis (Cambridge,

It is noteworthy that the new pattern established itself very
quickly after 1647 in Colyton. The change was abrupt and
decisive. Before this middle period and again for a time after it
the mean age for men and women differed very little, being in
each case 26–27, while in the latest sub-period and possibly also
in the earliest the more familiar pattern of men marrying
women younger than themselves is found. By the period 1825–
37 the mean age at first marriage for women had fallen to only
23, while that for men was 26, figures which appear to modern
eyes much more 'normal'.

TABLE II *Mean Age at First Marriage*

	Men		Women	
	No.	Mean	No.	Mean
1560–99	73	28·1	126	27·0
1600–29	124	27·4	162	27·3
1630–46	61	25·8	83	26·5
1647–59	38	26·9	48	30·0
1660–99	36	27·6	61	28·8
1700–19	35	28·1	27	30·7
1720–49	55	26·2	58	27·2
1750–69	35	25·0	46	26·3
1770–99	93	27·6	107	26·4
1800–24	67	25·6	100	24·9
1825–37	59	25·9	68	23·3

Changes in the median age at first marriage for women were
much less violent than the changes in the mean, while the
modal age did not change at all until the end of the eighteenth
century, being unaffected in the middle period, 1647–1719. The
commonest age at first marriage at that time remained about
23, but there was a much longer 'tail' to the right of the distribution. The contrast between different periods is well brought
out by a table showing the percentage of old and young brides
at different periods of Colyton's history. By the last decade of
the three centuries a quarter of the brides were teenagers, in the
period 1647–1719 only 4 per cent; while, on the other hand, 40
per cent were above 30 when they married for the first time in
the early period, compared with only 7 per cent in the later.

1964), esp. pp. 93–103, for a very interesting examination of the factors which
might induce men to take brides older than themselves in Norway in the late
eighteenth and early nineteenth centuries.

The male means, medians, and modes were notably 'sticky'.[1] Men entered married life at much the same time for almost three hundred years (only in the last few decades was there a slight fall in the male mean), but they proved remarkably flexible in their judgement of what constituted an acceptable age in their brides. A higher proportion of men married women older than themselves in the period 1647–1719 than either before or later. In the period 1560–1646 in 48 per cent of the

TABLE III *Women at First Marriage*

	−19		30+		40+	
	No.	%	No.	%	No.	%
1560–1646	24	6·5	95	25·6	18	4·9
1647–1719	6	4·4	54	39·7	14	10·3
1825–37	17	25·0	5	7·4	1	1·5

first marriages in which the age of both parties is known the man was older than the woman, in 47 per cent the woman was older than the man, and in 5 per cent their ages were equal. In the period 1647–1719 the percentages were 40, 55, and 5, while by the period 1800–37 the figures were 59, 29, and 12.

The figures of age at first marriage demonstrate immediately the great range of general fertility levels which might be found in pre-industrial communities. Other things being equal, the changes in mean age of marriage alone provided scope for a very wide range of rates of increase (or decrease) of population. In marriages not prematurely interrupted by death an average age at first marriage for women of, say, 24 might well produce two more children than marriages contracted at an average age of, say, 29. The most extreme female mean ages at first marriage found at Colyton (30·7 in 1700–1 and 23·3 in 1825–37) can easily result in average completed family sizes differing from each other by a factor of 2.

The details of age at first marriage in themselves go far towards explaining the changes in numbers of children baptized, which are apparent in the moving averages of crude totals of baptisms. However, any changes on the fertility side

[1] This may well be a very common feature of European demography in many centuries. See, for example, *Report of the Royal Commission on Population*, Cmd. 7695, p. 249, para. 25, for England in recent decades. See also E. A. Wrigley, *Industrial Growth and Population Change* (Cambridge, 1962), pp. 155–7, for nineteenth-century France and Germany.

of the population history of Colyton which arose from changes in the mean age of first marriage were considerably amplified by changes in fertility within marriage, as Table IV and Figure 2 will make clear.

TABLE IV　*Age-specific Marital Fertility (Children Born per Thousand Woman-years Lived)*

(In brackets the number of women-years on which the rate is based)

Colyton

	15–19	20–4	25–9	30–4	35–9	40–4	45–9
1560–1629	412 (17·0)	467 (205·5)	403 (473·5)	369 (561·5)	302 (517·0)	174 (443·0)	18 (383·5)
1630–1646	500 (4·0)	378 (63·5)	382 (120·5)	298 (107·5)	234 (55·5)	128 (23·5)	0 (16·0)
1647–1719	500 (4·0)	346 (52·0)	395 (187·5)	272 (253·5)	182 (258·5)	104 (249·5)	20 (200·5)
1720–1769	462 (19·5)	362 (69·0)	342 (164·0)	292 (216·0)	227 (203·0)	160 (156·0)	0 (138·0)
1770–1837	500 (34·0)	441 (279·0)	361 (498·0)	347 (504·5)	270 (430·0)	152 (224·0)	22 (186·0)

Crulai

	15–19	20–4	25–9	30–4	35–9	40–4	45–9
1674–1742	320 (65·5)	419 (305·5)	429 (599·0)	355 (633·0)	292 (588·5)	142 (505·5)	10 (205·5)

Note. The Crulai figures are taken from Gautier and Henry, *La Population de Crulai*, pp. 102 and 105, and Table VII, pp. 249–54. The Colyton rates are derived from marriages formed during the years specified, except that marriages which bridge the period 1630–1646 to 1647–1719 are divided at the end of 1646, data from before that date being allocated to the earlier period, beyond it to 1647–1719. The reason for this appears in the text below, pp. 169–170.

In the first period 1560–1629 the age-specific marital fertility rates in Colyton were high, being distinctly higher than those found at Crulai in the late seventeenth and early eighteenth centuries.[1] There is a marked decline of fertility in the last fifteen years before the plague of 1645–6, and this became more pronounced after 1646. Fertility remained low throughout the period marked also by an exceptionally high average age at first marriage for women.[2] During the period 1720–69 there was some recovery in the rates, while during the final period 1770–1837 the rates were much higher, though still not quite at the level attained in the sixteenth and early seventeenth centuries. There was therefore a cycle in marital fertility levels, passing

[1] The Crulai figures reveal in a very striking way the phenomenon of teenage subfecundity. This is absent in the Colyton figures, but its absence is not significant, because a very high proportion of first births in Colyton were pre-nuptially conceived (about a third until the nineteenth century, when the figure rose to about half). A large proportion of these in turn were born shortly after marriage (22 per cent of all first births were baptized within six months of marriage 1538–1799, 36 per cent 1800–37). Teenage brides, like others, were often pregnant at marriage, and since most births to teenage mothers were first births, the 15–19 rate is inflated as a result, and no valid comparison with Crulai can be made. The same is true to a lesser degree of the age-group 20–4.

[2] It is unfortunately not possible to estimate what changes took place in the proportions of women ever married at, say, 45.

from high through low to high once more during the three centuries under review. Both the transition from the initial high level to a lower level of marital fertility and the subsequent recovery in fertility levels are of the greatest interest, but in this article I shall concentrate chiefly on the change from high to low levels of fertility in the mid-seventeenth century,

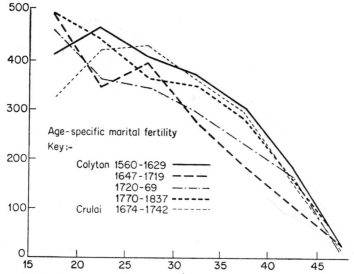

The horizontal axis shows age of women in years. The vertical axis shows the number of children born per thousand woman-years lived. Note 1630-46 omitted to avoid overcrowding the graph

FIGURE 2

though the rise in fertility during the eighteenth century is a matter of equal fascination. Comparison of the periods 1560–1629 and 1647–1719 reveals the fact that the relative difference between the five-year age-groups becomes more and more marked with rising age. With 1560–1629 as 100 in each case the figures for 1647–1719 are 74, 98, 74, 61, and 60 for the age-groups 20–4, 25–9, 30–4, 35–9, and 40–4 respectively. The anomalous figure for the 20–4 age-group may be explained perhaps by the small number of years in marriage from which it was derived, but apart from this the progressively greater gap is well marked. When represented graphically the curve of the period 1560–1629 is convex to the upper side, while the curve of the later period is slightly concave to the upper side in the later years of the fertile period.[1] Since the latter is often taken as an indication of the restriction of fertility within the family, it is important to look further into the fertility charac-

TABLE V

1560–1629[2]

No. of children	20–4	25–9	30–4	35–9	40–4	45–9	Total
0	1	2	6	16	34	61	120
1	1	16	19	24	32	6	98
2	6	31	49	35	9	0	130
3	2	9	14	9	4	0	38
4	0	2	0	3	1	0	6
5	1	0	1	0	0	0	2
Total	11	60	89	87	80	67	394
Average	2·18	1·88	1·84	1·53	0·83	0·09	

1647–1719

No. of children	25–9	30–4	35–9	40–4	45–9	Total
0	1	8	17	23	32	81
1	6	11	15	14	2	48
2	4	16	9	3	0	32
3	4	3	0	0	0	7
4	2	0	0	0	0	2
5	0	0	0	0	0	0
Total	17	38	41	40	34	170
Average	2·00	1·37	0·80	0·50	0·60	

teristics of women in the period 1647–1719. The reason why a concavity to the upper side of a curve representing age-specific marital fertility often indicates family limitation is, of course, that most married couples want some children but not as large a number as might be born to them without any limitation of

[1] The changes which took place at Colyton are very similar to those which took place at the same period in the Genevan *bourgeoisie*. See Henry, *Anciennes familles genevoises*, esp. pp. 75–81. The family limitation which began among the Genevan *bourgeoise* in the second half of the seventeenth century, however, became accentuated in the eighteenth, whereas in Colyton there was a reversion to the earlier fertility patterns.

[2] In this table and subsequently in Tables XI and XII the period 1560–1629 is used rather than 1560–1646 both because fertility was somewhat lower in 1630–46 and because of the problem of the 'bridging' families (see pp. 169–70 and Table VII below).

fertility. They will tend to concentrate their reproductive effort into the earlier part of the wife's fertile period. Age-specific fertility in the younger age-groups in these circumstances may remain high, but in the later age-groups there will be a progressively greater shortfall from the full fertility potential of the women in question, producing the characteristic concavity in the curve.

Table V shows the frequency with which women bore 0, 1, 2, 3, 4, or 5 children when living throughout a specified five-year age-group. At the foot of each column the average number of children born in the five-year period is shown. The figures when converted approximate closely to the rates shown in Table IV, as is to be expected (where they are a little lower it is because they largely eliminate the influence of the very short interval between marriage and first baptism – see p. 166, n. 1). It is possible to make an analysis of variance on the four age-groups over 30 in the two periods, with the following result.

	Sum of squares	Degrees of freedom	Estimate of variance	F
Total	490·00	475		
Age-groups	168·92	3	56·31	88·2
Periods	20·38	1	20·38	31·9
Error	300·70	471	0·6384	

A test for interaction produces an *F* which is not significant, and the assumption of additivity can be retained. The difference between the two periods is very highly significant (beyond the 0·1 per cent level), and we may therefore say with confidence that there was a fall in fertility above the age of 30 between the two periods.[1]

The possibility of the existence of some form of family limitation immediately suggests a comparison of the fertility rates in the age-groups 30–44 of those women marrying below the age of 30 with the rates for those marrying in their thirties. Since the former will already in most cases have borne children before entering their thirties, it is to be expected that their fertility rates will be lower than those of women marrying after 30, who will have less reason to seek to restrict the number of

[1] I am greatly indebted to Dr T. H. Hollingsworth for his advice on statistical technique in this article and for his comments generally.

their children. Table VI shows that the expected pattern is present, though it should not be forgotten that rather higher rates among those marrying at 30 or over are to be expected anyway, because the interval between marriage and the birth of the first child is much less than the later birth intervals, and

TABLE VI

Age-specific Marital Fertility (Children Born per Thousand Woman-Years Lived)

(In brackets the number of woman-years on which the rate is based)

1647–1719

Women marrying	30–4	35–9	40–4	45–9
−29	265 (215·5)	146 (191·5)	96 (146·0)	0 (108·5)
30+	316 (38·0)	284 (67·0)	116 (103·5)	43 (92·0)

this will cause the fertility rates of women bearing their first child after a marriage above 30 to appear higher than those who married younger, even if the true fertility position were the same. The differences, however, are much too large to be accounted for on this ground. It is of interest incidentally to follow the short-term experience of the couples who had married before the plague visitation of 1645–6 and who survived the terrible year. It has sometimes been supposed that the 'instinctive' reaction of a population after a heavy loss of life is to increase fertility to fill the gaps created by death. Table VII

TABLE VII   *Age-specific Marital Fertility (Children Born per Thousand Woman-years Lived)*

(In brackets the number of woman-years on which the rate is based)

	15–19	20–4	25–9	30–4	35–9	40–4	45–9
−1646	572 (3·5)	429 (28·0)	412 (51·0)	370 (40·5)	194 (15·5)	0 (4·0)	
1647+			174 (11·5)	247 (36·5)	154 (52·0)	127 (55·0)	0 (43·5)

shows the age-specific fertility rates of women in families which bridged the plague year and where the age of the wife is known. Some were at the beginning of their child-bearing period when the plague struck, others were near the end, which explains how there are rates on both sides of the temporal division for most age-groups. The numbers involved were, of course, small, but the picture which emerges is none

the less suggestive. Fertility rates dropped sharply and immediately to the levels which were to be characteristic of Colyton
for the next two or three generations, even though the women
in question had displayed a fertility well above the average in
the period before the swingeing losses of 1646.[1] The change
from a high to a low level of fertility within these families was
abrupt and complete, just as was the change to a later age at
first marriage for women.

TABLE VIII *Mean Birth Intervals (in Months)*

	0–1	No.	1–2	No.	2–3	No.	3–4	No.	Last	No.
1560–1646	11·3	87	25·2	87	27·4	84	30·1	77	37·5	76
1647–1719	10·3	23	29·1	23	32·6	26	32·1	18	50·7	34
1720–1769	11·9	24	25·1	24	29·8	24	32·9	22	40·6	24

Birth Intervals 1–4 Combined

	Mean	No.
1560–1646	27·5	248
1647–1719	31·4	67
1720–1769	29·1	70

Notes. The smaller number of intervals 3–4 arises because when the interval
3–4 was also the last interval it is not included in the 3–4 totals. The large number
of last birth intervals 1647–1719 and the reduced number 1560–1646 is a result
of splitting families which bridged the year 1646 in the way described above.

A difference of means test may be applied to the means of the last birth intervals
1560–1646 and 1647–1719. The difference in the two means is 13·1 months. The
standard error of the difference is 4·62 months. The difference of means is therefore
2·88 times the standard error of the difference, and the difference is significant
at the 1 per cent level. The same test applied to the means of all birth intervals
1–4 shows the mean of 1560–1646 to be significantly different from the mean of
1647–1719 at the 5 per cent level (difference of means 2·15 times the standard error of the difference).

The examination of mean birth intervals can also throw
much light on the question of family limitation. Table VIII
shows the mean birth intervals 0–1, 1–2, 2–3, 3–4, and penultimate to last of completed families of four or more children in
the three periods 1560–1646, 1647–1719, and 1720–69.[2] A com-

---

[1] It may be of interest to note that Creighton, in discussing the aftermath of
the Black Death, quotes a passage from the *Eulogium Historiarum* that 'the women
who survived remained for the most part barren during several years'. C.
Creighton, *History of Epidemics in Britain*, 2 vols (Cambridge, 1891, 1894), I,
p. 200. Creighton also quotes Piers the Plowman to much the same effect.

[2] The period 1770–1837 yields too few completed families to be worth including.

pleted family is one in which the woman reached the age of 45 in marriage, and would therefore in almost all cases have completed her child-bearing. Only those women who married under 30 are included in the table, since if family limitation was to be found in the period 1647–1719, it is in such families

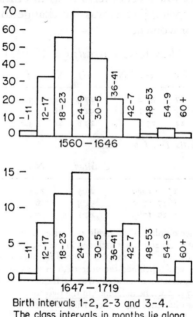

Birth intervals 1-2, 2-3 and 3-4.
The class intervals in months lie along
the horizontal axis. The vertical axis
shows the number in each class

FIGURE 3

that it would be most clearly apparent for reasons touched on above. To those in each group of whom the exact age at marriage is known have been added completed families[1] in which the age of the wife is not known when there were six or more children born to the marriage in the periods 1560–1646 and 1720–69 and where there were four or more children in the period 1647–1719, since in the vast majority of these cases the wife was under 30 at marriage. Including such marriages increases substantially the number of cases which can be studied

[1] Completed families here comprise any in which at least 27 years is known to have elapsed between the beginning and end of the marriage.

(by almost three-quarters). The most striking feature of this table is the contrast between the middle period and the other two in the mean interval between the penultimate and last births. A marked rise in this interval is typical of a community beginning to practise family limitation.[1] It rises in these circumstances, because even after reaching an intended final family size additions are nevertheless occasionally made either

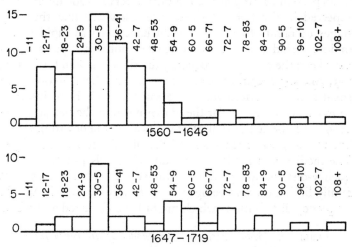

Final birth intervals. The class intervals in months lie along the horizontal axis. The vertical axis shows the number in each class

FIGURE 4

from accident (failure of whatever system of restriction is in use), from a reversal of an earlier decision not to increase family size, or from a desire to replace a child which has died. Figure 4 shows the distribution of final birth intervals of the two periods 1560–1646 and 1647–1719 in the form of a histogram. In the earlier period the distribution is unimodal with a fairly clear peak about the 30–35-month interval. In the later period this peak is again apparent, but there is also a suspicion of a second peak in the 54–65-month intervals, suggesting that while the 'natural' distribution continued to occur in some cases, there was superimposed upon it a different pattern which might be the result of family limitation.

[1] See Henry, *Anciennes familles genevoises*, esp. pp. 93–110.

Table VIII contains other points of interest. The mean interval between marriage and first baptism did not change materially over the two centuries covered by the table. The later birth intervals, 1–2, 2–3, and 3–4, were always higher in 1647–1719 than in 1560–1646, though, rather surprisingly perhaps, the difference showed no tendency to grow greater as the rank of birth increased. It is also surprising to find the higher mean present as early as the 1–2 birth interval. One might have expected in the light of experience elsewhere that the early stages of family formation would have been as rapid in the middle period as either earlier or later, but this appears not to have been the case. The frequency distribution of all births 1–2, 2–3, and 3–4 (taken together, since the numbers involved are small and the pattern much the same at each birth interval) shows that the reason for the higher mean in the period 1647–1719 does not lie in the shift of the peak frequency to the right but in the greater skewness of the distribution to the right. The median and modal figures underline this point. The frequency-distribution pattern is compatible with the view that family limitation was being practised. Some other changes in frequency distributions which might have occurred and which

TABLE IX *Means, Medians, and Modes of all Birth Intervals 1–4*

	Mean	Median	Mode
1560–1646	27·5	26·6	24·8
1647–1719	31·4	29·0	24·1

would have produced a higher mean would have shown a different pattern. For example, if there had been a general increase in the customary suckling period, which would have increased the mean birth intervals by prolonging the period of lowered fecundity in the mother, there would probably have been a shift in the peak frequency to the right.[1]

Another tell-tale sign of family limitation is a fall in the age

[1] See the searching discussion of this question and the data presented in Henry, *Anciennes familles genevoises*, Chaps. 4 and 5. It is of interest also to note that the mean birth interval after the death of the preceding child under 1 year of age (excluding last birth intervals) was 20·6 months in the period 1538–1646 (114 cases) and 22·7 months (15 cases) in 1647–1719 (data drawn from all families in which the date of the end of the union is known).

at which women bear their last child in families in which they are at risk to the end of the child-bearing period (45 years of age). This is likely to arise for the same reasons which tend to produce a very long final birth interval and will be most evident among women who marry young and have had several children well before the end of their fertile period. Table X

TABLE X

	−29	No.	30+	No.
1560–1646	39·8	50	40·5	25
1647–1719	37·6	22	42·7	14
1720–1769	40·4	14	41·4	5

shows the mean ages at the birth of the last child of women marrying above and below the age of 30. In the first of the three periods the mean age at birth of last child was much the same for women marrying −29 as for those marrying above 30, in each case about 40, and the same is true of the period 1720–69. But in the middle period the mean age at birth of last child for women marrying under 30 was lower than for those marrying over 30 and lower than for women in the same age-group in the other two periods. Both these features are to be expected if family limitation were taking place.[1] The fall between 1560–1646 and 1647–1719 in the mean for women marrying under 30 was 2·25 years. This in combination with a steep rise in the mean interval between the penultimate and last births underlies, of course, the very low age-specific fertility figures found in the age-groups 30–4, 35–9, and 40–4 for women marrying under 30 (see Table VI). The eighteenth century shows a reversion to the earlier pattern in age at birth of last child as in the other fertility characteristics considered.

A convenient measure which reflects the combined effects of the changes already discussed is the mean size of completed families. Table XI sets forth the chief statistics.

The extent of the decline between the first and second halves of the seventeenth century is underscored by the figures of

[1] The difference in mean age at birth of last child of women marrying under 30 between 1560–1646 and 1647–1719 is 2·25. The standard error of the difference of the two means is 1·24. The difference between the two means is therefore not significant at the 5 per cent level (the former is only 1·81 times the latter).

completed family size.[1] Figure 5 gives more detail of the distribution of family sizes in the form of a series of histograms.

TABLE XI   *Mean Completed Family Size*

	−24	25–29	30–9
1560–1629	7·3 ± 1·3	5·7 ± 1·1	2·7 ± 0·8
1646–1719	5·0 ± 2·0	3·3 ± 1·7	1·7 ± 0·9
1720–1769	5·8 ± 2·5	3·8 ± 1·7	2·4 ± 1·7
1770–1837	7·3 ± 1·6	4·5 ± 2·3	3·2 ± 0·9

Note. The figures after the means are the 95 per cent confidence intervals.

Perhaps the most striking single feature of the detailed distribution is that only 18 per cent of women marrying under 30 between 1647 and 1719 and living right through the fertile period had families of 6 children or more (3 in 17), compared with 55 per cent (29 in 53) in 1560–1629, 48 per cent (10 in 21) in 1720–69, and 60 per cent (12 in 20) in 1770–1837. Very large families, on the other hand, were rare at any time in Colyton, the largest during the full three centuries being only 13. Childless marriages were also rare in the period of high fertility before 1646. Of all marriages formed when the bride was under 35 and lasting till she was 45 or more, only 5 out of 70 were childless. Since a small number of marriages are infertile for physiological reasons, the position in the earliest period may well represent a figure close to the minimum which can be expected.[2] It is notably similar to the Crulai figure, and is found also in the latest period 1770–1837, when marital fertility was again high at Colyton. In the other two periods, 1647–1719 and 1720–69, the proportion of childless families was much higher. It is interesting that the period 1720–69, an intermediate period in most other respects, had such a high proportion of childless marriages, though the absolute numbers involved are not large and are subject to wide margins of error. The difference between the first period, 1560–1629, and the two

[1] The fall occurred at a time when age-specific death-rates, especially of young children, were rising so that the net reproduction rate fell even more sharply than the gross rate. It is doubtful whether the net reproduction rate of the population of Colyton reached unity during the period when fertility rates were at their lowest.

[2] See, for example, the tables of D. V. Glass and E. Grebenik reproduced in *The Cambridge Economic History of Europe*, Vol. VI, Pt. 1 (Cambridge, 1965), p. 114.

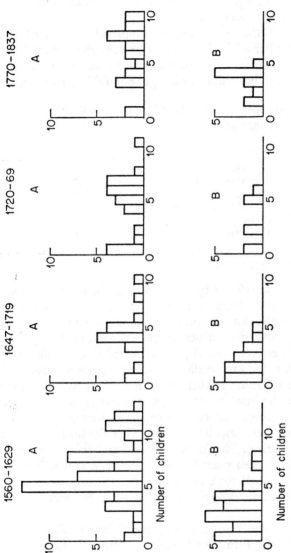

Number of children in completed families. A, where women married–29. B, where women married 30–9. The horizontal axis shows the number of children in the family. The vertical axis shows the number of families

FIGURE 5

succeeding periods, 1647–1719 and 1720–69, is, however, not significant at the 5 per cent level, even if the latter two periods are grouped together (χ^2 test).

Statistics of the mean size of completed families can, of course, be rather misleading, since many marriages were interrupted by the death of one of the partners before the wife had passed through her child-bearing period. Table XI shows, for

TABLE XII *Childless Completed Marriages (Wife Marrying –35)*

	Childless	Total	%
1560–1629	5	70	7
1647–1719	4	22	18
1720–1769	6	29	21
1770–1837	2	26	8
Crulai			
1674–1742	5	77	6

Note. The Crulai figure is calculated from Gautier and Henry, *La Population de Crulai*, Table VII, pp. 249–54.

example, that in 1560–1629 the mean sizes of completed families born to women marrying –24, 25–9, and 30–9 were 7·3, 5·7, and 2·7 respectively. But if to these families are added all those cut short before the wife reached 45 the mean sizes fall to 5·2, 4·9, and 2·4 respectively. Marriages contracted in early life are, of course, more likely to be affected, and the proportionate fall in family size is greater in their case. In all the tables expressing family size the importance of age at marriage is clear. At all periods the contrast between marriages contracted in the early twenties and those which took place when the bride was in her thirties is marked. The immense social and economic import of the fall of seven years in the average age at first marriage for women which took place between the beginning of the eighteenth and the early nineteenth century, therefore, is firmly driven home.

Before turning to the more general issues raised by the history of family formation in Colyton during the three centuries when the parish registers are the prime source of information about demographic changes it is appropriate to touch upon the question of the completeness of registration. This is too large a topic to be treated here in its entirety, but one issue must be mentioned. Since the foregoing tables have been cast in a form which makes it easy to compare Colyton with industrializing countries today or with historical studies of the type done on French parish registers, it is important to know how accurate the Colyton statistics are. It is evident that when the figures err they will err by understating rather than over-stating the levels of fertility reached. For example, although the families which are used for the calculation of age-specific fertility are subjected to a fairly rigorous test of presence in the parish,[1] there must be a small proportion of baptisms recorded in the registers of other parishes which should ideally have been included in the fertility data for Colyton families. In addition to small 'leakages' of this sort, there is a major source of 'leakage' which deserves attention. In some periods in English parishes many children who died soon after birth were never baptized,[2] and some of these were buried without benefit of church service. No system of correction can overcome the difficulties arising from under-registration entirely, but some idea of the order of magnitude of correction which seems appropriate can be gained from a consideration of infant mortality, and especially the frequency distribution of the apparent age at death of children dying under the age of 1.

TABLE XIII *Age at Death*

	1st d.	1–6 d.	1–4 w.	1 m.	2 m.	3–5 m.	6–11 m.	Total
A	33	28	21	9	8	20	21	140
B	35	19	27	16	9	15	24	145
C	19	18	20	26	7	24	24	138

A. St Michael le Belfrey, York, 1571–86
B. Colyton, 1538–99
C. Colyton, 1600–49

Table XIII shows the age at death of children dying under 1 for the parish of St Michael le Belfrey in York and for Colyton at two different periods. The register of St Michael le Belfrey during the years 1571–86 is very remarkable, in that an exact

[1] For details see Wrigley (ed.), *Introduction to English Historical Demography*, Chap. 4.
[2] It would be more accurate to say that they never appeared in the baptism register. In some parishes it was the custom to baptize privately in the home if the child were in danger of death, but only to record it in the register after a subsequent public ceremony if the child survived its first dangers.

age at burial is given (even down to an age in hours if the child died during its first day of life), and every care appears to have been taken to secure a complete coverage of vital events. The baptism register contains many entries of baptism by the midwife in the house, and the burial of unbaptized children is also scrupulously set down. In Colyton in the same period only an apparent age at death can be calculated by comparing the dates of baptism and burial. Comparison of the A and B lines in Table XIII at least does nothing to undermine the view that in the sixteenth century children in Colyton were normally baptized very soon after birth, and that consequently the 'leakage' was very slight. The comparatively high proportion of children buried on the day they were baptized is difficult to reconcile with any other view.[1] Line C in Table XIII, however, presents a very different picture. In the period 1600–49 the proportion apparently dying in the first week of life was much lower. In all probability this period sees the beginning of the custom of delaying baptism in Colyton. Two calculations may now be made, one of which probably underestimates the amount of correction necessary, while the other perhaps overstates it. The first assumes that the number of deaths above one week is correct, and a figure for deaths in the first week is calculated on the assumption that they form the same percentage of total deaths as at Colyton, 1538–99, or at St Michael le Belfrey. This assumption might give an approximately correct answer if baptism usually took place within a few days of birth, but would tend to be on the low side, since some of those apparently dying in the first week of life would in fact be more than a week old. Alternatively, a figure may be calculated on the assumption that half the children buried at an apparent age of less than one month were in fact more than a month old and that the resulting figure of deaths above a month old formed the same percentage of total deaths as at Colyton earlier or at St Michael le Belfrey. Like the first method, this gives, of course, only a very rough and ready

---

[1] It is interesting to note that at Crulai in the late seventeenth and early eighteenth centuries, where baptism is known to have taken place almost invariably on the first day of life, 30 per cent of all deaths under 1 were on the first day (99 in 331), compared with 24 per cent at Colyton, 1538–99. Gautier and Henry remark, however, that a proportion of these may well in fact have been born dead. Gautier and Henry, *La Population de Crulai*, p. 170.

correction, but this time probably on the high side. Use can also be made of the life-table mortality rates 1–4, 5–9, and 10–14 (a few of which are listed on p. 182, n. 1). Comparison of these with the United Nations specimen life-table rates also throws some light on the question of the likely order of magnitude of infant mortality rates.[1] These several exercises suggest that the fertility rates quoted in Table IV understate the true position by between 2 and 6 per cent, with a low figure appropriate for the first period, 1560–1629, and figures in the upper part of the range more likely in the later periods. It appears most unlikely that differences in the degree of under-registration at different periods can serve to explain any of the major changes which appear in tables in the earlier sections of this article.

III

I have so far written of the striking changes in marital fertility which took place in Colyton between the first and second halves of the seventeenth century as if they were the result of a system of family limitation deliberate in the sense that social or individual action caused fewer children to be born, or at all events to survive long enough to be baptized, than would have been the case without such restraints. But is this a correct assumption? And if so, what were the means employed to reduce fertility so drastically?

Any explanation other than family limitation must take account of the fact that fertility fell much more steeply in the later years of the fertile period than the earlier, of the remarkable change in the mean age at first marriage for women, and, if possible, of the later reversion to a position not unlike that of the late sixteenth and early seventeenth centuries. Some of the explanations which might be entertained on one score are unacceptable on other grounds. For example, a fall in marital fertility might simply reflect a change in suckling habits, but this would not explain the much more drastic fall in fertility in the higher age-groups. Perhaps the only explanation other than family limitation which might cover the known facts is an

---

[1] I hope to deal more adequately with the mortality experience of Colyton in a later article.

economic reverse of such severity that the physiological condition of women of child-bearing age was affected by it (either from simple undernourishment or from the absence in their diet of elements necessary for high fertility). This might plausibly be argued to be likely to affect the older age-groups more than the younger. Such an explanation has the additional attraction that it is fully consonant with the steep rise in child mortality which took place at that time.[1] This alternative explanation deserves further careful study, but suffers from several defects.

The first difficulty is that fertility in the higher age-groups was much higher among women who married late in life than among those who married early. This might be explained on the ground that those who had already borne several children were exhausted by this and that their physical condition deteriorated seriously as a result. But it is doubtful whether child-bearing would have had this effect on the mass of women. Gautier and Henry remark that this did not occur at Crulai, and that it is not apparent in modern Indian rural populations.[2] Again, the abrupt change to much lower fertility levels among the families which spanned the great mortality of 1645–6 creates a problem. It is difficult to imagine a change in economic conditions effecting such a swift and complete change in the absence of family limitation. It is possible, of course, that this fall in fertility was due to the after-affects of plague infection on the women who survived, but against this it must be noted that their fertility after 1647 was closely similar to the general pattern over the next two generations. But perhaps the most important difficulty is that although death-rates at all ages rose in the second half of the seventeenth century, and expectation of life fell by several years to the low thirties,[3] it was still as

---

[1] The late seventeenth century was much more unhealthy for young children at Colyton than the preceding century, as is shown by these life-table mortality rates (the figures in brackets for 1600–49 are the rates which result from eliminating the deaths from plague in 1645–6. Rates per thousand).

	1538–99	*1600–49*	*1650–99*
1–4	88	97 (85)	162
5–9	30	54 (30)	45
10–14	16	41 (19)	37

[2] See Gautier and Henry, *La Population de Crulai*, pp. 98–100.
[3] I hope to publish the evidence for this statement on a later occasion.

high in Colyton at this period as it was in Crulai at much the same time. Yet fertility rates at Crulai were almost as high as in Colyton in the sixteenth century, and moreover, the pattern of age-specific rates in Crulai shows no sudden dip in the thirties. This undermines a main base of the argument from a general worsening of economic conditions, unless indeed it is held that diet and other conditions of life in Colyton, though generally no worse than in Crulai, were nevertheless more deficient in certain vital constituents necessary for high fertility in women.

There are, however, difficulties also with the view that family limitation lay behind the change in fertility in Colyton. These difficulties fall under two main heads: the explanation of the rise in child mortality which accompanied the fall in fertility, and the question of the means which it is reasonable to envisage having been employed to secure a lower fertility. The first is a problem, because it might seem natural to suppose that if a population began to limit its fertility drastically it would take the better care of those children who were born. If child mortality changed it would fall rather than rise. The second is a problem for the reason that Malthus expressed succinctly when he referred to the 'passion between the sexes' as a potent and unchanging feature of behaviour. Yet if the passion between the sexes is given free rein within marriage how can one explain a sudden fall in marital fertility in a period long before modern mechanical and chemical methods of birth control were practised? Both these are objections of weight, and any answer to them is bound to be tentative. I am more concerned in this section of the article to set an argument in train than to suggest that a full answer can as yet be given.

It may be that the problem of the fall in fertility coinciding with a rise in child mortality is only a problem if viewed, anachronistically, in modern terms. If the reason for limiting family size had been prudential and consciously so rather in the way that a modern family may choose between an extra child or an expensive education for the existing children, then a concomitant rise in child mortality would be very surprising.[1]

[1] Unless indeed the change in economic conditions had been so catastrophic that not even a fall in marital fertility as steep as that which took place in Colyton could ensure as good a life for the children of the small families of the late seventeenth century as their parents and grandparents had enjoyed in the much larger families of their childhood. There is, unfortunately, very little evidence as yet

But the change may well have been of a very different type. It must be borne in mind that the view that pre-industrial societies normally did little or nothing to restrict the level of fertility within marriage is an extreme hypothesis. Societies at a low level of material culture frequently developed taboos upon intercourse during long periods of married life, and practised abortion or infanticide.[1] There is a very large literature about the connection between the social activities of animals and the maintenance of population size at a level substantially below the maximum number which their habitat could support.[2] Both in primitive human groups and in an enormous range of insect, fish, bird, and mammal species it is clear that methods developed within the group through social activity to prevent numbers from pressing too hard upon the food base confer a notable selective advantage. If numbers are allowed to grow too great the ecological balance of the area may be upset and the ability of the area to provide food for the population be impaired. Moreover, the group as a whole is more likely to be successful if its members are well fed and in good health than if the constant pressure of numbers makes it hard to keep adults vigorous. A tribe of Australian aborigines having only a limited food base on which to support itself behaves much as bird and animal communities do in similar circumstances. It throws up social controls which prevent so large a number of new mouths coming into existence as to prejudice the well-being of those already living. This may be done in animal populations either by preventing some adults from breeding in a given season or by delaying the entry of adolescents into the breeding population, or by restricting the number of viable offspring, or

---

about the state of the Colyton economy in the late seventeenth century. Study of the Exeter wheat price series suggests that living was dear in this region at the beginning of the period of low fertility, though prices had fallen to low levels well before its end (in 1647 wheat was 62·72 shillings per quarter at Exeter, a level not surpassed until 1795, and prices stayed high for much of the 1650s and 1660s – but they had been very high before this, reaching 62·94 shillings in 1596). The state of affairs in Colyton may, of course, have been either better or worse than in the county or country as a whole.

[1] See e.g., N. E. Himes, *Medical History of Contraception* (Baltimore, 1936), and F. Lorimer, *Culture and Human Fertility* (Paris, 1954).

[2] This subject is brilliantly reviewed in V. C. Wynne-Edwards, *Animal Dispersion in Relation to Social Behaviour* (1962). A. M. Carr-Saunders has also used this argument in *The Population Problem* (1922).

by causing the early death of many which are born, or indeed by many combinations and modifications of these methods. But in all cases the effect is to keep population numbers fluctuating some way beneath the maximum – that is at a level which neither prejudices the flow of food by creating too great a pressure on the available food base (over-fishing in Wynne-Edwards terminology; encroaching on capital rather than living off dividend in more familiar jargon) nor stunts the development of the adult members of the community but yet does not restrict numbers much below the level imposed by these desiderata. It is important to note that when a population has risen substantially above this level and a contraction of numbers is necessary it is normally secured, in part at least, by reducing the flow of new members into the community, and it is to be expected both that the number of births will fall and that the infant death-rate will rise. Conversely, if numbers fall below the optimum range it is probable that there will be both a rise in fertility and a fall in the wastage of life among the very young members of the population. If therefore a model drawn from the study of animal populations were made the basis of expectation, it would occasion no surprise that fertility and child mortality should change in Colyton in the way that they did in the later seventeenth century.[1] Such a model, incidentally, also makes the changes in mean age at first marriage of women (particularly the reversal of the usual age gap between the sexes at marriage) easier to understand, since this, too, is a reaction which might be expected in a population which was restricting its numbers to approach an optimum.

Populations whose economy is based upon hunting and the collection of food appear to conform closely in their methods of population control to the general model of animal communities. Pre-industrial populations whose economies are based upon the cultivation of the land are differently placed. In their case the food base may be substantially broadened from time to time by technological advance (for example, by the development of a more effective plough or the introduction of a new type of food crop). Their population control problems are much less

---

[1] The argument here is, of course, very general. Several other possible causes of higher child mortality can be envisaged. It may be, for example, that smallpox at this period was both more virulent and more widespread than earlier.

simple, since in periods following technological or organizational advance and an expansion of the food base they may be
able to allow populations to rise for several centuries with only
intermittent checks from epidemics and bad harvests, but they
will be brought up against the same problem once more when
the possibilities of any given advance in material culture have
been exhausted. The Malthusian model under which populations tend to approach a maximum rather than fluctuate well
below this is perhaps an aberration in the history of populations
from the more general model to which most animal societies
conform, rather as the classical model of full employment is
a limiting case of Keynesian employment theory. At times when
the potential of a technological or organizational advance has
been fully used up populations may well have to relearn
methods of social control of population size which could be
forgotten as long as an expansion in the food base had made
Malthusian behaviour for a time possible and even appropriate.[1] In the absence of much more empirical work much of this
discussion is inevitably speculative, but it may well explain why
populations in the late fourteenth and fifteenth centuries remained at a lower level than before the Black Death in spite of
the rise in real incomes which apparently took place among
the peasants. Upon Malthusian assumptions this should have
produced a fall in the age of marriage and a rapid rise in
population.[2]

All the foregoing, of course, does not imply that the individual man or woman was conscious of this range of issues in
the least, any more than the individual robin or rook is conscious of the problems of avoiding too large a population, but
like robins and rooks, people respond sensitively to social
pressures. It would be surprising if there were not present in

---

[1] The word Malthusian is not, of course, used here in the French sense. An
interesting example of this cycle of events is afforded by the Irish population in
the eighteenth and nineteenth centuries.

[2] In a recent article Bean argues that recurrences of plague in the fifteenth
century were not sufficiently severe to keep population down to post-Black
Death levels and that therefore it is reasonable to suppose that numbers were
increasing. This view is advanced with proper caution, but is interesting as an
illustration of the tendency to expect populations to rise unless some exogenous
agency keeps them down. See J. M. W. Bean, 'Plague, Population and Economic
Decline in England in the Later Middle Ages', *The Economic History Review*, 2nd
series, XV (1963), 431–6.

pre-industrial European populations a range of possible courses of social action which would secure a stabilization of numbers well short of the appalling conditions of control envisaged at times by Malthus. Populations before then and since have acted to secure this: it would be surprising if none in the intervening centuries had acted in the same way, and had done so not merely by altering socially acceptable patterns of age at marriage but by changing normal levels of fertility within marriage (perhaps in ways which bore more heavily upon the lower sections of the social pyramid), and even by changes in social custom likely to produce higher child mortality.[1]

There remains the second general problem in accepting at its face value the evidence for control of fertility within marriage at Colyton, the problem of the methods used to produce this result. Once more one can plausibly argue that this is a problem only if approached with preconceived ideas, or more properly, since this is to some extent inevitable, with a particular set of preconceived ideas. It is quite clear that European pre-industrial populations could severely restrict their family sizes, not merely in the wealthy and leisured families but throughout a whole community. When in the late eighteenth century rural populations in France still set in traditional economic ways began to limit the size of their families[2] they did not have at their disposal any of the modern chemical or mechanical means of contraception. They limited their families, so far as is yet known, by practising *coitus interruptus* or *reservatus*, and no doubt procuring many abortions, possibly also by infanticide. Any means which may have been available to French peasants of the Ile de France or Normandy at the end of the eighteenth century were also available to English communities a century and a half earlier – and indeed to European communities for many centuries before that.[3] Such means may perhaps be re-

[1] This possibility must have been in Krause's mind when he wrote: 'The usually cited infant death rates greatly exaggerate pre-industrial European infant mortality, especially among infants born to families which wanted to keep them alive' (J. T. Krause, 'Some Implications of Recent Work in Historical Demography', *Comparative Studies in Society and History*, II (1959), 177).

[2] See Gautier and Henry, *La Population de Crulai*, and J. Ganiage, *Trois villages de l'Ile de France au XVIIIe siècle*, I.N.E.D. Cahier No. 40 (Paris, 1963).

[3] Helleiner concluded recently that contraception and abortion may have been more widely practised in pre-industrial Europe than has usually been supposed. He takes issue with Mols on this question quoting literary evidence of *coitus*

garded as being permanently at the disposal of European pre-
industrial populations, requiring only the right sort of 'trigger'
to bring them forth. Circumstances in Colyton in the middle of
the seventeenth century appear to have been such as to produce
this change. The parish register of Colyton carries no clues to
the methods of family limitation used. These may never be
known with certainty, but it is likely that there was scope for
the quiet disposal outside the ecclesiastical purview of abortions, and indeed of the victims of infanticide if this was
practised. The early hours of a child's life provide many oc-
casions when it is easy to follow the maxim that 'thou shalt not
kill but needst not strive officiously to keep alive'. In the nature
of things there cannot be much evidence about the frequency of
coitus interruptus and similar methods of avoiding conception in
the absence of literary evidence on the subject. There is,
however, a good deal of evidence from more recent times of
the large scale upon which *coitus interruptus* may be practised
and that it is an effective means of controlling conception.[1]
Coitus interruptus may well have been the most important
method of family limitation in use in Colyton in the seventeenth and early eighteenth centuries.[2] It was probably widely
employed by French populations to secure a lower marital
fertility a century later.

---

interruptus from Germany in the sixteenth and eighteenth centuries. In comment-
ing on the big falls in births recorded during many French *crises* he writes, 'But
when all is said, the magnitude of the decline in births is such as to suggest to
most students of the phenomenon that people during crises had recourse on a
considerable scale to birth control or abortion.' K. F. Helleiner, 'New Light on
the History of Urban Populations', *Journal of Economic History*, XVIII (1958),
60-1.

[1] See, for example, Glass and Grebenik, *The Cambridge Economic History of
Europe*, Vol. VI, Pt. I, pp. 113-18, esp. footnote 1 on p. 118.

[2] Sutter remarks that *coitus interruptus* is a technique which has sprung up
independently in many places and at many times. He writes '*Chaque couple
pourrait l'inventer. Il ne nécessite, d'autre part, l'intervention d'aucun corps étranger, ni
d'aucune manœuvre féminine particulière*'. It is a technique '– *capable d'auto-apparition
et pouvant se diffuser sans propagande. Ce n'est pas une manifestation culturelle comme les
autres méthodes, il est propre à l'espèce humaine et n'est pas une caractéristique ethno-
logique spécifique*'. H. Bergues, P. Ariès, E. Helin, L. Henry, R. P. Riquet, A. Sauvy,
and J. Sutter, *La prévention des naissances dans la famille. Ses origines dans les temps
modernes*, I.N.E.D. Cahier No. 35 (Paris, 1959), p. 345.

It may be of some importance that *coitus interruptus* is essentially a male act,
since in animal populations in general the social activities which serve to maintain populations near an optimum are normally a male preserve.

IV

Before it can be known whether the population history of Colyton in the seventeenth century is typical of much of England or is an unusual variant from the normal pattern, very much work needs to be done. Family reconstitution is a laborious and expensive form of analysis, and it may be some time before detailed studies of fertility using this method have been done sufficiently often and widely to permit confident generalizations about regional or national trends. It is much simpler, of course, to assemble evidence about the changes in the balance between baptisms and burials derived from parish registers and reliable transcripts. The *Cambridge Group for the History of Population and Social Structure* has instituted a survey of this sort, depending largely upon the help of local historians, genealogists, and others interested in work of this type. Each volunteer fills in standard printed forms on which are recorded the monthly totals of baptisms, burials, and marriages in accordance with a cyclo-styled sheet of instructions. In this way it may be possible to compile, say, a 5 per cent sample of the totals of vital events for the three centuries between the institution of parish registers and the beginning of civil registration. Already returns for about 290 parishes are to hand. If it can safely be assumed that changes in the ratio of baptisms to burials similar to those which occurred in Colyton were produced by changes in fertility and mortality similar to those noted in Colyton, then it is already clear that the pattern of events in Colyton is repeated in other places. In a high percentage of the parishes for which returns are available the surplus of baptisms over burials was much less in the second half of the seventeenth century and the first few decades of the eighteenth than either earlier or later. In a substantial minority of parishes the change was sufficiently marked to produce surpluses of burials over baptisms for all or most of the decades during this period.[1] In general, it seems that the Colyton

[1] This pattern appears in the material which Drake analysed in the West Riding. He dealt with the parish of Leeds and a number of parishes in the wapentakes of Morley and Agbrigg. In them the change between the first and second halves of the seventeenth century is very striking. Population was rising rapidly in the first half of the century with surpluses of baptisms in most years. In the second half of the century the population appears to have been falling,

pattern was most commonly found and was most marked in certain parts of the west, north, and, surprisingly, in Kent, but is less obvious in the home counties and the Midlands. Perhaps the constant baptism deficit in London which required a countervailing surplus of baptisms to occur somewhere else may have had something to do with this. The systematic analysis of the returns, however, has not yet begun and all conclusions must remain tentative.

V

Colyton's population history shows that in pre-industrial English society a very flexible response to economic and social conditions was possible. This may well have important implications for the general course of social and particularly economic change in England in the seventeenth and eighteenth centuries. It is now often asserted that during the early decades of the Industrial Revolution it was largely rising home demand which sustained the increasing output of industrial goods.[1] It is arguable that the growing home demand occurred because of rising real incomes spread broadly through large sections of the community.[2] The changes in real incomes and in the level of production were not very dramatic or abrupt, but spread out over several decades. If the Malthusian picture of demographic behaviour were correct this type of slow sea change coming over an economy and eventually helping to provide conditions in which decisive industrial advance can take place is very difficult to credit since one would expect precarious gains in real incomes, however achieved, to be wiped out

---

and if the returns for all the parishes are added together it appears that in the period 1660–99 there were 72,310 burials compared with 70,723 baptisms. M. Drake, 'An Elementary Exercise in Parish Register Demography', *The Economic History Review*, 2nd series, XIV (1962), 427–45.

[1] Deane and Cole, for example, remark '. . . it seems that the explanation of the higher average rate of growth in the second half of the century should be sought at home rather than abroad' (P. Deane and W. A. Cole, *British Economic Growth, 1688–1959* (Cambridge, 1962), p. 85).

[2] This is the tenor of the argument used by Landes in a recent review of the Industrial Revolution in Britain. See D. S. Landes, 'Technological Change and Industrial Development in Western Europe, 1750–1914', in *The Cambridge Economic History of Europe*, Vol. VI, Pt. I (Cambridge, 1965), pp. 280–5.

quickly in a flood of additional babies produced by earlier marriages (and possibly by increased fertility within marriage). If, on the other hand, populations behaved in a manner more likely to secure optimum than maximum numbers the establishment and holding of gains in real income are much easier to understand. The course of events in Colyton shows this to be a possibility. The balance between fertility and mortality was probably at all times delicate and unstable under stress. Colyton itself shows that the very restrictive adaptation which appeared in the middle of the seventeenth century was beginning to give way after 1720 and that in the 1770s or 1780s demographic behaviour reverted to the sixteenth century type. Nevertheless, for three-quarters of a century in an extreme form and for well over a century altogether Colyton behaved demographically in such a way as to make possible an increase and even a steady growth in real incomes.[1] If changes in the economy and technology of the period made possible rising production and real incomes demographic behaviour was not such as to prejudice them immediately.

This forms an instructive contrast with the course of events in the sixteenth and early seventeenth centuries which do seem to fit what may be called a Malthusian model quite well. There is much evidence that over the country as a whole population in the sixteenth century was rising faster than production and that real incomes became depressed. One of the reasons why the 'industrial revolution of the sixteenth century' which Nef has documented had no chance of fructifying into a steady expansion in production and real incomes was that population behaved much in the way Malthus supposed to be almost inevitable. The sixteenth-century English economy and

[1] In this connection it is important to note that a decline of fertility as great as that which occurred in Colyton in the seventeenth century must have had a marked effect on the age-structure of the population. The proportion of the population of working age must rise and the burden of unproductive mouths be reduced. For example, the United Nations study, *The Aging of Populations and its Economic and Social Implications*, Department of Economic and Social Affairs, Population Studies No. 26 (New York, 1956), Table 15, p. 26, gives 58·8 as the percentage of a stable population in the age-group 15–59 when the gross reproduction rate is 2·0 and expectation of life at birth is 40 years, compared with 65·0% in the same age-group when the gross reproduction rate is 1·0 and expectation of life at birth is 30. The ratio of productive to non-productive people in the first case is 1·43:1·00, in the second 1·86:1·00.

population was 'over-fishing'[1] and paid the penalty, just as the Irish population of the late eighteenth and early nineteenth century was 'over-fishing'. As with animal populations in similar circumstances, a sharp adjustment was inevitable. It is possible that at times in the late eighteenth and early nineteenth centuries the same cycle of events came close to being repeated for the great surge of population increase towards the end of the eighteenth century caused serious difficulties of which contemporaries were keenly aware. But if the new pattern of behaviour which can be seen in Colyton in the intervening period proved fragile and eventually gave way to a reversion to the older pattern, it may have helped to win a vital breathing space in the interim. Contemporary French population behaviour appears to have been very different and much more Malthusian (in the sense in which I have used the adjective in this article). Sauvy has estimated that towards the end of the eighteenth century French population was 100 per cent above the optimum level.[2] In consequence, any adventitious increase in real incomes in the short term was not likely to be used to swell demand in the industrial sector but simply to secure a slightly better level of nutrition.

VI

In this article I have been unable to deal extensively with more than a small fraction of the interesting topics which spring to mind in studying the family reconstitution data of Colyton. Mortality remains largely untouched, and on the fertility side such things as pre-nuptial pregnancy rates, the interval between being widowed and remarrying, and bastardy rates. Moreover, though much has been written of the remarkable fall in fertility in the mid-seventeenth century, the equally remarkable recovery in the eighteenth century has not been fully analysed; nor have the implications of the high level of fertility during the reigns of Elizabeth and James I been sufficiently discussed.

[1] I have discussed some aspects of this elsewhere. See E. A. Wrigley, 'The Supply of Raw Materials in the Industrial Revolution', *The Economic History Review*, 2nd series, XV (1962), 1–16.

[2] A. Sauvy, *Théorie générale de la population*, 2 vols (Paris 1956, 1959), I, 186–7. Sauvy sets the optimum between 10 and 12 millions at most in 1790 against an actual population of 24 millions.

While the middle period is perhaps the most fascinating because it is the most unexpected, the significance of the earlier and later periods is also great. Each period is the more interesting and intelligible because a knowledge of the others provides a perspective in which to view it.[1]

The life of men in societies is a subtle and complex thing which can and does influence behaviour at marriage and within marriage. Since the disadvantages to society and to the individual of the unrestrained flow of births which it is within the physiological capacity of women to sustain are very great, societies take care at all times not to expose themselves to such strains. In comparing the sixteenth and the late seventeenth centuries in Colyton, the contrast is not between a society producing children at a maximum rate and a society imposing maximum restrictions but rather between two points on a spectrum of possibilities, each some way from the furthest extremes. In the earlier period the control appears to have lain largely in conventional ages at first marriage which were even then so late for women as to cause them to spend on an average at least a third of their fertile life unmarried. But once marriage had taken place, restraints upon fertility appear to have been slight. In the later period after the great plague visitation of the mid-1640s the restraint through age at marriage became more pronounced and was compounded by new restraints within marriage. These in combination lowered fertility to the point where increase stopped.

It is likely that among the circumstances which produce large changes in fertility economic conditions often bulk large, but it also seems probable that the relationship is not direct and simple but indirect and flexible. Societies are unwilling to allow matters to reach a Malthusian extreme. But the buffer provided by a society's socio-demographic organization to cushion the shock of harvest fluctuation and economic *débâcle*

---

[1] Colyton shows not only that it was within the power of pre-industrial communities to halt population growth, but also that their powers of growth were very remarkable. Over a period of about ninety years (1538–1629) when fertility was high and mortality comparatively low (expectation of life was about 40) baptisms stood to burials in the ratio of 1·61 : 1·00 – a ratio as high as this was common at this period. Rates of increase well above 1 per cent per annum were clearly possible – equivalent, say, to a doubling of population within about half a century.

may be either thin or thick, may be as inadequate as in parts of South-East Asia today or parts of the Beauvaisis in the seventeenth century, or so ample that the society has scope for further economic advance and is free from the periodic *crises démographiques* which are sometimes thought typical of all pre-industrial societies. The *mercuriale* may be a reliable guide to demographic fluctuations in parts of France in the seventeenth century, but some pre-industrial societies were much better buffered against the hazards of the weather than that. In the absence of a continuing advance in material culture a population will always find in time a rough equilibrium level of numbers, but the living standards which result from this will not be the same in all cases. Malthus proposed one limiting case, that in which living standards are minimized but numbers maximized. Other equilibria are also possible and will vary with the extent of the restrictions upon fertility developed within the society in question. If the restrictions are sufficiently severe the equilibrium may occur at a point substantially beneath the maximum level of population, with all that this implies for the likelihood of success in establishing a beneficent spiral of economic activity rather than becoming involved in that other chain of events which keeps the masses miserably short of food and prevents economic growth.

Select Bibliography

THE CHRONOLOGY OF THE DEBATE

Pre-history

1926

M. C. BUER, *Health, Wealth and Population in the Early Days of the Industrial Revolution* (London, 1926).

G. TALBOT GRIFFITH, *Population Problems of the Age of Malthus* (Cambridge, 1926).

1929

T. H. MARSHALL, 'The Population Problem During the Industrial Revolution. A Note on the Present State of the Controversy'. *Economic History* (Supplement to the *Economic Journal*), I (London, 1929), 429–56.

The Current Controversy

1950

K. H. CONNELL, *The Population of Ireland, 1750–1845* (Oxford, 1950).

1951

K. H. CONNELL, 'Some Unsettled Problems in English and Irish Population History, 1750–1845', *Irish Historical Studies*, VII, No. 28 (Dublin, 1951), 225–34.

1953

J. D. CHAMBERS, 'Enclosure and Labour Supply in the Industrial Revolution', *The Economic History Review*, 2nd series, V (Cambridge, 1953), 319–43.

H. J. HABAKKUK, 'English Population in the Eighteenth Century', *The Economic History Review*, 2nd series, VI (Cambridge, 1953), 117–33.

1954

G. UTTERSTRØM, 'Some Population Problems in Pre-industrial Sweden', *Scandinavian Economic History Review*, II (Stockholm, 1954), 103–65.

1955

THOMAS MCKEOWN and R. G. BROWN, 'Medical Evidence Related to English Population Changes in the Eighteenth Century', *Population Studies*, IX (London, 1955), 119–41.

G. UTTERSTRØM, 'Climatic Fluctuations and Population Problems in Early Modern History', *Scandinavian Economic History Review*, III (Stockholm, 1955), 3–47.

1956

D. E. C. EVERSLEY, 'A Survey of Population in an Area of Worcestershire from 1660–1850', *Population Studies*, X (London, 1956–7), 230–53.

1957

J. D. CHAMBERS, 'The Vale of Trent, 1670–1800, A Regional Study of Economic Change', *The Economic History Review*, Supplement 3 (London, 1957).

KARL F. HELLEINER, 'The Vital Revolution Reconsidered', *The Canadian Journal of Economics and Political Science*, XIII (Toronto, 1957).

T. H. HOLLINGSWORTH, 'A Demographic Study of the British Ducal Families', *Population Studies*, XI (London, 1957), 4–26.

1958

A. J. COALE and E. M. HOOVER, *Population Growth and Economic Development in Low Income Countries; a Case Study of India's Prospects* (Princeton, 1958).

H. J. HABAKKUK, 'The Economic History of Modern Britain', *Journal of Economic History*, XVIII (New York, 1958), 486–501.

J. T. KRAUSE, 'Changes in English Fertility and Mortality', *The Economic History Review*, 2nd series, XI (Utrecht, 1958), 52–70.

1959

J. T. KRAUSE, 'Some Implications of Recent Work in Historical Demography', *Comparative Studies in History and Society*, 1 (The Hague, 1959), 164–88.

J. T. KRAUSE, 'Some Neglected Factors in the English Industrial Revolution', *Journal of Economic History*, XIX (New York, 1959), 528–40.

1962

P. DEANE and W. A. COLE, 'Industrialization and Population Change in the Eighteenth and Early Nineteenth Centuries', in their *British Economic Growth, 1688–1959: Trends and Structure* (Cambridge, 1962), pp. 99–135.

M. DRAKE, 'An Elementary Exercise in Parish Register

Demography', *The Economic History Review*, 2nd series, XIV (Utrecht, 1962), 427–45.

T. MCKEOWN and R. G. RECORD, 'Reasons for the Decline of Mortality in England and Wales during the Nineteenth Century', *Population Studies*, XVI (London, 1962), 94–122.

1963

M. DRAKE, 'Marriage and Population Growth in Ireland, 1750–1845', *The Economic History Review*, 2nd series, XVI (Utrecht, 1963), 301–13.

H. J. HABAKKUK, 'Population Problems and European Economic Development in the Late Eighteenth and Nineteenth Centuries', *The American Economic Review*, LIII, 2 (Menasha, Wisconsin, May 1963), 607–18.

J. T. KRAUSE, 'English Population Movements between 1700 and 1850', *International Population Conference, New York 1961*, I (London, 1963), 583–90.

S. SOGNER, 'Aspects of the Demographic Situation in Seventeen Parishes in Shropshire, 1711–60', *Population Studies*, XVII (London, 1963–4), 126–46.

G. S. L. TUCKER, 'English Pre-industrial Population Trends', *The Economic History Review*, 2nd series, XVI (Utrecht, 1963), 205–18.

1964

T. H. HOLLINGSWORTH, 'The Demography of the British Peerage', Supplement, *Population Studies*, XVIII (London, 1964).

1965

ESTER BOSERUP, *The Conditions of Agricultural Growth: the Economics of Agrarian Change under Population Pressure*, (London, 1965).

M. DRAKE, 'The Growth of Population in Norway, 1735–1855', *Scandinavian Economic History Review*, XIII (Copenhagen, 1965), 97–142.

D. E. C. EVERSLEY, 'Mortality in Britain in the Eighteenth Century: Problems and Prospects', in P. Harsin and E. Hélin (eds.), *Problèmes de Mortalité*, *Actes du Colloque International de Démographie Historique* (Liège, 1965), pp. 351–67.

D. V. GLASS and D. E. C. EVERSLEY (eds.), *Population in History* (London, 1965), contains an introduction by D. V.

Glass and the following wide selection of articles on historical demography:

D. E. C. Eversley, 'Population, Economy and Society', pp.
23–69.

S. Peller, 'Births and Deaths among Europe's Ruling
Families since 1500', pp. 87–100.

J. Hajnal, 'European Marriage Patterns in Perspective', pp.
101–43.

D. V. Glass, 'Two Papers on Gregory King', pp. 159–220,
and 'Population and Population Movements in England
and Wales, 1700–1850', pp. 221–46.

J. D. Chambers, 'Three Essays on the Population and
Economy of the Midlands', pp. 308–53.

J. T. Krause, 'The Changing Adequacy of English Registration 1690–1837', pp. 379–93.

K. H. Connell, 'Land and Population in Ireland, 1780–1845',
pp. 423–33.

Louis Henry, 'The Population of France in the Eighteenth
Century', pp. 434–56.

Pierre Goubert, 'Recent Theories and Research in French
Population between 1500 and 1700', pp. 457–73.

J. Bourgeois-Pichat, 'The General Development of the
Population of France since the Eighteenth Century', pp.
474–506.

J. Meuvret, 'Demographic Crisis in France from the
Sixteenth to the Eighteenth Century', pp. 507–22.

G. Utterstrøm, 'Two Essays on Population in Eighteenth-
century Scandinavia', pp. 523–48.

Eino Jutikkala, 'Finland's Population Movement in the
Eighteenth Century, pp. 549–69.

Carlo M. Cipolla, 'Four Centuries of Italian Demographic
Development', pp. 570–87.

W. Koellman, 'The Population of Barmen before and during
the Period of Industrialization', pp. 588–607.

P. Deprez, 'The Demographic Development of Flanders in
the Eighteenth Century', pp. 608–30.

J. Potter, 'The Growth of Population in America, 1700–
1860', pp. 631–88.

The volume also contains reprints of Habakkuk (1953 and

1958): Helleiner (1957), Marshall (1929), McKeown and Brown (1955), Hollingsworth (1957), and Eversley (1956).

PETER LASLETT, *The World We Have Lost*, (London, 1965).

P. E. RAZZELL, 'Population Change in Eighteenth Century England: a Re-appraisal,' *The Economic History Review*, XVIII (Utrecht, 1965), 312–32.

1966

M. DRAKE, 'Malthus on Norway', *Population Studies*, XX (London, 1966–7), 175–96.

ERIC SIGSWORTH, 'A Provincial Hospital in the Eighteenth and Early Nineteenth Centuries', *College of General Practitioners, Yorkshire Faculty Journal*, June 1966, pp. 1–8.

E. A. WRIGLEY, 'Family Limitation in Pre-industrial England', *The Economic History Review*, XIX (Utrecht, 1966), 82–109.

E. A. WRIGLEY (ed.), *An Introduction to English Historical Demography* (London, 1966).

1967

COLIN CLARK, *Population Growth and Land Use* (London, 1967).

J. T. KRAUSE, 'Some Aspects of Population Change, 1690–1790', in E. L. Jones and G. E. Mingay (eds.), *Land, Labour and Population in the Industrial Revolution* (London, 1967), pp. 187–205.

P. E. RAZZELL, 'Population Growth and Economic Change in Eighteenth- and Early Nineteenth-century England and Ireland', in E. L. Jones and G. E. Mingay (eds.), *Land, Labour and Population in the Industrial Revolution* (London, 1967), pp. 260–81.

1968

DAEDALUS, *Historical Population Studies*, Vol. 97, No. 2, *Proceedings of the American Academy of Arts and Sciences* (Cambridge, Mass., 1968) contains an introduction by Roger Revelle and the following articles:

David Landes, 'The Treatment of Population in History Textbooks', pp. 363–84.

Louis Henry, 'Historical Demography', pp. 385–96.

J. A. Banks, 'Historical Sociology and the Study of Population', pp. 397–414.

T. H. Hollingsworth, 'The Importance of the Quality of the Data in Historical Demography', pp. 415–32.

Joseph J. Spengler, 'Demographic Factors and Early Modern Economic Development', pp. 433–46.

David M. Heer, 'Economic Development and the Fertility Transition', pp. 447–62.

John T. Noonan, Jr., 'Intellectual and Demographic History', pp. 463–85.

Etienne van de Walle, 'Marriage and Marital Fertility', pp. 486–501.

Paul Demeny, 'Early Fertility Decline in Austria-Hungary: a Lesson in Demographic Transition', pp. 502–22.

Massimo Livi-Bacci, 'Fertility and Population Growth in Spain in the Eighteenth and Nineteenth Centuries', pp. 523–35.

Jean-Noël Biraben, 'Certain Demographic Characteristics of the Plague Epidemic in France, 1720–22', pp. 536–45.

E. A. Wrigley, 'Mortality in Pre-industrial England: the Example of Colyton, Devon over Three Centuries', pp. 546–80.

D. V. Glass, 'Notes on the Demography of London at the End of the Seventeenth Century', pp. 581–92.

Pierre Goubert, 'Legitimate Fecundity and Infant Mortality in France During the Eighteenth Century: a Comparison', pp. 593–603.

Bernard H. Slicher van Bath, 'Historical Demography and the Social and Economic Development of the Netherlands', pp. 604–21.

Susan B. Hanley, 'Population Trends and Economic Development in Tokugawa, Japan: the Case of Bizen Province in Okayama', pp. 622–35.

M. DRAKE, 'The Irish Demographic Crisis of 1740–41', in T. W. Moody (ed.), *Historical Studies*, VI (London, 1968), 101–24.

JOSEPH LEE, 'Marriage and Population in Pre-Famine Ireland', *The Economic History Review*, 2nd series, XXI (London, 1968), 283–95.

1969

M. DRAKE, *Population and Society in Norway, 1735–1865* (Cambridge, 1969).